Colloquial
Thai

Use FS1 Thai first
with this

The Colloquial Series

Series adviser: Gary King

The following languages are available in the Colloquial series:

Albanian	Japanese
Amharic	Korean
Arabic (Levantine)	Latvian
Arabic of Egypt	Lithuanian
Arabic of the Gulf and Saudi Arabia	Malay
	Mongolian
Basque	Norwegian
Bulgarian	Panjabi
* Cambodian	Persian
* Cantonese	Polish
* Chinese	Portuguese
Croatian and Serbian	Portuguese of Brazil
Czech	Romanian
Danish	* Russian
Dutch	Slovak
Estonian	Slovene
Finnish	Somali
French	* Spanish
German	Spanish of Latin America
Greek	Swedish
Gujarati	* Thai
Hindi	Turkish
Hungarian	Ukrainian
Indonesian	* Vietnamese
Italian	Welsh

Accompanying cassette(s) (*and CDs) are available for all the above titles. They can be ordered through your bookseller, or send payment with order to Routledge Ltd, ITPS, Cheriton House, North Way, Andover, Hants SP10 5BE, or to Routledge Inc., 29 West 35th Street, New York, NY 10001, USA.

COLLOQUIAL CD-ROMs
Multimedia Language Courses
Available in: Chinese, French, Portuguese and Spanish

Colloquial
Thai

John Moore and Saowalak Rodchue

London and New York

First published 1994
by Routledge
11 New Fetter Lane, London EC4P 4EE

Simultaneously published in the USA and Canada
by Routledge
29 West 35th Street, New York, NY 10001

Co-published in Thailand with Asia Books Co. Ltd
5 Sulchumvit Road, Soi 61, Bangkok 10110

Reprinted 1995, 1996, 1997, 1999 (three times), 2000

Routledge is an imprint of the Taylor & Francis Group

© 1994 John Moore and Saowalak Rodchue

Typeset in 10/12pt Times Ten by Florencetype Ltd, Kewstoke, Avon

Printed and bound in England by Clays Ltd, St Ives plc

British Library Cataloguing in Publication Data
A catalogue record for this book is available from the British Library

Library of Congress Cataloguing in Publication Data
A catalogue record for this book has been applied for

ISBN 0–415–09574–3 (book)
ISBN 0–415–09575–1 (cassettes)
ISBN 0–415–09576–X (book and cassettes course)

Contents

Introduction

The country

A knowledge of Thai will enable you to communicate with over 85 per cent of the population of Thailand (currently about 58 million). Thailand is visited by over 5 million tourists a year. Many of those will not take the trouble to learn the language or find out about the country. The ones who do will find their efforts richly rewarded. Thailand, literally 'Land of the free', is the only South-East Asian country which has never been colonized or occupied by foreign powers except in war. Bangkok, the capital, which literally means 'City of angels', boasts probably the longest name of any city in the world:

Krungthepmahanakonbowornratanakosinmahintarayudyayama-
hadiloponoparatanarajthaniburiromudomrajniwesmahasatar-
namornpimarnavatarsatitsakattiyavisanukamphrasit

This is usually abbreviated to **krungthep**.

Geographically, Thailand has borders with Burma, Laos, Cambodia and Malaysia and is roughly the size of France though its shape makes it more like an elongated version of Italy. The central region around Bangkok is fertile and criss-crossed by the Chao Phraya river network. Northern Thailand (including the Chieng Mai region) consists of mountains and fertile valleys. The plateau region of the north-east (including Khong Kaen) is the poorest in the country. South of Bangkok, a narrow peninsula covered in rain forest leads down to the Malaysian border. Most of Thailand is hot all the year round (though it can be pleasantly cool in the mountains), with the rainy season concentrated between July and October. Tropical storms and consequently flooding are common, but droughts are also a problem in the north-east.

In terms of numbers, Bangkok overshadows the other towns, with a population of over one-tenth that of the whole country. This puts a real strain on roads and other public services and parts of Bangkok are very polluted. Chieng Mai, the second largest town, is way behind, with around 200,000 people. About 14 per cent of the population are Chinese and the north of the country is home for a number of hill-tribes with their own cultures and languages. Thailand has a literacy rate of well over 91 per cent and a life expectancy of 65 years, both of which figures are amongst the highest in the area.

Thailand is a constitutional monarchy with an Assembly consisting of a Senate and an elected House of Representatives. A multi-party system operates, with the military playing a leading role. Health compares favourably to that of other South-East Asian countries though health care is meagre. Education is free and compulsory between the ages of 7 and 15. The teaching of the Buddha is expressed in a concern for balance and elegance and an attachment to tradition. Thai architecture can best be seen in the multiple-structure temple grounds. Wood is the basic material here, and parts are lavishly decorated with glass mosaics, gold leaf and mother of pearl. Many temples have paintings with religious themes on their walls. Visitors will have plenty of opportunities to see the graceful traditional Thai dancing. The music, which uses an equi-distant scale, is based very much on an orchestra of gongs and xylophones with a few string and reed instruments. Tourists also have the chance to see Thailand's national sport – Thai boxing. This depends on agility rather than force and allows blows from the knees, legs, elbows and shoulders. Other sports include **takraw**, which uses a ball made of rattan, and kite flying. In recent years Thai food has achieved deserved popularity in the West. Liberal amounts of lemon grass, coriander, basil and chillies make Thai cuisine a mixture of sensations: spicy, sweet, sour and, thanks to the tiny chillies, just plain hot.

The economy

About 76 per cent of Thai labour is engaged in agriculture and only 7 per cent in industry. In addition to traditional exports like rice, sugar and rubber, the top twenty export earners include such things as computer parts and electronics, garments and footwear, gems and jewellery and toys.

Development strategies carried out over the years have resulted in the massive destruction of natural resources, especially land and forests. Since 1992 the Government has made a major effort towards environmental protection. Thailand's rapid growth has also put a strain on its infrastructure and human resources. The prospects for the economy, however, are promising: the Asian Development Bank has predicted, for example, that Thailand will be one of the economic stars of ASEAN in the 1990s.

History

Thailand has been inhabited continuously for over twenty thousand years. The Thais themselves originated from southern China and drifted down amongst the Mons, Khmer and Burmese in the eleventh and twelfth centuries. During the thirteenth century two Thai states emerged, centred in Sukothai and Chieng Mai. In 1350 the kingdom of Ayutthaya succeeded Sukothai and absorbed Chieng Mai, and remained the capital of the Thai kingdom until the end of the eighteenth century (with a gap of fifteen years when it was invaded by the Burmese). The Burmese, in fact, destroyed Ayutthaya in 1767 and the Rama dynasty, which still reigns in Thailand today, was established with the capital in Bangkok. The nineteenth century saw the reign of two great monarchs, Mongkut (Rama IV) and Chulalongkorn (Rama V). King Mongkut understood that to resist the influence of the French and English he had to modernize the institutions and administration. King Chulalongkorn carried through these reforms, adapting them to the needs, traditions and character of the people. Siam (as the country was called until 1939) took part in the First World War on the Allies' side and in 1932 there was a coup carried out by army personnel and students who had returned from their studies in Europe, and a liberal constitution was set up. In the 1930s the regime became increasingly military and authoritarian and during the Second World War Thailand was forced to align itself with the Japanese; but after their defeat democracy was restored. King Bhumibol came to the throne in 1946 and has reigned ever since. During the 1950s and 1960s the government was dominated by the military. After disturbances in 1973, the King launched the process that led to the inauguration of elected civilian government. A subtle and pragmatic approach to life has seen the country prosper, though there are not infrequent signs of strain: the 1991 coup was the seventeenth in fifty years and in May 1992 there were violent protests against the assumption of the Prime Minister's office by the head of the army.

Religion

The teachings of Buddha have shaped the way Thais think, feel and act. Clarac in his *Guide to Thailand* (p. 12) went so far as to say:

> The notion of worldly impermanence on which Buddhism is founded causes Thais to give facts and things minor significance; their conduct is but little burdened, at least in general, by cares of responsibility which Westerners suffer from; from this comes their carefree attitude, their flexibility, their lack of psychological tension, which gives the local atmosphere a happy-go-lucky easiness which strikes every visitor from the moment he sets foot in the country.

The religion is not confined to the innumerable temples; it is alive in every home, institution and business in the country. Most Thai men spend a time in a monastery. Early-morning monks in saffron robes stroll through the quiet streets receiving offerings from people who gain merit through their giving. Shops and businesses have little shrines with offerings of fruit and flowers.

Thai values

The fun-loving side of Thai people is counterbalanced by other equally important values. One of the most fundamental is respect (**napteuh**) whether for the monarchy, for one's elders, for one's boss or teacher. Thais like things to appear decorous and orderly (**riaproi**) – they are very neat in appearance and do not like behaviour that suggests a lack of order or discipline. Improper behaviour in public shows a lack of politeness and is not **supharp**. Public displays of affection, for example, are not **supharp**. This awareness of what is right in public is accompanied by consideration of the feelings of others: it is good to **kreng chai**, that is, to consider how what you would like to do may affect others.

Communicating with Thais

Typically Thais do not raise their voices and stay smiling even when they are seething inside. They often criticize **farang** (Westerners) for showing signs of anger or impatience. They can be quite blunt and to the point but always with a smile. A nervous laugh or giggle is often a sign of embarrassment, though, not of amusement. Thais have a ready sense of humour and enjoy teasing each other in conversation. Bargaining, for example, is always carried out with good humour. Don't think that you need walk on eggshells: there are not many taboos and Thais are famous for their tolerance. Some of the feelings you do need to take account of are to do with the uncleanliness of feet and footwear. You should always be ready to take off your shoes when entering someone's house; lounging in a café with your feet on chairs or thrust towards other people is definitely not **supharp**.

In formal situations you will see Thais greet each other by putting the palms of both hands together in the gesture known as a **wai**. There are elaborate conventions surrounding the use of the **wai**. One explanation offered is that 'the height of the hands is in inverse ratio to the age and social position of the participants'. You would not normally be expected as a foreigner to use this form of greeting but in the right situation its use would be appreciated. Informally Thais may give each other a light touch on the arm by way of greeting, but the sort of social kissing often used in the West is definitely out!

The Thai language

Thai belongs to the Sino-Tibetan group of languages and shares a number of features with Chinese. For the Western learner it has attractions as well as some difficulties. You do not have to learn complicated verb and noun endings. Nouns have no gender or number endings and there are no articles, so **rot** ('car') can mean 'a car', 'the car', 'cars' or 'the cars'. Verbs do not vary their ending with number, tense or person, so **rak** ('love') is the same whether it corresponds to 'love', 'loves', 'loved', or 'will love'. This means that you have to understand a sentence in Thai by reference to its context. When it is necessary to make the meaning explicit Thai uses separate words rather as we use modal verbs like 'can' or 'must' in English.

Now the difficulties. Most of the words are totally unconnected to their English equivalent, so there are no associations you can fall back on as in many European languages. **Narm** is not connected with any English word that is associated with water. Some of the words, particularly those of Indian origin, are long. The word for the month of May for example is **phreutsapharkhom**. One of the main difficulties for a Western learner is the use of tones. In English we use pitch (intonation) to add meaning to the words in a sentence: to express our attitude or make it a question, for example. In Thai, pitch is an integral part of the pronunciation of the word. The same combination of vowels and consonants with a different tone has a different meaning. For example, **phee** can mean 'fat', 'older sibling' or 'ghost' according to the tone you give it. You therefore need to learn the tone of a word as well as its pronunciation. You must also be careful not to use intonation as you would in English by, for example, adding a questioning intonation to a sentence.

There are five tones in Thai: mid (no tone mark), high (´), low (`), falling (^) and rising (˅). In this book the tone marks are given when a word is introduced and in the glossaries; however, they are not given each time the word is used as you should try to learn the tone with each new word and not rely on the tone marks themselves. You will find that Thais have considerable difficulty in understanding you when you get the tones wrong, so it is worth making the effort. There are considerable differences in Thai between the written and spoken forms of the language and between formal and informal speech. This book uses the sort of language that would be acceptable with strangers or acquaintances. Some formal and informal variants of the same word which are particularly common are introduced and the distinction between them is explained.

Transliteration

There are various systems for writing Thai in roman letters, each with its own advantages and disadvantages. This course uses the following:

Vowels

Transliteration	Sound (approximate) as in
e	hen
a	sun
i	sip
o	hot
ar	arm (without the 'r')
ai	Thai
ae	air

ao	cow
ee	fee
er	fern
oei	er-ee (without the 'r')
eu	ugh ! (short)
euh	ugh (long)
eua	ugh-a
iu	hue
oh	cone (but shorter)
or	born
oo	boot
u	book
oi	boy
ia	beer
aeo	air-o (without the 'r')
ieo	Leo
ua	tour
uey	oo-way
ui	phooey

Consonants

p	spy (i.e. a 'p' sound without the puff of air)
ph	pie (with the puff of air)
b	book
d	die
t	sty (without the puff of air)
th	tie (with the puff of air)
k	ski (without the puff of air)
kh	Korea (with the puff of air)
ch	*between* chest *and* jest
sh	*between* sheet *and* cheat

Other sounds (such as 'm', 'r', 'l') are not included in this list as they are not significantly different from the English. This system does not by any means capture all the subtleties of Thai pronunciation, but it will give you a guide as to the main features you should be aware of.

Pronunciation

The sound that is most different in Thai from English is *eu* (or its longer form *euh*). This is generally described as being like the sound in 'ugh!' Some sounds are slightly different: *p*, *t* and *k* for example are in between *p* and *b*, *t* and *d*, and *k* and *g*, respectively. Some of the diphthongs use vowels in slightly different combinations: *aeo* (pronounced 'air-o' without the 'r') and *oei* (pronounced 'er-ee' without the 'r'). The final *p*, *t* and *k* in a syllable are not released: the mouth just moves into the position to make the sound. The consonant cluster 'ng', which in English only occurs at the end of a syllable, in Thai can come at the beginning as in **ngai** ('easy' – which it is when you practise it).

The writing system

Thai uses forty-four consonant letters for twenty-one consonant sounds. Some sounds have more than one corresponding letter (*th* has six, for example). There are also thirty-two different vowel symbols. Some vowel symbols are written after the consonant they follow; some are written before it, some above it and some are a combination of symbols in two or three positions. There are a number of ways in which the writing system represents the tones. The rules are built on three different characteristics of syllables: (1) the initial consonant, (2) the vowel, (3) the syllable ending.

Consonants are grouped into three classes: low, mid and high. Vowels may be long or short.

If a syllable ends with the sound *m*, *n*, *ng*, *y*, *w* or with a long vowel it is known as 'live'. Syllables ending with a short vowel or p, t, k are called 'dead'.

Live syllables normally have a mid tone except for those beginning with a high consonant, which have a rising tone. Dead syllables have a low tone unless they start with a low-class consonant. In this case if the syllable has a short vowel it has a high tone; if it has a long vowel it will normally have a falling tone.

This description of the writing system and the tones will help you understand how the language works. You will not need it, however, to work out the tones of words introduced in this book (the tone marks given will be much more useful).

There are also four tone symbols which change the normal tone that would be given a syllable.

Using this course

Objectives:

- to handle common social courtesies such as greetings, saying you're sorry
- to converse with casual acquaintances on topics like food, your family, where you come from, what you do in your free time, holidays and holiday plans, etc.
- to make arrangements such as fixing a meeting with someone
- to read a note or letter someone might write you on such topics
- to write a simple note or short letter to a friend on such topics
- to read some common signs you might see in streets, etc.

You will not learn to read and write everything you say – the written form is limited to the most useful or straightforward forms.

Each lesson presents the language you will find most useful to talk about a common topic or situation. You will practise it in ways that will make it easy to use in real-life situations. The lessons follow this pattern:

Dialogue: new grammar and vocabulary in a realistic context.
Additional vocabulary for the exercises is presented separately.
Exercises to practise using the new language to communicate.
A further dialogue presents and practises more grammar and vocabulary on a related theme in the same way as the first.

In addition there are four other types of exercises:

Tone practice focuses on the tones of some new words introduced.
A vocabulary exercise practises word-building and relationships. Some exercises help you to combine words you already know in order to make new ones; others revise words you know by grouping them according to their meaning.
Reading and writing exercises introduce progressively the symbols of written Thai with examples drawn from words you already know.

Finally, a *comprehension passage* gives practice in reading (in transliteration) or listening to a stretch of natural spoken Thai. Tapes are also available and provide valuable opportunities for improving your ability to understand spoken Thai. There is also a key to the exercises at the back of the book to help you to check the work you have done. The book also includes a summary of grammar points introduced which you can refer to when you need to review what you have learnt. Finally, the book contains English–Thai and Thai–English glossaries.

1 thee opfit

Calling at the office

In this lesson you will learn how to:

- greet someone
- find out someone's whereabouts
- thank someone
- take leave of someone
- ask questions to check what you think

You will also learn how to respond in these situations

Dialogue 🔲

Ken is on holiday in Thailand. He is also hoping to do some business while he is there. One of the contacts he wants to make works in an office in Bangkok. He goes to his office to try to find him. The receptionist is rather busy so he has only a brief conversation with her

KEN:	sawatdee khrap.
RECEPTIONIST:	sawatdee kha.
KEN:	khorthoht khrap. khun Suporn yoo mai khrap?
RECEPTIONIST:	mai yoo kha. wannee mai mar tham ngarn kha.
KEN:	khorpkhun khrap.
RECEPTIONIST:	mai pen rai kha.

KEN:	*Hello.*
RECEPTIONIST:	*Hello.*
KEN:	*Excuse me. Is Suporn here?*
RECEPTIONIST:	*No, he's not. He didn't come to work today.*
KEN:	*Thank you.*
RECEPTIONIST:	*You're welcome.*

Vocabulary

sawàtdee	hello
khráp, kha	(polite particles)
khǒrthôht	excuse me
khun	(polite title)
yòo	to be somewhere, stay, live
mái	(question marker)
mâi	negative marker
khòrpkhun	thank you
mâi pen rai	It's all right, it doesn't matter, you're welcome
mar	to come
wannée	today
tham ngarn	to work (*lit.* do work)

Language points

Basic sentence patterns

In this lesson we will learn how to make some simple statements (affirmative and negative) and two ways of asking questions. We will also practise the appropriate short answers.

Affirmative statements

khun Malee *yoo.*	Malee *is here.*
khun Malee *tham ngarn.*	Malee *works* (is working).

Negative sentences

khun Malee *mai yoo.*	Malee *is not here.*
khun Malee *mai mar.*	Malee *is not coming.*

You make a sentence negative by adding **mai** immediately before the main verb. We will see the one exception to this rule in Lesson 3.

Yes/no questions

There are several ways of asking questions in Thai. We will see how their meanings differ according to the context. The simplest form of question is to use **mai** at the end of a statement:

khun Malee yoo *mai?*	Is Malee here?
khun Ken mar *mai?*	Is Ken coming?

Short answers

If you look back at how the receptionist answered Ken's question you will see there is no equivalent of the word 'no'. Neither, you might be surprised to know, is there an equivalent for 'yes'. There is no single word in Thai which corresponds to either 'yes' or 'no'. You give a short 'yes/no' answer to this sort of question by repeating the main verb:

Question	*Yes answer*	*No answer*
khun Malee tham ngarn mai?	**tham**	**mai tham**

Absence of pronouns

You will also notice from the receptionist's answer that she did not use a pronoun corresponding to 'he'. The use of the personal pronouns in Thai is optional – you use them normally if what you say would otherwise be ambiguous.

Verbs

You will have noticed that **mar** has been used to mean 'come' or 'has come'. You will also have seen that **tham ngarn** (lit. 'do work') can mean 'work' or 'is working'. There are no verb endings to show tense or aspect in Thai. Later on you will practise ways in which you can indicate these meanings in Thai.

Language and culture notes

sawatdee

sawatdee is the normal form of greeting, covering both formal and informal greetings. You can use it at any time of day (or night) – there are no separate words for 'good afternoon', etc.

khrap, kha

Politeness is an important ingredient of communication with Thais and you will learn several ways of making what you say sound polite. One of them is the use of the final particles **khrap** and **kha**. **khrap** is used by male speakers, **kha** by female. To start with you should use them in almost every sentence: later you will get a better idea of when to drop them. Talking to someone you do not know well without using them will make you sound a bit clumsy or even downright rude.

khorthoht

khorthoht is a useful phrase, roughly equivalent to 'excuse me'. Again it is a good way of sounding more polite especially when you are going to ask someone a question or a favour. If you are about to ask a personal question it can mean something like 'forgive me for asking, but ...' On its own, it's a convenient way of apologizing for something you have done.

mai pen rai

mai pen rai (literally 'there is nothing') is one of those key phrases with which foreigners like to sum up Thai culture. It's the normal way of responding when someone thanks you for something or apologizes for doing something. It is used more generally to mean 'it doesn't matter' or 'there's no need to worry about it.' As Thais use it a lot to reassure foreigners as well as themselves it is in a sense indicative of the tolerance and easy-going nature for which Thais are famous. It can sometimes be irritating when news of any disaster or misfortune that has befallen you is greeted with a stoical **mai pen rai**!

Addressing or referring to people: khun

Notice that Ken does not refer to Supòrn alone but to **khun Suporn**. The polite title **khun** is used to address people or refer to them (whether they are male or female). Notice that you use **khun** with the first name – Suporn would address or refer to Ken, for example, as **khun Ken**. Surnames are used only for official purposes, never to refer to someone or address them in normal conversation.

Exercise 1

Ask if these people are here:
Ken, Malee, Ena, Sakorn, Steve, Saowalak
Example: **khun Ken yoo mai?**
Now ask again adding **khrap** or **kha**.

Exercise 2

Now answer the questions you asked in Exercise 1. These people are here: Saowalak, Steve, Malee. The others are not.

Exercise 3

Use the cues to give short answers to these questions:

1 khun Ken yoo mai khrap? (yes)
2 khun John mar mai kha? (yes)
3 khun Saowalak tham ngarn mai? (no)
4 khun Sakorn yoo mai kha? (yes)
5 khun Saowalak mar mai? (no)
6 khun Steve mar tham ngarn mai kha? (no)

Exercise 4

Match the response on the right with the statement or question on the left:

1 sawatdee kha.	yoo, khrap.
2 khun malee mai yoo khrap.	mai yoo kha.
3 khorpkhun khrap.	sawatdee khrap.
4 khun Ena yoo mai kha?	khorpkhun khrap.
5 khun Ken yoo mai kha?	mai pen rai.

Exercise 5

How would you find out if:

1 khun Sawat is here
2 Steve is at work
3 Ken is coming
4 khun Sakorn is at work
5 khun Malee is coming

Exercise 6

Rewrite the dialogue at the beginning of this part to fit this situation. Mary calls at her friend Suchart's house. A man tells her that Suchart is there.

Dialogue 🔲

Ken goes back to the same office the following day looking for Suporn. He sees the same receptionist, who is as busy as ever.

KEN:	sawatdee khrap.
RECEPTIONIST:	sawatdee kha. khun Suporn mai yoo kha.
KEN:	yoo thee barn shai mai khrap?
RECEPTIONIST:	mai shai, kha. pai sanarmbin kha.
KEN:	khorpkhun mark khrap.
RECEPTIONIST:	mai pen rai kha.
KEN (AS HE LEAVES):	sawatdee khrap
RECEPTIONIST:	sawatdee kha.
KEN:	*Hello.*
RECEPTIONIST:	*Hello. Suporn is not here.*

KEN:	*Is he at home?*
RECEPTIONIST:	*No, he has gone to the airport.*
KEN:	*Thank you very much.*
RECEPTIONIST:	*You're welcome.*
KEN:	*Goodbye.*
RECEPTIONIST:	*Goodbye.*

Vocabulary

bârn	house	**pai**	to go
thêe	in	**sanǎrmbin**	airport
shâi mái	(question marker)	**mârk**	a lot, much
mâi shâi	(negative marker)		

Language points

Articles

The phrase **yoo thee barn** can mean 'to be at home' or 'to be in the house'. We will learn other words for places in this lesson such as 'hotel' and 'flat' and you will see that we do not use any articles with them. So the noun **barn** can mean 'house', 'a house' or 'the house'.

yoo thee

You have seen the verb **yoo** used in the dialogue to mean 'to be somewhere'.

> *yoo* **thee barn.** He *is at* home.

yoo thee can also mean 'to live somewhere':

> **khun Ken** *yoo thee* **London.** **Ken** *lives in* London.

Prepositions

You will have noticed that you do not need a preposition with **pai** to mean 'to':

> *pai* **London.** I'm going *to* London.

In informal speech **thee** can also be omitted:

> **yoo barn.** She's at home.

The question form shai mai

yoo thee barn shai mai?   Is she at home?

The question form **shai mai** serves to check what you think to be true. It often corresponds to question tags such as 'isn't it' as in 'She's at home isn't she?'. However, we also use **shai mai** where in English a simple yes/no question would be used. A question with **mai** can sometimes suggest intention so the question **pai London mai?** could mean '*Are you going* (or *intending*) to go to London?' The question **pai London *shai mai*?**, however, just asks for confirmation and can often be translated simply by '*Are you going* to London?'

Notice that you use the same marker to confirm a negative statement:

khun Ken mai yoo thee barn   Ken isn't at home *is he*?
   shai mai?

Short answers to shai mai *questions*

Question	*Affirmative answer*	*Negative answer*
khun pai London shai mai?	**shai, khrap.**	**mai shai, kha.**

Language and culture notes

sawatdee

As well as being used as a greeting, **sawatdee** can also be used to say goodbye to someone if you have said (or it is clear from the situation) that you are leaving.

Vocabulary

Khun malee mai yoo thee opfit. mai yoo thee rohng raem. mai yoo thee apartmen. mai yoo thee Chieng Mai. yoo thee krungthep.

opfit	office	**krungthêp**	Bangkok
rohng raem	hotel	**Chieng Mài**	(town in
apártmén	flat		northern Thailand)

Exercise 7

1 You are in the office when someone comes looking for three colleagues who are not there. One is in London, one in Chieng Mai and the other in Bangkok. What would he ask you and how would you tell him where they all are?
2 Someone comes to your flat looking for your flatmates. One has gone to the office, one to the airport and the third to the Oriental hotel. What would she ask you and what would you tell her?

Exercise 8

Your newspaper has given you an assignment to find out where some people are. You find that none of them are what they were thought to be. Use the notes below to report back.

Name of person	Where they were thought to be	Where they really are
Sakorn	London	Bangkok
Steve Hunt	The Oriental hotel	his house
Saowalak	her flat	the office
Ann Chambers	Bangkok	Chieng Mai

Exercise 9

What question would you ask to check whether these facts are true?

1 Saowalak tham ngarn thee London
2 Steve tham ngarn thee rohng raem Oriental
3 Sakorn mai yoo thee opfit
4 Steve pai krungthep
5 wannee Saowalak mai mar tham ngarn
6 Steve pai opfit

Exercise 10

Answer the questions in Exercise 9 as follows:
1 yes   2 yes   3 no   4 no   5 yes   6 no

Exercise 11 📼

Answer these questions about yourself:
1 tham ngarn thee London shai mai?
2 yoo thee krungthep shai mai?
3 tham ngarn thee opfit shai mai?
4 wannee pai sanarmbin shai mai?
5 wannee mar tham ngarn shai mai?

Exercise 12

Make as many sentences as you can by using these words:
>   rohng raem   shai   pai   mai
>   khrap   yoo   thee   sanarmbin

Exercise 13

What would you say if:
1 You telephone a friend. Someone else answers and you want to find out if he is at home.
2 You want to get on a crowded bus and someone is standing in your way.
3 You have had all your money stolen, you've missed the last bus and it starts to rain heavily but you want to tell your friend not to worry.
4 You want to see if you can guess where your friend is going – how many questions can you ask her?
5 A friend telephones you and asks if Malee is at home. You tell him she is at the office. He asks you if you are going to the office but you tell him you are staying at home.

Tone practice 📼

You will remember from the Introduction that every syllable has a tone (mid, low, falling, high or rising). Practise the tones in these syllables:
>   mar   yòo   mâi   pen   rai   pai   mârk   bârn

Practise the sequence of tones in these words and phrases:
>   sawàtdee   wanneé   rohng raem   khòrpkhun mârk
>   apártmén   sanǎrmbin   khǒrthôht

Vocabulary-building

A lot of Thai words are built up from smaller words. Here are some words which are contained in words you have learnt in this lesson. See if you can match them to their English equivalent.

tham	this
wan	to ask for
thoht	work
bin	day
nee	to fly
ngarn	to do
khor	punishment

Reading and writing

In this lesson you will learn to read six consonants and three vowels. These will first be introduced individually and then in words you will have met in this lesson. You will also practise reading and writing some new words. At this point don't worry about the meaning of any new words. You will meet them in subsequent lessons.

Consonants

ค ท บ น ม ป

d   th   b   n   m   p

Vowels

You will remember from the Introduction that vowels can come in different positions in relation to the consonant they follow phonetically. In this lesson you will practise one vowel written above the consonant, one written before and one written after it.

ดี   ไป   มา

ee   ai   ar

Exercise 14

Write these words in transliteration:

ดี มี มา นาน ไป บาท

Exercise 15

Write these words in Thai script:

  1 **dee** 2 **mar** 3 **pai** 4 **mee** 5 **bart** 6 **narn**

Dialogue ▢▢

Ken goes to another office where he has been given the names of four more people to contact

Comprehension

Note where Sakorn, Saowalak, Saowanee and Manat all are.

RECEPTIONIST:	sawatdee kha.
KEN:	sawatdee khrap. khun Sakorn yoo mai khrap?
RECEPTIONIST:	khun Sakorn, reuh. khun Sakorn mai yoo kha. wannee mai mar tham ngarn kha.
KEN:	khorpkhun khrap. lae khun Saowalak, yoo mai khrap?
RECEPTIONIST	mai yoo kha.
KEN:	yoo thee London shai mai khrap?
RECEPTIONIST:	mai shai kha. yoo thee Paris kha.
KEN:	khun Saowanee yoo mai khrap?
RECEPTIONIST	mai yoo kha. wannee pai tham ngarn thee sanarm-bin.
KEN:	mai pen rai, khrap. khun Manat yoo opfit shai mai khrap?
RECEPTIONIST:	khorthoht kha. mai yoo kha. wannee tham ngarn thee rohng raem Hilton. khorthoht kha.
KEN:	mai pen rai khrap.

2 phóp phêuan

(handwritten annotations: meet, friend, = hâ)

Meetings and greetings

In this lesson you will learn how to:

- ask how someone is
- find out where someone is going
- take leave of someone
- ask more questions for confirmation
- ask questions to check what you think

You will also learn how to respond in these situations

Dialogue 🔛

Ken catches sight of his friend Saowanee. She is obviously in a hurry so they have only a fleeting conversation

KEN:	sawatdee khrap, khun Saowanee.
SAOWANEE:	sawatdee kha, khun Ken. khun sabai dee mai?
KEN:	sabai dee khorpkhun khrap. khun la khrap?
SAOWANEE:	sabai dee kha.
KEN:	pai nai khrap?
SAOWANEE:	pai talart kha.
KEN:	shohk dee na khrap.
SAOWANEE:	khorpkhun kha. laeo cher kan na kha.

KEN:	*Hello, Saowanee.*
SAOWANEE:	*Hello, Ken. How are you?*
KEN:	*I'm fine, thank you. How are you?*
SAOWANEE:	*I'm fine.*
KEN:	*Where are you going?*
SAOWANEE:	*I'm going to the market.*
KEN:	*Good luck!*
SAOWANEE:	*Thanks. See you.*

Vocabulary

sabai dee	to be well
na	('filler' word used to make what you say sound more polite and draw attention to what you are saying)
năi	where
talàrt	market
shôhk	luck
khun	you
khun la?	what about you?
cher kan	see you (*lit.* **cher** 'to meet', **kan** 'together')
laéo	so, and
dee	good

póp kan (handwritten)

Language points

Talking about where you are going

pai talart.　　　　　　　　I'm going to the market.

You will remember from Lesson 1 that you can omit not only the pronoun and the article but also the preposition 'to'.

You should have no difficulty with question and negative forms with **pai** as they are exactly the same as with **yoo**:

pai **talart mai?**　　　　　Are you *going* to the market?
mai *pai* **talart.**　　　　　I'm not *going* to the market.

We have already seen that the same sentence in Thai can mean different things according to the context.

A question like **pai talart mai?** can also suggest 'Do you want to go the market?' or 'Shall we go to the market?'

You will remember from Lesson 1 that to confirm what you think you would use **shai mai**:

pai talart *shai mai?*　　　You're going to the market *are you?*

Asking where someone is or is going

pai *nai?*　　　　　　　　*Where* are you going?
khun Saowanee yoo *nai?*　*Where* is Saowanee?

Notice that the question word **nai**, like other question words in Thai, comes at the end of the sentence.

You can also use **thee nai** instead of **nai**:

khun Saowanee yoo *thee nai?* *Where is* Saowanee?
pai *thee nai?*　　　　　　*Where* are you going?

thee nai usually suggests you are asking for more precise information, as in the English 'whereabouts'.

Personal pronouns

In this dialogue we see the word **khun** which we learnt as a title now used as a personal pronoun to mean 'you'. Like the other pronouns it can be omitted when the meaning is clear. Here are the other personal pronouns which you will find used gradually in the dialogues:

phǒm	I (male speaker)
shán	I (female speaker)
khun	you (male or female, singular or plural)
kháo	he, she, they
ráo	we

People often use names when in English we would use 'I' or 'you'. Malee talking to Ken might say **Malee yoo thee barn**, for example. She might also say **Ken** or **khun Ken** instead of 'you'.

Language and culture notes

dee

dee means 'good' in the sense of morally good or something that makes you feel good; you do not use it in the sense of 'being good at' which we will see in Lesson 4. Like a number of languages, Thai does not have an all-purpose word for 'bad'. The commonest way of translating this is simply to say **mai dee**.

Asking if someone is well

sabai dee are the words you normally use to ask if someone is well or say that you are well. **sabai** on its own is a very important word – we will see it used in the sense of 'feeling comfortable', 'taking things easy' and other related meanings.

Initiating conversation

A common way of greeting people is to ask where they are going or have been – it is often little more than a polite enquiry to initiate the conversation. **pai nai?** can often suggest not just 'Where are you going?' but 'What are you going to do somewhere?'

sawatdee

Notice that if you know someone's name it is usual to greet them with it. Because you want to sound particularly polite when you are greeting someone you should use **sawatdee** with **khrap** and preface the person's name with **khun**.

Wishing someone good luck

shohk dee ('good luck!') is a common way of parting and not only a way of specifically wishing someone good luck. It can also be used to refer to good luck. 'Bad luck' is **shohk mai dee**.

Vocabulary

khun malee pai sanarmbin. pai London. mai pai thura. pai thieo.

pai thúrá	to go on business
pai thîeo	to go somewhere for pleasure

(You can also say **mar thura** or **mar thieo**.)

Exercise 1

How would you tell someone that you are going to the market/office/Bangkok/Chieng Mai/London/the airport/the hotel/the apartment

Exercise 2

Ask someone if they are going to the same places.

Exercise 3

Use these cues to answer the questions:

1 pai talart mai? (rohng raem)
2 pai nai khrap? (opfit)
3 khun malee yoo thee nai kha? (krungthep)
4 pai opfit mai? (talart)
5 pai thura mai? (thieo)
6 pai nai khrap? (sanarmbin)

Exercise 4

Now use the same cues to make dialogues like this:

khun pai talart shai mai kha?
mai shai khrap. pai rohng raem. khun la khrap?
pai talart kha.

Exercise 5

Rewrite the dialogue between Malee (who speaks first) and Akorn.
Malee is going to the office and Akorn to the airport.

Exercise 6

Ask a question with **nai** or **thee nai** in response to these statements:

1 khun Saowanee mai yoo thee barn.
2 phom mai pai sanarmbin.
3 shan mai pai opfit.
4 khun Malee mai yoo thee London.
5 rao pai sanarmbin.

Exercise 7

How would you respond to the following:

1 khun sabai dee mai?
2 shohk dee na kha.
3 pai nai khrap?
4 khun yoo thee nai?
5 khorthoht kha.

Dialogue 🔲

Ken meets Sakorn and they arrange to go for a meal together

KEN: sawatdee khrap Sakorn.
SAKORN: sawatdee khrap Ken. khun sabai dee reuh?
KEN: sabai dee, khorpkhun khrap.
SAKORN: pai nai khrap?
KEN: pai kin khao khrap. pai duey kan mai?
SAKORN: dee see khrap.

KEN: *Hello, Sakorn*
SAKORN: *Hello, Ken. How are you?*
KEN: *I'm fine, thanks.*
SAKORN: *Where are you going?*
KEN: *I'm going to have something to eat. Shall we go together?*
SAKORN: *Fine!*

Vocabulary

rĕuh	question marker	**kin khâo**	to have something to eat
kin	to eat, drink	**duêy kan**	together
khâo	rice	**dee see**	Fine!

Language points

Forms of address

As Ken and Sakorn are friends, they address each other by their names alone without adding **khun**.

Questions and answers with reuh

The use of **reuh** is very similar to **shai mai**. It suggests you want to check whether something is the case.

khun Ken pai London *reuh*?	Ken is going to London *is he*?
khrap/kha.	Yes.
mai shai.	No.

Like **shai mai** you can use it in negative questions:

khun mai pai opfit *reuh*?	You're not going to the office, *then*?

Implications of questions with mai

We have seen that a question like **pai talart mai?** can suggest that you are asking about the other person's intention. In **pai duey kan mai?** the implication is that you are making a suggestion.

Using more than one verb together

You will have noticed in Lesson 1 that we can use two verbs together without any linking words:

pai tham ngarn	to go to work
mar tham ngarn	to come to work
pai kin khao	to go and eat

You will find this very common in Thai. Sometimes a number of verbs are used together in this way to convey the meaning of one English verb.

Language and culture notes

Eating and drinking: kin khao

The particular meaning of **khao** is 'rice' but in the phrase **kin khao** it refers more generally to having a meal (rice being an almost essential ingredient of any Thai meal).

kin is used informally between friends and can mean either 'eat' or 'drink'. You need to add another word to it to show which you mean.

Vocabulary

A: pai nai khrap?
B: pai talart kha. pai seuh khorng. khun la kha?
A: pai kin karfae thee rohng raem Oriental.

seúh	to buy	seúh khŏrng	shopping
khŏrng	things	karfae	coffee

pai kin khao. pai kin karfae duey. mai pai talart. mai pai seuh khorng duey.

dûey	as well, either

Exercise 8

Respond to these statements by asking a question with **reuh**.

1 shan pai tham ngarn.
2 phom pai talart
3 shan pai sanarmbin
4 khun Malee mai yoo kha.
5 khun Sakorn yoo thee barn.
6 shan pai rohng raem Oriental.

Exercise 9

How would you check if the following are correct using **shai mai** or **reuh**?

1 Suchart works in the Hilton hotel
2 Malee is at home
3 Saowanee is not at the office
4 Suchart does not work in the airport
5 Sakorn is going to the airport
6 Malee is not going to the market

Exercise 10

What question would you use in the following situations?

1 You want to find out if Dusit is intending to go to work.
2 You want to check that Saowanee works at the airport.
3 You want to check that Dusit is going to work today.
4 You want to suggest that your friend comes with you to the hotel.
5 You want to check that Saowanee is at the market.

Exercise 11

Answer these questions about yourself:

1 khun tham ngarn thee London shai mai?
2 wannee khun yoo barn mai?
3 khun yoo thee Paris shai mai?
4 khun pai kin khao reuh?
5 khun tham ngarn thee sanarmbin reuh?
6 wannee khun pai seuh khorng mai?

Exercise 12

How would you tell your friend you are going to these places and suggest he might like to come with you?

1 to the market
2 to the airport
3 shopping
4 to have a coffee
5 to the office
6 to London

Exercise 13

Rewrite the dialogue at the beginning of this part. Malee meets her friend Sue and they decide to go shopping together.

Exercise 14

1 You meet a friend when you are going shopping and you'd like her to join you. What do you say?
2 You are on your way to have a coffee in the Hilton hotel when you meet a friend who asks where you are going. What do you say to him? What do you say when he asks if he can join you?
3 You've had a brief chat with a friend but you have to go now as you are going to the market.
4 You are in a taxi on the way to Bangkok airport. You are going to London on business. The taxi driver makes a cynical remark about foreigners having the time and money to go on pleasure trips. What do you say?

Tone practice

Practise the tones in these syllables:

dee phǒm shán kháo khǎo dûey

Now practise the sequence of tones in these words:

sabai dee   sabai dee mái   sabai dee rěuh   pai kin khâo   pai séuh khǒrng   khǒrthôht khráp   khǒrthôht kha

Vocabulary building

Look through the whole lesson and note down:

1 all the words and phrases you can find containing **dee**
2 all the words you can find referring to places

Reading and writing

Consonants

ร ก ง

r   k   ng

Vowels

In this lesson we will practise two vowels written above the consonant as well as a letter representing a vowel plus a consonant.

กิน   กัน   ทำ

i   a   arm

Exercise 15

Write these words in transliteration:

ทำ ไร กิน งาน กัน บิน รัก มาก

Exercise 16

Write these words in Thai script:

1 **kin**   2 **tham**   3 **kan**   4 **rak**   5 **mark**   6 **ngarn**   7 **bin**   8 **rim**

Dialogue

Steve is waiting for a bus when he sees his friend Saowanee come out of her house

SAOWANEE: sawatdee kha khun Steve.
STEVE   sawatdee khrap khun Saowanee. khun sabai dee mai khrap?
SAOWANEE: sabai dee khorpkhun kha. khun la kha?
STEVE: sabai dee. khorpkhun mark khrap. khun Saowanee pai talart reuh khrap?
SAOWANEE: mai shai, kha. wannee shan mai pai talart kha. mai pai

	opfit duey. pai sanarmbin. pai London.
STEVE:	Mm. pai thieo shai mai khrap.
SAOWANEE:	mai shai kha. Pai thura. khun la kha? pai nai kha?
STEVE:	pai rohng raem Hilton. pai kin khao. khorthoht khrap, khun manat yoo thee barn shai mai khrap?
SAOWANEE:	mai yoo, kha. yoo thee London. pai seuh khorng thee London.
STEVE:	dee khrap. laeo cher kan na khrap. shohk dee na khrap.
SAOWANEE:	khorpkhun mark, kha. sawatdee kha khun Steve.
STEVE:	sawatdee khrap.

Comprehension

1 where are Saowanee and Akorn going?
2 where is Saowanee's husband Manat?

3 phoot khui reuang khon 1

Talking about people (1)

In this lesson you will learn how to:

- talk about nationalities and where someone comes from
- describe people using simple adjectives
- indicate possession and relationships

Dialogue 🔲

Ken stops off for a beer in a café and starts chatting to the waitress

WAITRESS: khorthoht kha khun pen khon amerikan shai mai kha?
KEN: mai shai khrap. pen khon angkrit, khrap. mar chark London. khun mar chark krungthep reuh khrap?
WAITRESS: mai shai kha. mar chark Chieng Mai. khun mar krungthep thammai? mar thura reuh?
KEN: mai shai, khrap. mar thieo.
WAITRESS: sanuk mai?
KEN: sanuk mark.

WAITRESS: *Excuse me. You're American aren't you?*
KEN: *No, I'm English. I'm from London. Are you from Bangkok?*
WAITRESS: *No, I'm from Chieng Mai. What have you come to Bangkok for? On business?*
KEN: *No, I'm on holiday (for pleasure).*
WAITRESS: *Are you enjoying it?*
KEN: *Yes, very much.*

Vocabulary

pen	to be (followed by a noun)	**angkrìt**	English
khon	person, people	**thammai**	what for, why?
amerikan	American	**sanùk**	enjoyable, fun

Language points

Adjectives of nationalities

Notice that the Thai equivalent of 'He is American' is 'He is person American' (**pen khon amerikan**). Adjectives follow the noun they modify:

khon thai	a Thai
khon amerikan	an American

Saying where you are from (mar chark + *town or country*)

shan *mar chark* **London.** I am *from* London

khun *mar chark* **thee nay?** Where are you *from*?

The use of pen ('to be')

When the predicate contains a noun you use the verb 'to be', **pen**:

khao *pen* **khon thai.** He *is* Thai.

khun *pen* **khon angkrit shai mai?** *Are* you English?

Negative statements with mai shai

We saw in Lesson 1 that you make a negative statement by putting **mai** before the verb.

khun Malee *mai yoo.* Malee *isn't* here.

If you want to make a sentence with **pen** negative, however, you use **mai shai** instead of **pen**:

phom *mai shai* **khon angkrit.** *I'm not* English.

Questions with thammai

pai thammai? Why are you going? (i.e. What are you going for?)

thammai can be used (like the question word 'why') either when you want an explanation or when you want to know the purpose of something. When it is used at the end of the sentence, as in this dialogue, it often asks for the purpose of something ('what ... for?'). To ask for an explanation, you normally use **thammai** at the beginning of the sentence.

Language and culture notes

sanuk

sanuk is another of those words or expressions (like **mai pen rai**) which are often used to sum up Thai culture. It often means 'fun' but can also cover what in English we would describe as 'enjoyable'

or entertaining. Things that can be **sanuk** include an entertaining
film, a readable book, a good game of football, a pleasant evening at
a restaurant with friends, an interesting lecture, etc. Thais are
famous for enjoying life and wanting to have fun so you will often
find that the first question you are asked about something is
whether it was **sanuk**. And to say something is **mai sanuk** is strong
criticism indeed!

Vocabulary

Adjectives for nationalities

1 Saowalak pen khon thai. Ming pen khon cheen. Dulip pen
khon lao. Wan Omar pen khon malesian. Rico pen khon yeepun.
Yves pen khon farangset. Ed pen khon amerikan.
2 khao pen khon thai shai mai? mai shai. pen farang.

thai	Thai	**yêepùn**	Japanese
cheen	Chinese	**faràngsèt**	French
lao	Laotian	**amerikan**	American
malesian	Malaysian	**faràng**	foreigner (westerner)

Note: you will hear **farang** used very commonly to refer to any
European- or American-looking foreigner.

Names of countries

In informal speech the same word is often used for the adjective of
nationality and for the country. It is more correct, however, to use
the word **meuang** ('country') first. In some cases the use of **meuang**
or an equivalent is necessary, as with **meuang thai**:

meuang thai	Thailand
angkrìt	England or English
amerikar	America
yêepùn	Japan
ìtarlêe	Italy

Exercise 1

Respond to these statements by giving the person's nationality:

1 khun Dusit mar chark krungthep.
2 Philip mar chark London.
3 Don mar chark Washington.
4 Yves mar chark Paris.
5 Wu Tan mar chark pakin.
6 Wan Omar mar chark Kuala Lumpur.

Exercise 2

Ask if these people come from the capital of the country concerned.
Use **shai mai** or **reuh**.

1 phom pen khon farangset.
2 phom pen khon thai.
3 shan pen khon amerikan.
4 khao pen khon malesian.
5 shan pen khon angkrit.
6 rao pen khon cheen.

Exercise 3 ▮▮

Answer these questions about yourself:

1 khun tham ngarn thee London shai mai?
2 khun pen khon cheen reuh?
3 khun pai thieo krungthep shai mai?
4 khun mar chark New York shai mai?
5 khun pen khon angkrit reuh?
6 khun mar chark thee nai?
7 khun pen farang shai mai?

Exercise 4

Correct these statements:

1 Yves pen khon cheen.
2 Wan Omar pen khon angkrit.
3 Saowalak pen khon lao.
4 Steve pen khon thai
5 Wei Lin pen khon farangset.

Exercise 5

Say which country the following people come from:

1 Ken mar chark Leeds.
2 Manat mar chark krungthep.
3 Rico mar chark Tokyo.
4 Ed mar chark New York.
5 Tino mar chark Rome.
6 Ena mar chark Khon Kaen.

Exercise 6

See how many sentences you can make with this table:

Ken	pai thieo		angkrit
Ena	mar chark	meuang	itarlee
Manat	pai thura thee		thai
Suchat	yoo thii		amerikar
			yeepun
			lao

Exercise 7

How would you ask someone why they:

1 are going to the market
2 have come to London
3 are going to the airport
4 are going to Bangkok
5 are going to the hotel

Exercise 8

Answer the questions you asked in Exercise 7.

Exercise 9

See how many sentences you can make from these words. You can use any word more than once.

pai   mai   thammai   London   mar   shai   chark   yoo   thee

Exercise 10

Complete these dialogues:

Dialogue 1
A: pai _____ khrap?
B: _____ kha.
A: _____ thammai.
B: pai _____.
A: _____.
B: khorpkhun mark kha.

Dialogue 2
A: _____ pen khon _____ shai mai?
B: _____ khrap. _____ angkrit _____?
A: _____ cheen.

Exercise 11

Rewrite the dialogue above to take place between Lisa and Suchat. Lisa is an Italian woman on business in Bangkok and is not enjoying it.

Dialogue 🔲

Ken carries on talking to the waitress, who asks him about his family

WAITRESS: shan mee pheuan. yoo thee London. khao pen khon ruey mark. mee faen duey. faen pen khon angkrit. khorthoht kha, khun mee faen mai kha?
KEN: mee khrap.
WAITRESS: pen khon angkrit shai mai kha?
KEN: shai khrap.
WAITRESS: khun mee look mai kha?
KEN: mai mee khrap. mai mee look.

WAITRESS: *I have a friend. He lives in London. He's very rich. He has a wife as well. She's English. Excuse me, have you got a wife?*
KEN: *Yes.*
WAITRESS: *Is she English?*
KEN: *Yes, she is.*
WAITRESS: *Do you have any children?*
KEN: *No, we don't have any children.*

Vocabulary

faen	boyfriend, girlfriend, husband, wife	**ruey**	rich
		mee	to have
lôok	child, children	**phêuan**	friend

Language points

Use of adjectives

phom ruey.   I am rich.

Notice that you do not use the verb 'to be' with adjectives: the adjectives can actually be used like verbs, so that **ruey** can mean 'rich' or 'to be rich'. Singular and plural forms of adjectives are exactly the same. In questions and negatives the adjectives function exactly like verbs:

khun ruey mai?   Are you rich?
shan mai ruey.   I'm not rich.

We saw earlier in this lesson that adjectives of nationality follow the noun they modify. Other adjectives are used in the same way:

khao pen *khon ruey*   He's a *rich man*.

Indicating possession (mee)

mee can mean 'to have' when referring to relationships as in the dialogue.

mai *mee* look.   I don't *have* children.

It also means 'have' in the sense of possession:

khun *mee* barn mai?   Do you *have* a house?

You can also use it to mean 'there is' or 'there are':

mee rohng raem mai?   Is *there* a hotel?
mai *mee* khon.   *There's* nobody here.

Omission of articles and determiners

mee look mai? Do you have any children?

Notice that, just as Thai does not use definite or indefinite articles, there is no need to use words like 'some' or 'any':

mai mee look. I don't have any children.

You can see that the same few words can mean a lot of different things, depending on the context. **mee look** can mean 'I or you or somebody else has a child or children'!

Language and culture notes

faen

faen originally meant 'admirer' and came from the English word 'fan'. It then passed into colloquial use as 'boyfriend' or 'girlfriend'. In very informal speech, however, it can also be used to refer to your partner or spouse. You will in due course learn more formal words for 'husband' and 'wife'.

Topics of conversation

Thais will often start a conversation by asking where you are from or about your family. You should treat these conversation openers as polite enquiries not an attempt to pry into your personal life. There is one topic of conversation which figures much less prominently than in England, for example, and that is the weather. Only if it is exceptionally hot or there is a particularly heavy downpour will Thais bother talking about the weather. We will, however, practise some useful language for these occasions in Lesson 6.

Vocabulary

Adjectives referring to people

1 Dusit pen khon kae.

Saowalak pen khon sao. Steve pen khon num. Saowalak suey. Steve nar kliat. Cholada nar rak.

kàe	old
sǎo	young (for a female)
nùm	young (for a male)
sǔey	pretty
nâr klìat	ugly, disgusting
nâr rák	lovely (used, for example about a young child)

Notes: You will encounter a number of expressions containing the word **nar**. **nar** often indicates what in English can be conveyed by the present participle '-ing'. For example, **beua** alone means bored; **nar beua** means boring.

nar kliat often refers to physical appearance ('ugly'). But it can also be used to condemn something or some behaviour you disapprove of. Someone who is unwashed, gets drunk, or refuses to lend a friend some money can be described as **nar kliat**.

2 krungthep sanuk. London nar beua.

nâr bèua	boring, not fun

3
Steve pen khon ruey. mee ngern mark. Brian mai mee ngern. pen khon chon. Ken mee ngern nitnoi.

ngern	money	**chon**	poor
nítnòi	a little		

Both **mark** and **nitnoi** can be used to qualify nouns as well as adjectives: **suey mark**, **nar beua nitnoi**. We saw in Lesson 1 that Thai often repeats words for extra effect.

On its own, **mark** can be used to qualify an adjective and means 'very'. **dee mark** means 'very good'. You can use **mark mark** to emphasize this: **dee mark mark** means something like 'very, very good'. When you use **mark** with a noun such as **ngern** or **khon** it means 'a lot' and again **mark mark** makes the quantity even more impressive. You cannot, however, do this with **nitnoi**.

Exercise 12

Use the cues to practise asking and answering questions like this:
kae _____ kae mai? mai kae. sao.

1 dee
2 sao
3 sanuk

4 ruey
5 nar kliat
6 nar beua
7 chon
8 suey
9 num

Exercise 13

Now practise asking and answering questions using **pen khon** with these adjectives: **pen khon kae mai? mai shai. pen khon sao.**

1 dee
2 sao
3 ruey
4 thai
5 cheen
6 chon

Exercise 14

Give a short answer to these questions:

1 khun mee faen mai?
2 khun mee look mai?
3 krungthep mee sanarmbin mai?
4 khun mee ngern mai?
5 khun mee pheuan mai?
6 krungthep mee rohng raem mai?
7 khun mee apartmen mai?

Exercise 15

You start chatting to someone in a café. How many questions can you ask her about her work and where exactly she comes from?

Exercise 16

1 khun Suchart is a very successful businessman and a family man. Using words you have learnt so far tell someone as many things as you can think of that he has.
2 Martin lives alone in a squat in London and is broke. Tell some-one what a miserable time it is for him.

Exercise 17

How would you ask someone if they have:

1 a wife/husband
2 children
3 money
4 a house
5 an apartment
6 a job

Exercise 18

Say whether you think these are enjoyable or boring:

1 tham ngarn nak
2 yoo thee barn
3 yoo thee London
4 yoo thee krungthep
5 yoo thee rohng raem
6 pai talart
7 pai sanarmbin
8 pai thura
9 pai thieo

Now repeat the exercise underlining what you are saying with **mark**
or **mark mark** or qualifying it with **nitnoi**.

Exercise 19

Answer the questions on these short passages:

1 Why doesn't Saowalak like Bangkok?

KEN: khun Saowalak mar chark thee nai?
SAOWALAK: mar chark Chieng Mai khrap. tham ngarn thee
              krungthep.
KEN: sanuk mai?
SAOWALAK: mai sanuk. mai mee pheuan.

2 Why doesn't Saowalak live in a house ?

KEN: khun Saowalak yoo barn shai mai?
SAOWALAK: mai shai kha. yoo apartmen.
KEN: dee mai?

SAOWALAK: mai dee. shan mai mee ngern.

3   How do you know Steve is rich?

Steve mai tham ngarn. mee barn thee London. mee apartmen thee Paris. yoo New York. mai mee faen. wannee pai thieo yeepun.

Exercise 20

Match the sentences which make sense when used together:

khun Ken mar chark London	mai mee ngern
khun Martin pen khon chon	nar beua
khun Saowalak mai kae	pen khon ruey
khao mai shai khon chon	pen khon sao
yoo thee apartmen mai sanuk	pen khon angkrit

Exercise 21

Complete these dialogues with any words that fit:

Dialogue 1

KEN: _____ khun Manat.
MANAT: _____Ken. pai _____?
KEN: pai _____
MANAT: _____yoo thee nai?
KEN: yoo _____

Dialogue 2

A. khun _____ ngern _____?
B. _____ khon ruey. khun la khrap?
A. mee _____ mai _____ khon chon.

Exercise 22

1 How would you tell someone that you are fed up with your job, you don't have any friends and you haven't any money?
2 How would you ask someone where she comes from, where she works and whether she enjoys her job?
3 How would you tell someone that your boyfriend/girlfriend is Chinese and comes from Hong Kong? He/she lives in London and works in Oxford.
4 Your friend, who is twenty-three, pretty but broke, and works in

a hotel, has just married a particularly unattractive fifty-year-old millionaire who has a flat in three capitals. How would you describe them?

Vocabulary building

Thai contains many long words or compound nouns which can be built up from smaller ones. Here is a reminder of some words we have met in the first two lessons:

> **thee tham ngarn barn khon rohng raem** (*lit.* a place for guests) **suey dee pheuan**

Can you guess the meanings of these words?

1 khon tham ngarn
2 tham suey
3 ngarn barn
4 thee thamngarn
5 tham dee
6 pheuan barn

Tone practice

Practise the tones in these words:

lôok sǔey nâr khȉat nâr bèua phêuan nâr rák nítnòi

Reading and writing

Consonants

ค ล ส ช

kh l s ch

Vowels

ลูก

oo

The letters 'w' ว and 'y' ย can be used as consonants or as vowel substitutes. Here they are used as vowels:

ลาว รวย

Here they are used as consonants:

วัน   ยา

wan   yar

Omission of vowels

Although there are some consonant clusters in Thai there are many common words where the vowel between two consonants in omitted. In words consisting of one syllable where there is no vowel between the consonants you usually insert the sound 'o'. For example:

จน

chon

Exercise 23

Write the transliteration for these words:

ลูก ลาว สูบ คน สวย จีน วัน

ทำไม   สาว จน

Exercise 24

Write these words in Thai script:

1 **khon**   2 **yar**   3 **suey**   4 **nom**   5 **ruey**   6 **doo**   7 **cheen**
8 **long**   9 **lao**   10 **wan**

Dialogue 📻

You overhear two people chatting at the next table in a café. They start off complaining about their work and then talk about their families

DUSIT: sawatdee khrap

SUTHAEP:	sawatdee khrap. khun sabai dee mai?
DUSIT:	sabai dee, khorpkhun khrap. khun la khrap?
SUTHAEP:	sabai dee. tham ngarn mark. khun la khrap?
DUSIT:	tham ngarn nitnoi, mai mark. mai mee khon. mai dee.
SUTHAEP:	khun tham ngarn thee nai?
DUSIT:	tham ngarn thee sanarmbin. mai sanuk. ngarn nar beua. khorthoht khrap, khun tham ngarn thee rohng raem Hilton shai mai khrap?
SUTHAEP:	mai shai, khrap. tham ngarn thee rohng raem Oriental.
DUSIT:	mm. khun mee ngern mark.
SUTHAEP:	mee nitnoi khrap.
DUSIT:	khun pen khon angkrit shai mai khrap?
SUTHAEP:	mai shai, khrap. pen khon amerikan. mar chark Boston. khun mee look mai?
DUSIT:	mai mee khrap. mee faen.
SUTHAEP:	faen pen khon thai shai mai khrap?
DUSIT:	mai shai, khrap. pen khon angkrit, mar chark Sheffield. yoo thee London. faen khun yoo thee nai?
SUTHAEP:	yoo thee London duey. look phom yoo thee amerikar. tham ngarn thee New York. mee ngern mark mark. pen khon ruey. thee New York mee apartmen suey mark.
DUSIT:	dee mark, khrap. OK. phom pai na khrap. laeo cher kan na khrap.
SUTHAEP:	shohk dee na khrap.

Comprehension

As you are naturally curious, make a note, in English, of where they work, where they are from and any other information they give about themselves and their families. How well do they know each other? What do they have in common?

4 phoot khui reuang khon 2

Talking about people (2)

In this lesson you will learn how to:

- use the numbers up to 100
- use the classifier **khon**
- ask about numbers of people
- indicate possession
- talk about someone's age
- give someone's occupation

Dialogue 📼

Ken continues his conversation with the waitress by asking about her family

KEN: khorthoht khrap. khun mee look mai?
WAITRESS: mee kha
KEN: mee look kee khon khrap?
WAITRESS: sorng khon, kha.
KEN: chingching reuh. pen phooshai reuh phooying?
WAITRESS: phooshai khon neung, phooying khon neung kha.
KEN: aryu thaorai khrap?
WAITRESS: phooying sarm khuap, phooshai sip see pee kha.

KEN: *Excuse me, do you have children?*
WAITRESS: *Yes.*
KEN: *How many?*
WAITRESS: *Two.*
KEN: *Really! Are they boys or girls?*
WAITRESS: *One boy and one girl.*
KEN: *How old are they?*
WAITRESS: *The girl is three, the boy is fourteen.*

Vocabulary

sǒrng	two
kèe	how many
chingching	really
phoôshai	boy
phoôyǐng	girl
nèung	one
aryú	age
thaôrài	how much
sìp sèe	fourteen
khuap, pee	year

Note: **khuap** is used for children under twelve. **pee** is used for any-one over twelve and is also the general word for year.

Language points

Numbers

The numbers 1 to 11 have to be learned individually:

1	2	3	4	5	6	7	8	9
nèung	**sŏrng**	**sǎrm**	**sèe**	**hâr**	**hòk**	**chèt**	**pàet**	**kâo**

10	11
sìp	**sìp èt**

Once you have learned these you can say any number up to 99! – with one exception: 20 (**yêe sip**). The others are all formed on the pattern **sip sorng**, **sip sarm** or **see sip, har sip,** etc. Learn one more – **roi** (100) – and you have every number up to 999!

The classifier khon

You will have noticed from the dialogue that Thai has a special way of referring to one or more persons (or things). Instead of saying, as in English, 'I have two children', Thai puts this as follows:

I have children two		persons
mee look	**sorng**	**khon**
noun	*number*	*classifier*

The word **khon** in this case is known as a classifier because there are different words for different sorts of nouns. In English we use a similar way of counting uncountable nouns. For example we usually say two bottles or glasses of milk rather than two milks. Thai uses the same system for all nouns. You can use the classifier **khon** for all people except monks and royalty (you should get by the first lessons of this book at least without needing this!). In later lessons we will gradually learn the other classifiers you need with other sorts of nouns.

kee ('how many')

Notice the word order in questions asking how many:

mee look *kee* **khon?** You have children *how many* people?

Since **kee** is automatically referring to a number of people or things you always use it with the appropriate classifier.

Language and culture notes

Polite responses: chingching reuh

> **phom pen khon ruey.**   I am a rich man.
> **chingching reuh.**   Really?

We saw in Lesson 3 that Thai often repeats a word for extra effect (as in **mark mark**). On its own, **ching** means 'true'. You can use **chingching** to mean 'for sure' or 'really' etc. as in:

> **phom pen khon ruey chingching.**   I *am* rich (It's true!)

As in English, **chingching reuh** can be used ironically as well as being a polite acknowledgement of what someone has said.

phooying, phooshai

These words really correspond to 'male' and 'female' as they cover not only 'boy' and 'girl' but also 'man' and 'woman'.

Vocabulary

> shan mee look sorng khon. phooshai khon neung. phooying khon neung.
> look shai aryu sip har pee. look sao aryu sip chet pee.

lôok shai	son
loôk săo	daughter

Exercise 1

Use the notes to answer the questions:

	people
hotel	9
airport	10
house	5
office	3
apartment	6

1   thee rohng raem mee kee khon?
2   thee sanarmbin mee kee khon?
3   thee barn mee kee khon?

4 thee opfit mee kee khon?
5 thee apartmen mee kee khon?

Exercise 2

Use the notes to tell someone how many friends/children/sons/
daughters these people have:

	Friends	*children*	*sons*	*daughters*
Suchart	2	7	5	2
Naowalak	10	4	1	3
Martin	0	0	0	0
Malee	3	1	0	1
Harry	6	5	1	4

Exercise 3

How would you ask someone how many of the following they have:
boyfriends/children/sons/daughters/friends/friends in the office/
people in their house:

Exercise 4

How would you tell someone these people's ages?

Cholada	2
Manop	47
Ena	23
Malee	35
Alex	6

Exercise 5

What question would you ask in these situations? You're not sure
whether:

1 someone is staying in the Hilton or the Oriental;
2 someone works at the airport or in a hotel;
3 someone's husband is from Bangkok or Chieng Mai;
4 someone is Thai or Lao;
5 there are four or five people in the house;
6 someone has sons or daughters (you know the children are the
  same sex).

Exercise 6

Match the numbers on the left with the figures on the right:

1	sarm sip kao	69
2	har sip hok	11
3	hok sip kao	48
4	chet sip et	39
5	see sip paet	56
6	sip et	71

Exercise 7

Here are the winning numbers in a lottery. Tell a friend who bought a book of tickets what they are:

a) 1734   b) 2686   c) 9424   d) 5317   e) 2746

Exercise 8

Answer these questions on the following dialogues:

1   How many men and women work in Suchart's office?

A: thee opfit mee khon tham ngarn kee khon khrap?
S: mee har sip khon khrap. phooying yee sip khon, phooshai sarm sip khon.

2   What does Martin tell Sakorn about his friends?

S: khun Martin mee faen mai khrap?
M: mee khrap. mee pheuan mark mark duey.
S: pheuan pen phooying reuh phooshai khrap?
M: phooying kao sip kao khon. phooshai khon neung.
S: phooshai tham ngarn thee opfit shai mai khrap?
M: mai shai, khrap. tham ngarn thee sanarmbin.

Exercise 9

Complete this dialogue:

A: _____, khun mee faen _____?
B: _____ mee look _____.
A: khun mee _____ khon?
B: har _____.

A: pen phooshai _____?
B: _____ phooying.
A: _____ !

Dialogue

The waitress tells Ken some more about her family in Chieng Mai

WAITRESS: lookshai shan pen nakrian. yoo thee Chieng Mai. yoo
kap khun mae. pai rohng rian, sabai sabai.
KEN: keng mai?
WAITRESS: keng mark kha.
KEN: khun phor khun tham ngarn shai mai khrap?
WAITRESS: shai, kha. pen tamruat kha. khun mae shan tham ngarn
duey. pen khroo.
KEN: lookshai khun rian kap mae khun duey shai mai?
WAITRESS: plao kha. khit war mai dee.

WAITRESS: *My little boy is a student. He is in Chieng Mai. He stays
with my mother. He goes to school. He's OK.*
KEN: *Is he clever?*
WAITRESS: *Very clever.*
KEN: *Does your father work?*
WAITRESS: *Yes. He's a policeman. My mother works as well. She's
a teacher.*
KEN: *Is your son in your mother's class (lit. learn with your
mother)?*
WAITRESS: *Oh, no. I don't think that's a good idea (lit. not good)*

Vocabulary

nákrian	student, pupil	**kèng**	clever, good at
mâe	mother	**phôr**	father
kàp	with	**tamrùat**	policeman
rohng rian	school	**khroo**	teacher
sabai sabai	(idiomatic phrase	**plào**	(negative particle)
	meaning something	**khít**	to think
	like 'no problem',	**wâr**	that
	'take it easy', 'It's OK'		

Language points

Possessives

In the dialogue you saw one way of indicating possession without any overt marker:

khun phor shan   my father (*lit.* father me)
khun mae Suchart   Suchart's mother (*lit.* mother Suchart)

You will see in Lesson 5 that you sometimes use a marker to show possession but this is optional in most cases.

Giving someone's occupation

As we saw in Lesson 3, **pen** is used as an equivalent of 'to be' when the subject complement is a noun. In Lesson 3 we saw this used to give someone's nationality. In this lesson we practise it to talk about occupations:

khao *pen khroo*.   He/she *is a teacher.*
khun Dusit *mai shai tamruat*.   Dusit *is not a policeman.*

The negative particle plao

Plao can be used in answer to all types of questions to show strong disagreement or correct firmly what someone has said.

khun pen khon angkrit reuh? plao kha!

Notice how you answer negative questions:

mai pai reuh?   You're not going then?

Confirming: **khrap** No, I'm not going.
Denying: **plao** On the contrary, I am going.

Vocabulary

Occupations

Khun Suporn pen mor. look shai khun Suporn pen nak thurakit. look sao pen lekharnukharn. faen khun Suporn pen mae barn.

| mǒr | doctor |
| nák thúrákìt | businessman |

(We will find **nak** used in a number of compounds to mean a person.)

| lekhǎrnúkarn | secretary |
| maê bârn | housewife |

Other words and expressions

khun manat pen mor. khun Jim ko pen mor

| kô | too |

A: shan mee looksao khon neung lae lookshai khon neung.
B: pen pai mai dai!

| laé | and |
| pen pai mâi dâi | That's not possible! |

Note: 'And' is used much less in Thai than in English. Very often it is omitted; you will also see there are ways of replacing it with other words. Thai has two words for 'and'. If you are enumerating each item in a list you use **lae**. If you are giving typical examples you use **laéo ko**.

Exercise 10

How would you ask someone if they are:

1 a teacher
2 a doctor
3 a housewife
4 a secretary
5 a businessman
6 a policeman
7 a waitress

You guessed wrong in each case. Suggest an answer for each of the questions you asked above.

Exercise 11

Invent three characters for a novel and describe them using the words you have learnt in this lesson and Lesson 3. Say where they come from, what their job is and describe them.

Exercise 12

Give short answers to these questions about yourself:

1 ngarn khun mai sanuk reuh?
2 khun pen khon ruey shai mai?
3 khun mae khun tham ngarn reuh?
4 khun mee look mai?
5 faen khun mai shai khon amerikan reuh?
6 khun yoo kap khun phor khun mae khun shai mai?
7 khun mai keng reuh?

Exercise 13

Use this table to ask six different questions:

khun mae		pen	khon angkrit	
khun phor	khao		mor	shai mai
look sao			nak thurakit	
look shai	khun		khon lao	reuh

Exercise 14

You have a very interesting family. Respond to these statements by saying that a member of your family does or is the same.

1 khun phor khun Saowalak pen nak thurakit.
2 khun mae khao yoo thee amerikar.
3 look shai khun Sakorn pai sanarmbin
4 ngarn shan nar beua mark.
5 look shan keng.

Exercise 15

How many sentences can you make from these jumbled words:

sao   khun   mai   pen   look   shan   mor   mae   barn   keng shai

Exercise 16

See if you can describe an unusual family. Perhaps there is something strange about their ages, their occupations, their nationalities or where they live. You should use only words that you have learned so far.

Exercise 17

Your friend is asking a lot of questions about someone you know only a little. Answer his questions by saying what you think to be the case.

1 khao pen khon amerikan reuh?
2 khao mee faen mai?
3 mee look kee khon?
4 khao yoo thee nai?
5 tham ngarn thee nai?
6 khao pen khon ruey shai mai?

Exercise 18

1 You are at the doctor's. The doctor asks your friend how many children she has, how old they are and where they are. Write what the doctor might ask and her replies.
2 How would you check if someone's mother is a secretary?
3 Someone thinks that your child goes to school. Correct them strongly and explain that the child stays at home with your friend quite happily.

Tone practice

Practise the tones in the numbers:

neung sŏrng sărm seè hâr hòk chèt paèt kâo sìp

Now practise the tone sequences in these numbers:

paèt sìp hâr	**sărm sìp sèe**	**yêe sìp hòk**
chèt sìp kâo	**hâr sìp sŏrng**	**yêe sìp sărm**

Vocabulary building

We saw in Lesson 3 that we can join words together to make compounds with new meanings. This exercise practises identifying the small words which have been joined together to make larger ones. First a reminder of some words we have met:

sanarmbin rohng rian nar kliat nar bue nar rak chingching

In the above words find a word which means:

1 to hate
2 to fly
3 to learn
4 a building
5 bored
6 a field
7 to love
8 true

Reading and writing

Consonants

ต ห ผ ฉ

t   h   ph   sh

Vowels

สอง

or

In Lesson 3 we saw that you sometimes have to add the vowel 'o' between consonants. On other occasions you have to add the vowel 'a':

ตลาด   สบายดี สนามบิน

Exercise 19

Practise writing these words in transliteration:

ผม ฉัน สาม หก มอง ตลาด สบายดี   สิบหก

Exercise 20

Practise writing these words in Thai script:

1 **hok**   2 **phom**   3 **sorng**   4 **shan**   5 **tok**   6 **morng**

Reading sentences

One of the difficulties in reading Thai script is that there is no space between words. You have to learn how to recognize separate words in a continuous sequence of letters.

Exercise 21

Here are some examples with words you already know. Write them in transliteration.

ผมไปสนามบิน   คนจีนมาทำงาน

ทำไมลูกทำงานนาน   ฉันรักคนจีนมาก

Dialogue

Jo and her family are living in Bangkok. Jo goes to see a doctor who first asks her about her family

MOR: khun aryu thaorai khrap?
Jo: sarm sip har pee kha.
MOR: faen khun tham ngarn thee krungthep shai mai khrap?
Jo: shai kha. pen mor.
MOR: khun mee look kee khon?
Jo: mee look sarm khon kha.
MOR: chingching reuh? phooying reuh phooshai?
Jo: phooying kha
MOR: phooying sarm khon reuh?
Jo: kha.
MOR: phom ko mee looksao sarm khon.
Jo: chingching reuh.
MOR: look sao khun aryu thaorai khrap?

Jo: aryu sorng khuap, see khuap lae hok khuap.
MOR: chingching reuh! look sao phom ko sorng khuap, see khuap
lae hok khuap. khun jo mar chark thee nay?
Jo: mar chark Manchester kha.
MOR: faen phom ko mar chark Manchester.
Jo: pen pai mai dai!
MOR: chingching khrap.

Comprehension

Make a note of what information Jo gives about the members of her family. Also note the various coincidences which emerge.

5 phoot khui reuang sing khorng

Finding out about things

In this lesson you will learn how to:

- ask what something is
- describe things using simple adjectives
- ask what something is like

Dialogue 🔘

Manat is taking Ken to his house. They are in the car on the way and Ken is interested in the surroundings

KEN: nan teuk arai khrap?
MANAT: nan wat khrap.
KEN: suey mark khrap.
MANAT: nee barn khorng phom khrap.
KEN: yai mark, khrap.
MANAT: mai shai lang nan khrap.
KEN: barn khun lang nai khrap?
MANAT: barn lang lek khrap.
KEN: barn yai khorng khrai khrap?
MANAT: mai sarp, khrap. khit war khon ruey mark.

KEN: *What's that building over there?*
MANAT: *It's a temple.*
KEN: *It's beautiful.*
MANAT: *This is my house.*
KEN: *Mm, it's very big.*
MANAT: *No, not that one.*
KEN: *Which house is yours?*
MANAT: *The little one.*
KEN: *Oh. Who lives in the big house?*
MANAT: *I don't know. Somebody very rich, I think.*

Vocabulary

teùk	building	**nán**	that
arai	what	**lék**	small
née	this, this is	**khrai**	who
khǒrng	(marker of possession)	**nǎi**	which
yài	big	**sârp**	know
lǎng	(classifier for houses)		

Language points

Classifiers

In Lesson 4 we saw the classifier for people (**khon**). We also use classifiers with concrete nouns. This is more complicated than talking about people as you use a different classifier with different types of objects. **lang**, for example, is used with houses, apartments. You will learn two other classifiers in this lesson and others later. The classifiers are used:

to indicate plurals:

> **mee barn sorng *lang*.**   There *are* two houses.

to specify what you are talking about:

> **barn *lang* nai?**   *Which* house?

to refer back to a noun you have mentioned:

> ***lang* nan.**   *That* one (i.e. that house).

Demonstratives

nee – near the speaker:

> **tamruat khon *nee***   *this* policeman

nan – away from the speaker:

> **tamruat khon *nan***   *that* policeman

nohn – further away but within view:

> **tamruat khon *nohn***   *that* policeman over there

Saying where something is

> **ngern yoo thee nai?**   Where's the money?
> **yoo thee *nee*.**   It's *here*.
> **yoo thee *nan*.**   It's *there*.
> **yoo thee nohn**   It's *over there*.

Possessives

We saw in Lesson 4 one way of expressing possession. A more explicit way is to use the word **khorng** ('belonging to'):

    ngern *khorng* phom   *my* money

khorng is optional unless the noun you are referring to is omitted:

    ngern *khorng* khrai?   *Whose* is the money?
    ***khorng* phom.**   *Mine.*

Questions with arai

arai normally has the same position in the sentence as the noun it refers to (this is usually at the end of the question):

    khun kin ***arai*?**   *What* are you drinking?
    kin karfae.   I'm drinking coffee.

Note an idiomatic phrase:

    pen arai?   What's the matter?

Questions with khrai

Like **arai**, **khrai** has the same position in the question as the word it refers to:

    barn lang nan khorng khrai?   Whose is that house?
    khrai yoo thee barn lang nan?   Who lives in that house?

Language and culture notes

The Buddhist temple

wat refers to a Buddhist temple compound which includes a number of buildings for religious offices and the daily life of the monks who live there. **wat** are referred to by their own individual name: **Wat Pho**, **Wat Arun**, etc.

Vocabulary

mee rohng phayarbarn sorng haeng, mee thanarkharn sarm haeng.

haèng	(classifier for buildings)
rohng phayarbarn	hospital
thanarkharn	bank

Exercise 1

You're standing on a hill showing your friend your home town. Near you is the school and your office. A little further away there is your house, the Shangri-La hotel and a bank. In the distance you can see the airport, the market and a hospital. Point them all out to him.

Exercise 2

You've just been on holiday and you're telling your friend about the place you visited. Tell her how many there were of the following (you can use the same classifier for all of them):

1 hotels
2 markets
3 banks
4 hospitals
5 airports
6 temples

Exercise 3

You do not always need to use the classifier with **nai**. In this exercise you will practise **nai** without the classifier. Respond to these statements by asking which one the person is going to.

1 khun phor phom pai sanarmbin
2 pheuan phom pai rohng phayarbarn
3 khao pai thanarkharn
4 look sao shan pai rohng rian
5 phom pai rohng raem
6 pheuan phom pai wat

Exercise 4

What question would you ask your friend in these situations:

1 She is chewing something – you're not sure what.
2 He's in the next room making a lot of noise and you want to know what he's up to.
3 She's about to hand over some money in a shop.
4 He's looking intently out of the window.
5 She's got a puzzled look on her face.
6 He doesn't look well.

Exercise 5

You are responsible for a group of tourists who have to go to different places. How would you ask them who is going:

1 to the airport
2 to the hotel
3 to the hospital
4 to have a coffee
5 shopping
6 to the bank

Exercise 6

In this conversation between three friends, what do B and C disagree on?

A: nan teuk arai khrap?
B: mai sarp khrap. khit war rohng phayarbarn.
C: mai shai rohng phayarbarn. pen thanarkharn amerikan. teuk suey mark khrap.
B: khit war mai suey khrap. teuk nan nar kliat khrap.

Exercise 7

Answer the questions on these short dialogues.

A: barn khun Malee yai mai kha?
B: yai mark kha.
A: barn khun saowalak yai mai kha?
B: mai yai kha.

1 barn khorng khrai yai?
2 barn khorng khrai lek?

A: faen khorng Saowanee kae shai mai kha?
B: mai shai khrap.
A: pen nak thurakit shai mai kha?
B: mai shai khrap. pen tamruat.
A: faen khorng Malee kae shai mai kha?
B: shai khrap.
A: pen mor shai mai kha?
B: mai shai, khrap. pen nak thurakit.

3 faen khorng khrai pen nak thurakit?
4 faen khorng khrai num?
5 faen khorng khrai kae?
6 faen khorng khrai pen tamruat?

Dialogue

*Janet is looking for a house to rent and has been to see one.
Saowanee asks her about it*

SAOWANEE: barn pen yangngai barng kha?
JANET: nar son chai kha. barn mai. suey.
SAOWANEE: yoo klai mai kha?
JANET: mai klai kha.
SAOWANEE: yai mai kha?
JANET: mee horng norn sorng horng. mee horng nang len
 duey.
SAOWANEE: horng khrua yai mai kha?
JANET: mai yai tae sa-art.
SAOWANEE: mee ae mai kha?
JANET: mee kha.
SAOWANEE: mee horng narm kee horng kha?
JANET: mai sarp, kha. mai hen.
JANET: phaeng mai kha?
SAOWANEE: phaeng nitnoi kha. sarm phan har roi bart.

SAOWANEE: *What is the house like?*
JANET: *It's interesting. It's new. It's pretty.*
SAOWANEE: *Is it far?*
JANET: *No, it's not.*
SAOWANEE: *Is it big?*

JANET:	*There are two bedrooms and a sitting room as well.*
SAOWANEE:	*Is the kitchen big?*
JANET:	*No, it's not but it's clean.*
SAOWANEE:	*Is it air-conditioned?*
JANET:	*Yes.*
SAOWANEE:	*How many bathrooms are there?*
JANET:	*I don't know. I didn't see.*
SAOWANEE:	*Is it expensive?*
JANET:	*It is a little. Three thousand five hundred bart.*

Vocabulary

pen yangngai		**nárm**	water
bârng?	what's it like?	**hôrng nárm**	bathroom, toilet
nâr sǒn chai	interesting	**hôrng khrua**	kitchen
mài	new	**tàe**	but
klai	far	**sa-àrt**	clean
hôrng	room, classifier for	**hěn**	see
	rooms	**phaeng**	expensive
norn	to lie down, sleep	**phan**	thousand
hôrng norn	bedroom	**bàrt**	(unit of Thai
nâng	to sit		currency)
lên	to play	**ae**	air conditioning
hôrng nâng lên	sitting room		

Language points

Noun compounds

A large number of noun compounds are formed in Thai by adding a verb or verbs to a base noun:

horng norn	(room for sleeping)
horng nang len	(room for sitting and playing)

Classifiers with compounds

With some compound nouns the classifier is the same as the base word in the compound:

horng norn	bedroom
mee horng norn sarm horng.	There are three bedrooms.

Expressing contrast

horng khrua lek tae sa-art.   The kitchen is small but clean.

Numbers over 1000

In Lesson 4 you learned the numbers up to one thousand. With only four more words you can say any number you are likely to need.

neung phan	1000
sorng phan	2000
neung meun	10,000
neung saen	100,000
neung larn	1,000,000
sorng larn	2,000,000

Language and culture notes

Currency

Bart is probably the only word to do with currency that you will need for prices. There are 100 **satangs** in a **bart** and there are still 25 and 50 **satang** coins but you can't buy very much with them.

Vocabulary

Steve pai khap rot. Saowalak pai chort rot.
rot khorng Steve mai suey. kao. sokkaprok duey.
barn khorng Steve yoo klai. barn khorng Saowalak yoo klai.
barn khorng Saowalak mee sanarm yar. barn nar yoo.
Steve pai doo barn Saowalak.

rót	car	**klâi** (high tone)	near
sòkkapròk	dirty	**sanǎrm yâr**	garden
kào	old	**nâr yoo**	*lit.* good to stay in
khàp	to drive	**doo**	to look
chòrt	to park		

thee barn mee ae. mee thohrasap. mee too yen duey.

thohrasàp	telephone
tôo yen	fridge (*lit.* cold cupboard)

Exercise 8

Your friend has been to see a house you are interested in. Ask if there are any of the following:

1 garden
2 garage
3 telephone
4 air conditioning
5 fridge

Exercise 9

Your friend has been to the house of a very famous person. Ask what these are like:

1 his house
2 his car
3 his wife
4 the kitchen
5 the sitting room
6 the bathroom
7 his children

You've been to see a friend who has been showing off her family and possessions. Some you were impressed with, some less so. Answer the same questions that you asked above.

Exercise 10

Use the notes to answer the questions.

1 barn phaeng mai?	5,000,000	bart
2 rot phaeng mai?	80,000	bart
3 apartmen phaeng mai?	17,000,000	bart
4 thee rohng raem Hilton horng phaeng mai?	2,450	bart
5 rohng rian phaeng mai?	2,710,000	bart
6 krungthep yai mai?	4,900,000	people
7 London yai mai?	19,000,000	people
8 Chieng Mai yai mai?	175,000	people

Exercise 11

Match the items in the first column with a contrasting item from the second column and connect them using **tae**.

barn kao	sokkaprok
rohng raem phaeng	keng
rot mai	suey
rohng phayarbarn yai	mai phaeng
khao pen tamruat	mai mee ngern
faen khorng khun Saowalak pen khroo	mai dee
khao pen khon ruey	mai keng
phooying suey	pen khon sao
khao pen mor	dee

Exercise 12

The following noun compounds are composed of words which you already know. Try to guess the meaning of the compound.

1 horng rian
2 rohng ngarn
3 khon rak
4 khon khap rot
5 khorng len

Exercise 13

1 Give a brief factual description of your house.
2 Now describe it to someone you badly want to sell it to.
3 Describe it to someone who wants to rent it but whom you would like to put off.

Exercise 14

Your friend has just moved into a new flat. How many questions can you ask her about it?

Exercise 15

How many questions can you make from these words?

khrai pai arai seuh thammai nai rot mai khun yoo thanarkharn

Tone practice 📼

Practise the difference between **klai** and **klai**.
Now practise the tones in these words

mâi pen rai   năi   yài   khrai
hôrng norn   hôrng nâng lên   hôrng nárm   hôrng khrua

Vocabulary building

1   Match the words with contrasting meaning:

mar	khroo
mark	sokkaprok
thura	kao
nar beua	pai
kae	phooying
nar rak	phor
ruey	nitnoi
phooshai	thieo
looksao	tham ngarn
nakrian	chon
mae	lookshai
sa-art	narkliat
mai	nar son chai
len	num

2   Find words in these lists which have something in common:

talart	thee thamngarn
khao	khroo
sanuk	rohng phayarbarn
ruey	seuh khorng
suey	nar son chai
rohng rian	horng khrua
mor	ngern
lekharnukarn	nar rak

Exercise 16

1   How would you explain to a friend who tells you that he's going
to the bank that there are five banks here and you'd like to know
which one he's going to?

2 You're in a strange town and someone asks you the way to the school.
3 You want to find out who owns a beautiful house that has just been built in your neighbourhood.
4 Your friend has just bought a car. Ask her what it's like, whether it's new and if it was expensive.
5 You're interested in a flat your friend knows about. How would you find out about the garage?

Reading and writing

The tone mark '

This tone mark changes the tone of a syllable to a falling or low tone depending on the class of the consonant (see p. 8). This book will not enable you to read Thai words that you do not know so you do not need at this stage to try to work out the tone from the written Thai.

Vowels

เล่น   แปด   เป็น
เ   แ   เ

len   paet   pen

Consonants

พ   พัน

ph   phan

Exercise 17

Write these words in transliteration:

สี่ พ่อ แม่ เวลา เห็น เย็น
เล็ก แพง แก่ แต่

Exercise 18

Write these words in Thai script:

1 **phor**   2 **yen**   3 **phaeng**   4 **len**   5 **lek**   6 **tae**   7 **phoot**

Dialogue 🔲

Janet is looking for a house to rent. Malee has a friend with a house that she's renting. Janet is asking her about it

JANET: barn pen yangngai barng kha?
MALEE: suey mark kha.
JANET: phaeng mai kha?
MALEE: phaeng nitnoi kha.
JANET: thaorai kha?
MALEE: har phan sarm roi bart kha.
JANET: phaeng mark.
MALEE: phaeng tae suey.
JANET: yai mai kha?
MALEE: yai mark kha. mee horng norn sarm horng. horng nang len
         sorng horng, horng narm see horng.
JANET: horng nang len pen yangngai kha?
MALEE: nar yoo kha. suey kha.
JANET: mee thee chort rot mai kha?
MALEE: mee kha. mee sanarm yar duey.
JANET: sanarm yar pen yangngai kha?
MALEE: lek, tae suey kha.
JANET: barn khorng khrai kha?
MALEE: khorng pheuan shan kha.
JANET: thammai pheuan khun mai yoo thee barn nan kha?
MALEE: khao tham ngarn thee London kha.
JANET: barn yoo klai mai kha?
MALEE: klai nitnoi kha. yoo klai rohng phayarbarn. pai doo mai
         kha?
JANET: pai see kha.
             . . .
JANET: barn yoo klai mai kha?
MALEE: mai klai kha. khun hen teuk nan mai kha?
JANET: hen kha. nan teuk arai kha?
MALEE: nan rohng phayarbarn kha. klai rohng phayarbarn mee
         barn sorng lang. barn khorng pheuan shan lang nan.

JANET: mm. nar yoo mark kha.

Comprehension

Make a note of the details Malee gives of the house.

6 khreuang deuhm lae aharn

Food, drink and other essentials

In this lesson you will learn how to:

- express likes and dislikes
- order food and drink in a restaurant
- ask what is available
- express quantity

Dialogue 🔊

Akorn has invited Ken out for a meal

AKORN: khun shorp aharn thai mai khrap?
KEN: shorp khrap.
AKORN: thee nee mee plar aroi khrap.
KEN: mai kin plar, khrap. mai kin neua sat. kin tae phak khrap.
AKORN: ching ching reu. (*to the waitress*) khor tom yam kung lae phak ruam sorng charn khrap.
KHON SERP: kha. khun deuhm arai mai kha?
AKORN: khor bia sorng khuat khrap.

AKORN: *Do you like Thai food?*
KEN: *Yes, I do.*
AKORN: *The fish here is very good.*
KEN: *I don't eat fish. I only eat vegetables.*
AKORN: *Really! (to the waitress) A prawn soup and two mixed vegetables, please.*
WAITRESS: *Do you want anything to drink?*
AKORN: *Two bottles of beer, please.*

Vocabulary

shôrp	to like	**khǒr**	to request, ask for
ahǎrn	food		
plar	fish	**tôm yam**	spicy soup
aròi	delicious, good (of food)	**kûng**	prawn
		ruam	mixed
nêua	beef	**charn**	plate
nêua sat	meat	**bia**	beer
phàk	vegetables	**khùat**	bottle

Language points

Expressing likes and dislikes

shorp ('to like') can be followed by a noun or a verb phrase:

shorp **aharn farangset.**	I *like* French food.
shorp **pai talart.**	I *like* going to the market.

mai shorp is used in the same way:

> ***mai shorp* aharn cheen.**   I *don't like* Chinese food.

To say how much you like something you can use **nitnoi** or **mark**:

> **shorp aharn thai mai?**   Do you like Thai food?
> **shorp *mark*.**   I like it *a lot*.
> **shorp *nitnoi*.**   I like it *a little*.

Requesting something

khor (*lit.* 'I request') is often used to ask for or order something.

> ***khor* bia khrap.**   A beer *please*.

Notice that in spoken Thai there is no simple equivalent of 'please'. Politeness is signalled by the use of **khrap/kha** and words like **khor**.

'Anything', 'anyone' and 'anywhere'

We saw in Lesson 5 the use of the question word **arai** to mean 'what'. When **arai** is used with another question marker such as **mai** it means 'anything':

> **deuhm *arai*?**   *What* are you drinking?
> **deuhm *arai mai*?**   Are you drinking *anything*?

With a negative marker it means 'nothing':

> **mai *mee arai***   There's *nothing*.

khrai and **nai** are used in the same way:

> **mai *mee khrai***   There *isn't anybody*
> **pai har *khrai* mai?**   Are you going to see *anybody*?
> **pai *nai* mai?**   Are you going *anywhere*?
> **mai pai *nai*.**   I'm not going *anywhere*.

Uncountable nouns

In English we often use a word like 'piece of' or 'glass of' to refer to one or more units of an uncountable noun. Thai uses equivalent words in the same way:

> **khor bia *sorng khuat*.**   *Two bottles* of beer, please.
> **khor khao *sorng charn*.**   *Two plates* (portions) of rice, please.

Asking about types or numbers of things

We use **arai** when we are referring to one thing:

khun seuh *arai*?	What are you buying? (assumes you are buying one particular thing)
khun seuh *arai* barng?	What are you buying? (assumes you may be buying several things)

We use the same construction to ask for a list of what is available:

mee phak arai barng?	What vegetables are there?

Asking what is available

We have seen that **mee** ('to have') is also used to mean 'there is/are':

mee kung mai?	Are there any prawns?

Language and culture notes

Talking about food

Thais eat out a lot as there is a vast range of reasonably priced restaurants and stalls. The two key words to know are **aroi** and **phet**. To tell someone you are enjoying the food, just say **aroi!** ('it's good, delicious'). You will often be asked: **aroi mai?** ('do you like it?'), to which the polite answer is **aroi mark khrap/kha!** You will also be asked if you like your food **phet** (spicy). Thai food is famous for its mouth-numbing use of chillies and Thais will be delighted (and surprised) if you like your food **phet**.

Vocabulary

pai kin khao thee rarn aharn thai. hiu. hiu narm duey. aharn thai phet.

khor phonlamai ruam lae narm sorng kaeo lae karfae thuey neung.

rárn ahǎrn	restaurant	**phǒnlamái**	fruit
hǐu	hungry	**kâeo**	glass
hǐu nárm	thirsty	**thûey**	cup
phèt	spicy		

khor khao phat kai charn neung.

phàt	fry, fried
kài	chicken

Exercise 1

Ask if any of the following are available:

1 beer
2 vegetables
3 prawns
4 chicken
5 mixed vegetables
6 fish
7 water

Exercise 2

You have run out of everything except vegetables and water. How would you answer the questions in Exercise 1?

Exercise 3

Answer these questions giving your own likes and dislikes:

1 shorp aharn cheen mai?
2 shorp kin bia mai?
3 shorp yoo thee barn mai?
4 shorp ngarn khorng khun mai?
5 shorp pai seuh khorng mai?
6 shorp khon angkrit mai?
7 shorp khap rot mai?

Answer the questions again saying how much you like each.

Exercise 4

Ask a follow-up question using **shorp**

1 shan pai deuhm karfae.
2 shan pai tham ngarn.
3 shan pai talart.
4 phom pai thieo krungthep.

5 phom pai rarn aharn yeepun.
6 phom pai rohng rian.

Exercise 5

You are on your own in a restaurant and you're starving. Order six different things to eat and at least two to drink.

Exercise 6

Now you are with a group of friends who have persuaded you to take charge of the order for them. Here is what you have to order:

1 two bottles of water
2 three glasses of beer
3 four cups of coffee
4 five portions of mixed fruit
5 three plates of prawn fried rice
6 four bowls of chicken soup

Exercise 7

1 Your friend is being particularly uncommunicative on the phone. Ask him if he is going anywhere, going to eat or drink anything, if he's doing anything and if there's anyone at home with him.
2 Your friend is sulking – how would he answer 'no' to all the questions you asked him.

Exercise 8

In each of the following situations you assume there will be more than one thing, place or person involved. How would you ask someone:

1 who is at home with them
2 what they are going to buy in the market
3 what places they are going to
4 what fruit there is in the house
5 what vegetables there are in the market
6 what fish there are in the restaurant

Exercise 9

From the following dialogue, answer these questions:

1 Where is Steve going and why?
2 What are his opinions of Thai food?

AKORN: khun Steve pai nai khrap?
STEVE: pai rarn aharn thai khrap
AKORN: hiu may khrap?
STEVE: mai hiu, hiu narm.
AKORN: khun Steve shorp aharn thai shai mai?
STEVE: shorp nitnoi khrap. phet mark.
AKORN: mai shorp tom yam reuh?
STEVE: mai aroi. phet mark!
AKORN: shorp phonlamai thai mai?
STEVE: shorp mark khrap.

Dialogue 🔘🔘

Ken decides to try some fruit in a street market

KEN: saparot bai nee thaorai khrap?
STALLHOLDER: bai neung yee sip bart. warn kha. ao mai kha?
KEN: ao sorng bai khrap. mamuang khai yangngai khrap?
STALLHOLDER: kiloh la hok sip bart.
KEN: thammai phaeng khrap?
STALLHOLDER: mai phaeng rok kha. duen nee mee mamuang noi. fon mai tok. nao mark duey.
KEN: warn mai khrap?
STALLHOLDER: warn mark kha. thot lorng mai kha?
KEN: khorpkhun khrap. aroi khrap. khor kiloh neung khrap.

KEN: *How much are the pineapples?*
STALLHOLDER: *Twenty bart each. They are sweet. Would you like some?*
KEN: *I'll have two. How much are the mangoes?*
STALLHOLDER: *Sixty bart a kilo.*
KEN: *Why are they (so) expensive.*
STALLHOLDER: *That's not expensive. This month there are only a few mangoes. There's no rain. It's cold as well.*

KEN: *Are they sweet?*
STALLHOLDER: *Very sweet. Would you like to try one?*
KEN: *Thank you. Yes, it's good. I'll have a kilo.*

Vocabulary

sàparót	pineapple	**fǒn**	rain
bai	(classifier for fruit)	**tòk**	to fall
wǎrn	sweet	**fǒn tòk**	it's raining, it rains
ao	to take, have	**nǎo**	cold
khǎi	to sell	**thot lorng**	try
mamûâng	mango	**ròk**	(particle used to
kiloh	kilo		show polite
kiloh la	a kilo		disagreement or
nói	a few		contradiction)

Language points

Expressing quantity

We saw in Lessons 4 and 5 that words indicating quantity are used
with the appropriate classifier:

mee khon *lai khon.*	There are *several/many* people.
mee khon *barng khon.*	There are *some* people.
mee khon *noi khon.*	There are *few* people.
mee barn *lai* **lang.**	There are *several/many* houses.
mee barn *barng* **lang.**	There are *some* houses.
mee barn *noi* **lang.**	There are *few* houses,,

More on classifiers

The classifier **bai** is used with fruit as well as containers and docu-
ments or sheets of paper. We saw in Lesson 5 that classifiers are used
when you need to specify an object or indicate a number of objects:

mee saparot kee bai?	How many pineapples are there?
mee saparot sorng bai.	There are two pineapples.
saparot bai nai dee?	Which pineapple is good ?
saparot bai nee dee.	This pineapple is good.

The classifier can also be used in the same way as 'one' when it is clear what you are referring to. For example, you have mentioned or you are looking at two pineapples and you ask:

bai nai warn?   Which one is sweet?

Hot and cold

nao ('cold') and **rorn** ('hot') can be used to mean either 'It's hot' or 'I'm hot', 'he's hot', etc:

rorn mark!   It's very hot!
nao mai?   Are you cold?

Language and culture notes

Polite contradictions

Adding **rok** to the sentence when you are disagreeing with, correcting or contradicting something softens what you are saying so as to make it more polite. Without it you could sound rather abrupt or even rude:

suey na kha.   Mm, that's pretty.
mai suey rok   No, it isn't.

Talking about the weather

As we said in Lesson 3, Thai weather is not changeable enough to make it the staple topic of conversation it is in England, for example. Thais will, however, often complain if it is particularly hot or raining particularly heavily.

Vocabulary

mee phonlamai lai bai. mee kluey, taeng moh, som, laeo ko malakor. som mai warn. prieo.

klûey	banana	**malakor**	papaya
taeng moh	water melon	**prîeo**	sour
sôm	orange		

A: rap arai kha?

B: ao khao phat moo. mai ao khorng warn. kep satang duey khrap.

mǒo	pork	**khǒrng wǎrn**	dessert
ráp	(*lit.* receive)	**kep satang dûey**	bill, please!

wannee mai nao. rorn.

rórn   hot

Exercise 10

1 Describe the composition of this college using the words of quantity you learned in this lesson:

khon cheen	25
khon thai	150
khon amerikan	750
khon malesian	27
khon angkrit	650
khon yeepun	175

2 Describe the number of buildings there are in these cities

	A	B	C
hospitals	2	5	17
hotels	75	7	35
banks	3	85	25
restaurants	280	45	7

Exercise 11

How would you ask the price of:

1 the fruit
2 the fish soup
3 the pineapples
4 the mangoes
5 the beer
6 the coffee
7 the water

Exercise 12

You are making a large fruit salad for a party. How would you ask for:

1 three bananas
2 four mangoes
3 five pineapples
4 two water melons
5 three papayas
6 four oranges

Exercise 13

What would you ask someone in these situations:

1 She has just started on a tasty looking dish of fried rice.
2 He has taken his first bite of a juicy mango.
3 Her face is getting red as she eats her prawn soup.
4 An expression of disgust crosses his face as he tries an exotic delicacy.
5 She claims she hasn't eaten all day.
6 His eyes light up when he sees a pub.
7 She grimaces as she tries a green mango.
8 He licks his lips as he finishes off some gigantic prawns.
9 She is shivering as the air conditioning has been turned up.
10 He is perspiring in the midday sun.

Exercise 14

Steve is trying to do some shopping. Why is he unsuccessful?

STEVE: malakor rarkhar thaorai khrap?
STALLHOLDER: bai la sip bart kha.
STEVE: thammai phaeng?
STALLHOLDER: mai phaeng rok. duen nee mee malakor noi.
STEVE: mee som mai?
STALLHOLDER: mee tae mai warn kha.
STEVE: thammai mai warn khrap?
STALLHOLDER: fon mai tok mark kha. rorn mark.
STEVE: mee taeng moh mai khrap?
STALLHOLDER: mai mee kha.
STEVE: thammai khrap?
STALLHOLDER: fon tok mark kha. mai mee taeng moh.

Exercise 15

Complete this dialogue at the fish stall:

STEVE: _____ kung _____ khrap?
STALLHOLDER: kiloh _____ khrap.
STEVE: thammai _____?
STALLHOLDER: _____ phaeng _____
STEVE: _____ mai khrap?
STALLHOLDER: aroi _____ kha. _____ mai kha?
STEVE: _____.

Tone practice 🔲

Practise the tones in these words and phrases:

**shôrp   ahǎrn   kûng   phàk   phèt   kaêo   thûey   aròi   nǎo
rórn   hǐu   hǐu nárm   plar   wǎrn   aròi mârk   nǎo mârk
rórn mârk   hǐu mârk   hǐu nárm mârk   wǎrn mârk**

Vocabulary building

Find the odd one out in these groups of words:

1 **phonlamai   mamuang   taeng moh   khao   som**
2 **kai   neua   moo   kung**
3 **phak   plar   shorp   kluey**
4 **kluey   kung   malakor   bai   narm**
5 **thohrasap   khuat   charn   thuey   kaeo**
6 **too yen   horng khrua   rarn aharn   charn   thee chort rot**
7 **neua   kai   phonlamai   pla   phak   khorng warn**
8 **klai   aroi   phet   warn   prieo**

Reading and writing

The tone mark ◌ั

We saw in Lesson 5 that the tone mark **'** changes the tone of a syllable. The tone mark **◌ั** is used in the same way; it changes the tone in a syllable or word with a low-class consonant to a high tone. With other consonants it changes it to a falling tone.

Consonants

ช   บ

shorp   khao

Vowels

โ   โรงแรม   มะม่วง   กุ้ง

oh   a   u

rohng raem   mamuang   kung

Exercise 16

Write these words in transliteration:

กุ้ง   ผู้ชาย   ห้องนอน   ห้องนั่งเล่น

ห้องครัว   ห้องน้ำ   น้ำส้ม   แตงโม

Exercise 17

1 Write these words in Thai script:

hotel   prawn   Good luck!   bottle   orange juice   papaya
mango

2 Write a menu with the words for food and drink that you know in
Thai script.

Dialogue ▣▣

Suporn has invited his friend Janet out for a meal

SUPORN:	rao cha kin arai?
JANET:	mee arai barng?
SUPORN:	mee khao phat kung, khao phat kai, mee tom yam duey.
JANET:	shan mai kin kung. mai shorp.
SUPORN:	reu? mai shorp aharn thai reuh?
JANET:	shorp nitnoi. phet mark.

SUPORN: mee khao phat moo khrap.
JANET: mai shorp moo kha. shan mai hiu.
SUPORN: (*to the waitress*) khun khun!
KHON SERP: sawatdee kha. khun rap arai kha?
SUPORN: khor khao phat kung charn neung, laeo ko ...
JANET: shan mai kin arai. mai hiu.
KHON SERP: deuhm arai mai?
SUPORN: khor karfae thuey neung lae narm khuat neung
JANET: mee khorng warn arai barng?
KHON SERP: mee tae phonlamai kha.
SUPORN: mee phonlamai arai barng?
KHON SERP: mee taeng moh, saparot, mamuang laeo ko malakor.
JANET: kluey mee mai ?
KHON SERP: mai mee kha.
JANET: shan mai shorp phonlomai thai.
SUPORN: khor phonlamai ruam charn neung.
JANET: mamuang warn mai?
KHON SERP: mai warn kha. prieo.
JANET: mai ao mamuang.
SUPORN: kep satang duey khrap.

Comprehension

1 What is on the menu?
2 What does Janet like and not like?
3 What do they order?

7 tharm reuang thanon hon tharng

How to get there

In this lesson you will learn how to:

- ask for and give directions
- say where something is located
- tell someone to do something
- say what you have done or been doing
- talk about a journey

Dialogue 🔲

Manat has invited Ken to his house. Ken has never been before so he has to find out where to go

KEN:	khun phak yoo thee nai khrap?
MANAT:	phak yoo thanon Tarksin soi 13 khrap.
KEN:	Tarksin soi 13 yoo trong nai khrap?
MANAT:	khun roochak rohng phayarbarn Kungton mai khrap?
KEN:	roochak khrap.
MANAT:	khun dern pharn rohng phayarbarn pramarn har narthee laeo ko hen soi 13.
KEN:	yoo tharng sai reuh tharng kwar?
MANAT:	yoo tharng sai khrap.

Later in the taxi coming from the other direction

KHON KHAP ROT TAEKSEE:	trong nai khrap?
KEN:	trong pai khrap. korn rohng phayarbarn lieo kwar. chort trong nee khrap.

KEN:	*Where do you live?*
MANAT:	*Tarksin Street, sidestreet 13.*
KEN:	*Where is that?*
MANAT:	*Do you know the Kungton hospital?*
KEN:	*Yes.*
MANAT:	*You walk past the hospital for about five minutes and you'll see sidestreet 13.*
KEN:	*Is it on the left or the right?*
MANAT:	*On the left.*

Later in the taxi coming from the other direction

TAXI DRIVER:	*Which way?*
KEN:	*Straight on. Turn right before the hospital. Stop here.*

Vocabulary

phák	stay	**trong**	straight, right
thanǒn	street, road	**trong nǎi**	where exactly
soi	sidestreet off a **thanon**	**róochàk**	to know

dern	to walk	**sa̱i**	left
phàrn	after	**kwǎr**	right
narthee	minute	**trong pai**	straight ahead
pramarn	about	**liéo**	to turn
tharng	way	**kòrn**	before

Language points

Imperatives

You can make an imperative sentence by using the main verb alone:

pai!	Go away!
mar thee nee.	Come here.

This is fine in a neutral situation like giving directions (or with children, close friends, etc.) but would not work if you want to ask someone politely to do something. Ways of making imperatives polite will be dealt with in Lesson 8.

Negative imperatives

Imperatives can be made negative by adding **yar**:

yar **mar thee nee.**	*Don't* come here.

Again, you would not use this form alone to ask someone politely not to do something.

Directions

As in English you can give directions by using the normal affirmative form:

khun dern pharn rohng phayarbarn.	You walk past the hospital.

Adverbials of location and direction

Here is a summary of the expressions introduced so far in the lesson:

sai	(to the) left
kwar	(to the) right

tharng sai/kwar	on the left/right
pharn	after
korn	before
trong pai	straight on

'To know': sarp *and* roochak

There are several words in Thai which correspond to 'know'. **sarp** and **roochak** are amongst the most common. **sarp** means to know a fact, i.e. to know whether something is true. **roochak** is used in the sense of being acquainted with someone or somewhere. For example:

khao phak yoo thee nai?	**mai sarp.**
barn khao pen yangngai?	**mai sarp** or **mai roochak.** (i.e. I don't know his house)

sarp is a rather formal word. You will see an informal equivalent in Lesson 15.

Language and culture notes

thanon *and* soi

There are two kinds of streets in Thai towns. **thanon** are the main roads and **soi** are the sidestreets that branch off them. **soi** are usually numbered but some have a name as well.

Vocabulary

pam namman Esso yoo trong kharm rarn aharn thai. satharn thoot angkrit yoo klai rohng nang Century.

trong khârm	opposite	**sathǎrn**	place
pám námman	petrol station	**thôot**	Ambassador
námman	petrol, oil	**rohng nǎng**	cinema
sathǎrn thôot	Embassy	**nǎng**	film

Exercise 1

You have a particularly headstrong taxi driver. How would you tell him not to:

1 stop here
2 turn left
3 turn right
4 stop opposite the school
5 turn right after the hospital

Exercise 2

Look at the plan

A How would you ask a taxi driver to stop at each of the numbered positions?
B How would you tell him to take the next turning after each position/the turning before each position?

Exercise 3

Look at the plan below. Tell your friend how long it would take her to walk to the following places from the place before.

1 The British Embassy
2 St James school
3 The Chinese restaurant
4 The Golden cinema
5 The French bank

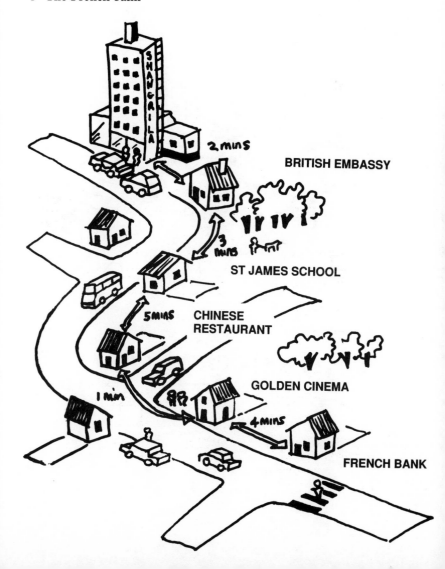

Exercise 4

From the following dialogue, mark on the plan the location of the following:

1 Suchart's house
2 the Italian Embassy

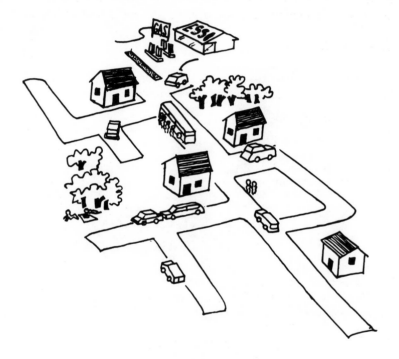

KEN:	khun Suchart phak yoo thee nai khrap?
SUCHART:	yoo thanon Tarksin soi sarm sip har khrap.
KEN:	soi sarm sip har yoo trong nai khrap?
SUCHART:	khun roochak pamnarmman Esso mai?
KEN:	roochak khrap.
SUCHART:	pharn pamnarmman lieo kwar laeo ko lieo sai. barn khorng phom yoo tharng sai.
KEN:	barn yoo klai satharn thoot itarlee shai mai khrap?
SUCHART:	shai khrap. barn yoo trong kharm satharn thoot itarlee.

Exercise 5

Your friend has just moved into a house in an area he does not know. Look at the plan and tell him how to get from his house to:

1 The Japanese bank
2 The Rex cinema
3 The airport
4 The French Embassy
5 The Thai restaurant

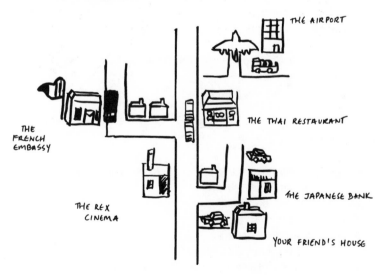

Exercise 6

Your friend gives you particularly vague directions how to get to her house. You have to keep asking her to be more precise. Write a dialogue.

Exercise 7

Ken had an unfortunate experience yesterday when he was trying to get directions. Summarize in English what happened. Ken is standing opposite the Rex cinema.

KEN: khorthoht khrap satharn thoot yeepun yoo thee nai?
A: mai sarp khrap.
KEN: yoo klai satharn thoot amerikan. khun roochak mai khrap?
A: mai roochak khrap.
KEN: khorthoht khrap. khun roochak satharn thoot yeepun mai khrap?
B: roochak. khun pharn satharnthoot amerikan lae ko lieo kwar.
KEN: yoo klai satharn thoot amerikan reuh khrap?
B: plao khrap. khun dern parn satharn thoot amerikan see sip har nathee. satharn thoot yeepun yoo trong kharm thanarkharn farangset.

Later, opposite the French bank

KEN: khorthoht khrap satharn thoot yeepun yoo trong nai?
C: satharn thoot yeepun, reuh. klai mark. khun roochak rohng nang Century mai khrap?
KEN: roochak.
C: satharn thoot yeepun yoo trong kharm rohng nang.
KEN: nan teuk arai khrap?
C: nan rohng rian yeepun, khrap.

Dialogue ▭

Saowanee has been away for a few days. Ken is asking her about it
KEN: pai nai mar khrap?
SAOWANEE: pai Phuket mar kha.
KEN: sanuk mai?
SAOWANEE: sanuk mark kha.
KEN: khun tham arai barng?
SAOWANEE: pai shai thale kha. pai thieo Ko Phi Phi. pai reua.
KEN: khun yoo thee nan kee wan khrap?
SAOWANEE: sorng wan thaonan kha.
KEN: pai yangngai khrap?
SAOWANEE: pai khreuang bin kha.
KEN: khreuang bin sia welar thaorai khrap?

SAOWANEE:	sia welar neung shuamohng kha.
KEN:	reo na khrap. khar tua phaeng mai khrap?
SAOWANEE:	mai phaeng kha. see phan bart thaonan kha.

KEN:	*Where have you been?*
SAOWANEE:	*I've been to Phuket.*
KEN:	*Did you enjoy it?*
SAOWANEE:	*Yes. Very much.*
KEN:	*What did you do?*
SAOWANEE:	*I went to the seaside. I went out by boat to Phi Phi Island.*
KEN:	*How long did you stay there?*
SAOWANEE:	*Only two days.*
KEN:	*How did you go?*
SAOWANEE:	*By plane.*
KEN:	*How long did the plane take?*
SAOWANEE:	*One hour.*
KEN:	*That's quick. Is the ticket expensive?*
SAOWANEE:	*No, it's not. Only four thousand bart.*

Vocabulary

pai nǎi mar?	where have you been?	**sǐa welar thâôrài?**	how long does it take?
shai thale	seaside	**shûamohng**	hour
kò	island	**thâô nán**	only
reua	boat	**tǔa**	ticket
khrêûang bin	aeroplane	**khâr tǔa**	fare
sǐa	to spend, waste	**reo**	quick
sǐa welar	to take time		

Language points

pai . . . mar

mar used after the main verb corresponds to the present perfect in English:

pai nai *mar*?	Where *have* you been?
pai seuh khorng *mar*.	I've *been* shopping.

Just as in English this is used to refer to the indefinite past and you do not use definite time expressions in conjunction with **mar** in this sense. **mar** is often omitted from the answers when the time reference is clear from the context:

pai nai mar?	Where have you been?
pai thieo.	I've been out.

Talking about means of transport

Notice that you do not need a preposition in sentences when saying how you travel somewhere:

pai khreuang bin.	I went by plane.

Language and culture points

Travel

A boat journey is often necessary to get to smaller islands around the coast of Thailand. They are also useful in Bangkok – the city is cut across by numerous canals (**khlorng**) as well as the river Chao Phraya so boats are a common and convenient form of transport. Taxis and buses are also cheap and plentiful in Bangkok (and other towns) as are three-wheel **samlors** or **tuk-tuk** and motorbike taxis. Buses and coaches go practically everywhere in Thailand, and many places are connected by rail or air.

Vocabulary

1 Forms of transport

pai rot taeksee phaeng. pai rot me mai phaeng. pai rot mortersai reo.

rót taéksêe	taxi
rót me	bus
rót mortersai	motorcycle

2

pai rot sia welar khreung shuamohng. pai rot tua sia welar sorng shuamohng khreung.

khrêung	half
rót tua	coach

3

A: shan yoo thee Chieng Mai sorng deuan.
B: rohng raem phaeng mai?
A: deuan la sarm phan bart
B: phom yoo thee Chieng Mai sorng arthit.

deuan	month
deuan la	per month (note you can also say **wan la**, **arthit la**)
arthít	week

4

  pai rot me narn. rot me shar. rot tit.

narn	(to take) a long time
shár	slow
tìt	to stick, get stuck

rot tit can mean either 'There's a traffic jam' or, more generally, 'the traffic's bad'.

5

A: shan mai pai thieo. mai mee ngern.
B: nar sia dai khrap!
A: khun pai thieo shai mai kha?
B: nae norn

nâr sǐa dai	What a pity!
nâe norn	sure, of course

Exercise 8

How do you tell your friend where you have been when she comes across you in the following situations:

1 you're holding a large wad of banknotes
2 you're at the wheel of a brand new car
3 you're laden down with shopping bags
4 you've got your arm in a sling
5 you're complaining of having stomach ache
6 you're jet-lagged
7 you're looking sun-tanned

Exercise 9

Complete this dialogue:

A: pai nai _____ kha?
B: _____ talart mar kha.
A: pai _____
B: pai _____ khorng kha.
A: seuh _____ kha?
B: seuh _____ kha.
A: pai _____ kha ?
B: pai reua kha.

Exercise 10

Your friend has had a horrendous journey. He started by plane, then had to transfer to a boat. Then he got a train. When the train broke down he continued by bus. The bus had an accident so he got a taxi. Ask him how long each took.

Exercise 11

How would he tell you that the plane took five hours, the boat three and a half hours, the train ten hours, the bus seven and a half hours and the taxi twenty-five minutes?

Exercise 12

How would you ask someone:

1 how many years she lived in Paris
2 how many days he walked
3 how many years she worked in a bank
4 how many minutes he stayed in the cinema
5 how many hours she stayed in hospital
6 how many weeks he worked in the French Embassy

Exercise 13

Find a question to fit these answers:

1 pai satharn thoot angkrit mar.
2 pai har pheuan.

3 nak thurakit khon cheen yoo thee barn lang nan.
4 pai rot sia welar see shuamohng.
5 khar tua rot me hok sip bart.
6 pai rot fai kha.
7 sorng arthit kha.

Exercise 14

Rewrite the conversation at the beginning of this part between Suchart and his friend Anna, who has just been on a coach trip to Paris.

Exercise 15

You are trying to explain to a friend how to get to your house. Answer her questions.

1 khun phak yoo thee nai khrap?
2 yoo klai mai khrap?
3 yoo klai rohng phayarbarn shai mai khrap?
4 pai yangngai khrap?
5 pai rot taeksee phaeng mai khrap?
6 sia welar thaorai khrap?
7 rot tit mai khrap?
8 dern narn mai khrap?
9 barn khorng khun yoo tharng sai reuh tharng kwar khrap?

Tone practice

Practise the tones in these words:

**liéo sái   liéo kwǎr   trong pai   trong khârm   sathǎrnthôot
rohng nǎng   sǐa welar thâòrài   shuâmohng**

Vocabulary building

1 Match the words with opposite or contrasting meanings:

reo	**warn**
kwar	**rorn**
korn	**shar**
nao	**sai**
prieo	**pharn**

2 How many words can you find in the lessons you have studied so far relating to travel and transport? To time?

Exercise 16

1 How would you tell your taxi driver (a) to stop opposite the Japanese restaurant? (b) Not to turn right after the petrol station?
2 How would you tell someone that you've just got back from holiday? You had a terrible time and a dreadful journey to get there.
3 How would you tell someone the advantages of going to see you by taxi?
4 Your friend has been on a walking holiday. Ask her how many hours a day she walked.

Reading and writing

Consonants

ฟ   กาแฟ ฝ   ฝน

f   karfae f   fon

Vowels

เิ-- เดิน

     dern

The tone mark ๋

This changes the tone of all syllables to a high tone.

The initial consonant substitute อ

We saw this symbol used as a vowel in Lesson 4. It can also be used to replace a consonant at the beginning of a word which would otherwise start with a vowel e.g. อะไร

In Thai script every word begins with a consonant letter or the

letter ย. There are two common words beginning with the sound of the letter ย which also start with the letter อ :
   อยู่ and อย่า (**yar**, 'don't').

Exercise 17

1 Write these words in transliteration:

ฝนตก   ไฟ ('light', 'fire') ไฟฟ้า ('electricity')

เดิน   เป็นคนฝรั่ง   อัฟริกัน   อัฟริกา อายุ

อิ่ม   ('to be full') เงิน เริ่ม ('start') อิตาลี

2 Answer these questions on the short texts below:

1 Where is the hotel?
2 Where is the hospital?
3 Where is Shartree?
4 How do you get to the airport?
5 Where is the market?

โรงแรมอยู่ตรงข้ามปั๊มน้ำมัน

โรงพยาบาลอยู่ผ่านโรงแรม

ชาตรีอยู่ที่ชายทะเล ตลาดอยู่ถนนตากสิน

ไปสนามบินเดินผ่านโรงแรมเดินตรงไป

Exercise 18

Look at the plan and write instructions to your friend on how to get
to your house.

Dialogue

*Ken is surprised to discover that Akorn does not live in the centre of
Bangkok*

KEN: khun phak yoo thee nai khrap?
AKORN: yoo Langsit khrap.
KEN: klai mai khrap?
AKORN: klai mark khrap.
KEN: thammai yoo thee nan khrap?
AKORN: barn mai phaeng khrap.
KEN: barn khorng khun pen yangngai barng khrap?
AKORN: yai mark khrap. suey duey. mee sanarm yar, mee thee chort rot.
KEN: barn mai shai mai?

AKORN: shai khrap. sorng pee laeo.
KEN: mee ae shai mai khrap.
AKORN: nae norn khrap!
KEN: pai tham ngarn yangnai?
AKORN: pai rot fai khrap.
KEN: rot fai sia welar thaorai?
AKORN: pramarn khreung shuamohng.
KEN: narn, ching ching. khar tua thaorai?
AKORN: deuan la hok roi bart.
KEN: phaeng mark khrap. khun mai mee rot reuh khrap?
AKORN: mee khrap.
KEN: thammai mai khap rot pai tham ngarn khrap?
AKORN: rot khorng phom kao laeo. kin namman mark. khar nam-man phaeng. rot tit mark duey. shar mark. phom khit war rot fai reo.
KEN: nar sia dai mai dai tham ngarn thee Langsit na khrap.

Comprehension

1 Why does Akorn live in Langsit?
2 What is his house like?
3 Why does he go to work by train and not use his car?

8 tharm reuang pheuan

Asking about people

In this lesson you will learn how to:

- introduce yourself and other people
- refer to future time
- identify someone
- refer to things that have already happened or not yet happened
- use some basic courtesies
- ask and talk about someone's health

Dialogue 🔲

Ken arrives at Malee's house. Malee's husband, Akorn, arrives later

KEN: sawatdee khrap. phom sheuh Ken. pen pheuan Anthony.
MALEE: sawatdee kha. shern kha. shern nang kha.
KEN: khorpkhun mark khrap.
MALEE: Anthony pen yangngai barng kha?
KEN: sabai dee. tham ngarn thee London. pen nak thurakit.
sarmee khun pai tham ngarn reuh khrap?
MALEE: shai kha. yang mai klap barn. eek har narthee cha mar
laeo kha. nan rot khao kha ... (*to her husband*) nee
pheuan khorng Anthony.
KEN: sawatdee khrap. phom sheuh Ken.
AKORN: sawatdee khrap. yindee thee dai roochak. khun pen
pheuan khorng Anthony reuh khrap?
KEN: shai khrap.
AKORN: phom khit theung khao mark. deuhm karfae mai khrap?
KEN: khorpkhun khrap. deuhm laeo khrap.

KEN: *Hello. My name is Ken. I'm a friend of Anthony's.*
MALEE: *Hello. Come in. Please sit down.*
KEN: *Thank you.*
MALEE: *How is Anthony?*
KEN: *He's fine. He's working in London. He's a businessman.*
Your husband has gone to work, has he?
MALEE: *Yes, he's not back yet. He'll be here in five minutes ... Ah,*
that's his car. (to her husband) This is a friend of Anthony's.
KEN: *Hello. I'm Ken.*
AKORN: *Hello, pleased to meet you. So you're a friend of Anthony's?*
KEN: *Yes. I am.*
AKORN: *I miss him a lot. Will you have some coffee?*
KEN: *No, thank you. I've had some already.*

Vocabulary

shêuh	to be called	**klàp bârn**	to go, come home
shern	to invite, please	**cha**	(marker of future time)
nâng	to sit, sit down	**laéo**	already
sǎrmee	husband	**yindee thêe dâi**	pleased to meet you
yang	still	**róochàk**	
yang mâi	not yet	**khít thěung**	to miss someone

Language points

Future with cha

We have seen that in many cases you do not need any explicit marker of past, present or future time in Thai. There are, however, one or two markers which you can use to make the reference more obvious. The question **pai nai** can, as we have seen, refer to past, present or future time. If you want to make it clear you are referring to the future, you should use **cha pai nai. cha** comes immediately before the main verb.

yang *('still' or 'not yet')*

yang **yoo thee krungthep**	He *still* lives in Bangkok.
yang **mai klap barn**	He hasn't come home *yet*.

laeo *('already')*

kin *laeo*	I have had something to eat/drink *already*.

laeo indicates an action that has already taken place. In English we can do this through the verb form alone (e.g. 'John has gone'). Since Thai does not have verb forms which indicate tense or aspect, **laeo** is sometimes used where we would not need to add 'already':

Steve mar laeo	Steve has come.

Language and culture notes

Saying 'please'

Just as there is no simple equivalent in Thai for 'yes' and 'no', neither is there for 'please'. If you are inviting someone to do something you can use **shern** in front of the verb:

shern nang khrap	Please sit down (go ahead and sit down).

shern on its own means 'go ahead'.

Formal and informal words

Like other languages Thai has formal words and informal words which express the same thing. **deuhm** is the formal word for drink; **kin** is the informal one and is used between people who know each other. **faen** in the sense of 'husband' or 'wife' is informal. **sarmee** is a more formal word as is the word for 'wife' which we meet later in this lesson. You need worry about this distinction only if you are likely to find yourself in very formal situations, however.

Vocabulary

phrungnee phom cha pai har mor. cha seuh buree.

phrûngnée	tomorrow	**burèe**	cigarette
hăr	to see, visit, call on		

Manat pen sarmee khorng Malee. Malee pen phanrayar khorng Manat. Manat mee phee norng sorng khon, phee sao khon neung, norng shai khon neung.

phanrayar	wife	**phêe săo**	elder sister
phêe nórng	brothers and sisters	**nórng shai**	younger brother

wannee phanrayar phom mai pai tham ngarn. mai sabai. pen wat. puat hua duey. phom ko mai pai tham ngarn. puat thorng. thorng sia.

mâi sabai	not well	**pùat**	ache
pen wàt	to have a cold	**thórng**	stomach
hŭa	head	**thórng sĭa**	upset stomach, diarrhoea

Exercise 1

Each of your friends is telling you where they are going tomorrow. Make a note of those who might see each other.

1 phrungnee shan cha pai seuh khorng
2 phrungnee shan cha pai har mor.
3 phrungnee phom cha pai London.
4 phrungnee phom cha pai rohng phayarbarn.
5 phrungnee shan cha pai sanarmbin.
6 phrungnee phom cha pai talart.

Exercise 2

Ask a follow-up question using **cha**.

1 phom cha pai seuh khorng.
2 shan cha pai rohng phayarbarn.
3 phom cha pai sanarmbin.
4 shan cha pai har pheuan.
5 phom cha pai kin khao.
6 phom cha pai thanarkharn.

Exercise 3

Your friend asks you what you're going to do when you leave work.
Tell her you're:

1 going home
2 going out for pleasure
3 going to see the doctor
4 going to buy a car
5 going to have something to eat

Exercise 4

You are a busy executive. You had asked one of your staff to go and
have lunch early, do some errands for you and come back to the
office. He hasn't returned. List all the things he has not done yet.

Exercise 5

You want to refuse these invitations by saying that you've already
done what is being suggested. What do you say?

1 kin karfae mai khrap?
2 kin khao mai kha?
3 soop buree mai khrap?
4 pai talart duey kan mai kha?
5 pai doo nang duey kan mai khrap?
6 deuhm bia mai khrap?

Exercise 6

Arrange these sentences to make a dialogue:

mai sarp khrap.
yang mai mar khrap.
phrungnee khao cha pai rohng phayarbarn shai mai kha?
khun Naowalak yoo mai kha?
eek sip narthee cha mar laeo.

Exercise 7

1 From this conversation find out who is unwell and what the matter is:

JANET: *phanrayar* khun pen yangngai barng kha?
MANAT: mai sabai khrap.
JANET: pen arai kha?
MANAT: *pen wat* khrap.

Now rewrite the conversation changing the italicized words and asking about Manat's elder sister/younger sister/elder brother/younger brother/father/mother.

2 Now do the same with this conversation:

JANET: *phanrayar* khun yang mai sabai yoo reuplao kha?
MANAT: shai khrap.
JANET: pen arai khrap?
MANAT: *puat thorng* khrap.

Exercise 8

A young man from Thailand calls on you claiming to be a friend of a friend. What questions could you ask him to see if he really knows your friend?

Dialogue ◖◗

Ken and Akorn have been invited to a party. Instead of circulating they start discussing some of the people around them

KEN: khon nan khrai khrap? khun roochak khao mai?
AKORN: khon nai khrap?
KEN: khon thee phoot kap Steve.
AKORN: khon uan shai mai? mai sarp. khit war pen khon mao.
KEN: khun roochak phanrayar khorng Steve mai?

AKORN: roochak khrap. khao mar thee nee reuplao?
KEN: plao khrap. khao pai thieo. cha klap barn phrungnee.
AKORN: khun roochak phooying thee deuhm pepsi mai?
KEN: roochak. sheuh Saowanee.
AKORN: taeng ngarn laeo reu yang khrap?
KEN: mai sarp. tharm thammai khrap?
KEN: khit war mar khon dieo.

KEN: *Who is that man over there? Do you know him?*
AKORN: *Which one?*
KEN: *The one who's talking to Steve.*
AKORN: *Oh, the fat one. I don't know. I think he's drunk.*
KEN: *Do you know Steve's wife?*
AKORN: *Yes. Did she come (tonight)?*
KEN: *No she's away on holiday. She's coming back tomorrow.*
AKORN: *Do you know the girl who's drinking Pepsi?*
KEN: *Yes. She's called Saowanee.*
AKORN: *Is she married?*
KEN: *I don't know. Why do you ask?*
AKORN: *I think she came alone.*

Vocabulary

thêe	who, which	**tàeng ngarn**	to marry, be married
phôot	to talk, speak	**laéo réu yang**	(question marker)
ûwan	fat	**thǎrm**	to ask
mao	drunk	**khon dieo**	alone
thêe nêe	here		
réuplào	(question marker indicating past time)		

Language points

Relative clauses with thee

thee corresponds to 'who', 'which' or 'where':

phooying thee phoot kap Steve suey.　The girl who is talking to Steve is pretty.

phooying thee khun roochak suey.　The girl you know is pretty.

barn thee khun seuh suey	The house you bought is nice.
barn thee yoo klai rohng phayarbarn suey.	The house which is near the hospital is nice.
rohng rian thee khao pai dee.	The school he goes to is good.

Questions with reuplao

The literal meaning of **reuplao** is 'are you . . . or not?' Although not as firm as the literal English equivalent it is a more insistent way of asking a question.

reuplao is the question word normally used when you are asking about the past. Notice how you give a short answer to a question with **reuplao**:

khun pai reuplao?	Are you going?
pai khrap.	Yes.
mai pai khrap	No.

Negatives with mai dai

mai dai is often used instead of **mai** to negate action verbs, verbs of motion, **pen** and **sheuh**.

pai thanarkharn reuplao?	Did you go to the bank?
mai dai **pai.**	*No, I didn't go.*

It is often used to refer to past time and in present situations which are contrary to expectations:

khao *mai dai* **sheuh Steve.**	He's *not* called Steve.
nar sia dai *mai dai* **tham ngarn thee Langsit.**	It's a pity *you don't* work in Langsit.

Questions with laeo reu yang

The question words **laeo reu yang** (*lit.* 'already' or 'not yet') are used rather like **reuplao** to ask whether something has been done. Like **reuplao** it is a fairly insistent way of asking a question.

khun kin khao *laeo reu yang*? Have you eaten *yet*?

Vocabulary

Steve mai shai khon uwan. pen khon phorm. mai tia. pen khon soong. sai waen tar.

phŏrm	thin	**sài**	to wear, put
tîa	short	**tar**	eye
sŏong	tall	**wâen tar**	glasses, spectacles

Steve pai thanarkharn tae mai mee ngern. Steve kroht.

kròht   angry

Exercise 9

Give short answers to these questions:

1 khun taeng ngarn laeo reu yang?
2 khun kin khao laeo reu yang?
3 khun deuhm karfae laeo reu yang?
4 wannee khun khap rot laeo reu yang ?
5 khun seuh barn laeo reu yang?

Exercise 10

Look back at Exercise 4. Your helper has returned. How would you check that he has done everything you asked him to? (Use **laeo reu yang**.)

Exercise 11

Your friend thinks you are so predictable that he knows what you did yesterday. Give short answers to these questions. (You have given up smoking and drinking, you worked hard in the office and had no time to eat. On the other questions he is correct.)

1 khun pai thanarkharn reuplao?
2 khun seuh buree reuplao?
3 khun pai doo nang reuplao?
4 khun pai har pheuan reuplao?
5 khun norn thee opfit reuplao?
6 khun tham ngarn thee barn reuplao?
7 khun pai kin khao thee rohng raem Hilton reuplao?
8 khun phoot kap Malee reuplao?
9 khun mao reuplao?

Exercise 12

Your friend was supposed to get some money, go shopping, see the doctor and then go for a night out with a friend yesterday. How many questions can you ask her to see what she did?

Exercise 13

Ken and Akorn are still discussing the other guests at the party. Make a note of who is doing what.

KEN: khun hen khon nan mai khrap?
AKORN: hen khrap.
KEN: khon nan khrai khrap?
AKORN: khon thee soop buree shai mai khrap?
KEN: shai khrap.
AKORN: khon nan sheuh Saowalak.
KEN: khon thee pai sanarm yar sheuh arai khrap?
AKORN: sheuh Steve khrap.
KEN: khun roochak phooying thee nang klai Naowalak mai khrap?
AKORN: khit war sheuh Saowanee khrap.

Exercise 14

How many sentences can you make from these examples?

A:

rot		shan		phaeng
barn		phom	pai	mai dee
thanarkharn	thee	looksao phom	doo	suey
rohng rian		mae shan	seuh	
rohng phayarbarn				

B:

phooying		seuh	rot phom	keng
phooshai	thee	mar doo	barn shan	mai dee
khon		pai	kap Steve	suey
		phoot	doo nang	pen khon mao
				pen khon kae
				kroht

Exercise 15

Complete this dialogue:

A: khorthoht khrap. khon _____ sarmee _____ khun shai mai?
B: mai shai kha. _____ taeng ngarn.
A: khon _____ khrap?
B: khon thee _____ shai mai kha?
A: mai shai khrap. khon thee _____.
B: _____ war _____ Manat. _____ thammai?
A: khit war _____.

Exercise 16

You are at a party and you are trying to find out who some of the people round you are. Your friend is not sure who you are asking about and gets the wrong person. Correct him.

1 khon nai khrap? khon uwan shai mai?
2 khon soong shai mai?
3 phooying suey shai mai?
4 khon phorm shai mai?
5 khon kae shai mai?
6 phooshai tia shai mai ?

Exercise 17

1 Introduce and give a short description of yourself.
2 You witnessed someone stealing a handbag. Write a description of the individual for the police.

Exercise 18

Write a short dialogue to fit these situations:

1 You are with your friend at a party. You know everyone and she knows no one. You point out some of the guests to her.
2 You introduce yourself to a girl you think is Thai and ask what her friend is called. It turns out that she is with her mother who is a policewoman. When you ask her name you realize she's English.

Exercise 19

1 A Thai friend of your mother arrives at your house. How would you invite her in and introduce her to your husband/wife?
2 Your friend's husband has been very busy recently. How would you ask after him?
3 How would you offer someone a Pepsi?
4 How would you ask someone if she misses her husband?
5 You are at a party. How would you ask someone if they came alone and if they are going to visit Malee tomorrow?

Vocabulary

It is useful to learn words which come together, either in set phrases or in commonly made associations. What word would you expect to come in place of the gaps?

1 _____ thee dai roochak.
2 cha _____ barn phrungnee.
3 look shan mai yoo barn. khit _____ mark.
4 khao mar laeo reu _____ ?
5 nar _____ dai!
6 nae _____ .
7 _____ tit.
8 sia _____ thaorai?
9 _____ kwar
10 _____ pai
11 _____ phat.
12 fon _____
13 seuh _____

Tone practice ▓▓

Practise the tones in these words:

**shêùh   nâng   phôòt   thêe nêê   wǎen   sǎrmee   phrûngnée
ûwan   thǎrm   sǒong   hǎr   khít thěung   phǒrm**

Reading and writing

Vowels

ชื่อ   ตึก   โ-   เดือน   เ-า   เรา

sheuh   teuk   deuan   rao

Notice that when the vowel symbol is not followed by a consonant the letter อ is used.

Consonants

ชื่อ   ณ   คุณ

seuh   khun

The initial ห หนึ่ง

When ห appears at the beginning of a syllable before another consonant it makes a low-class consonant behave like a high-class consonant (see p. 8)

Exercise 20

1 Write these words in transliteration:

เนื้อ   เสื้อ   เรือ   คิ่มเหล้า   เพื่อน   หนังสือ

มะละกอหวาน   ลืมแว่นตา   ชื้อบุหรี่

2 You have been away for a few days and find that your Thai flat-mate has left you some notes. What do they mean?

ชาตรียังไม่กลับบ้าน จะชื้อหนังสือพรุ่งนี้

ชาตรีแต่งงานแล้ว ผมคิดถึงคุณ

ผมไปหาลูกสาวของผมอายุสิบสองปี

Exercise 21

Write a note for your flatmate telling him/her that you will be coming home tomorrow and that today you went to the cinema to see a Chinese film. You enjoyed it.

Dialogue 🔲

Ken was in Thailand a few years ago and met some of Akorn's friends. Now he wants to catch up with news of them

KEN: pheuan khorng khun tham arai barng khrap?

AKORN: khon neung tham ngarn thee satharnthoot yeepun. khon neung tham ngarn thee pamnamman Esso thanon Tarksin. khun roochak Sombat mai?

KEN: Sombat pen khrai?

AKORN: khon thee seuh barn yai thanon Tarksin.

KEN: roochak. taeng ngarn leao reu yang?

AKORN: taeng ngarn laeo. mee look see khon.

KEN: pen pai mai dai!

AKORN: lae Suthaep pen tamruat.

KEN: Suthaep reuh? khon tia sai waen tar, khon khee mao shai mai khrap?

AKORN: shai khrap.

KEN: khrai thamngarn thee satharnthoot yeepun khrap?

AKORN: sheuh Suporn. khun roochak khao reuplao?

KEN: mai sarp. pen khon uwan shai mai?

AKORN: mai uwan. phorm.

KEN: khon thee mee phanraya suey mark shai mai?

AKORN: shai khrap.

KEN: roochak. kae laeo shai mai khrap?

AKORN: shai khrap. laeo ko Manop pai amerikar

KEN: pai thammai?

AKORN: pai tham ngarn reuang namman.

KEN: ching ching reuh.

AKORN: khao cha klap krungthep phrungnee

KEN: reuh? pai har khao duey kan mai?

AKORN: pai see khrap.

Comprehension

Make notes on how each person is described and the news Akorn gives Ken about them.

9 hai lae rap

Giving and getting

In this lesson you will learn how to:

- talk about things you did in the past
- identify and describe some common objects
- talk about giving, receiving, buying and selling, losing and finding things

Dialogue ▭

Suporn goes to see Janet on her birthday

SUPORN: nee khorng khwan hai khun khrap.
JANET: khorpkhun mark kha. khun chai dee mark. nee arai kha?
SUPORN: mai bork. pert doo see khrap.
JANET: roop nee suey chang loei kha.
SUPORN: shorp mai khrap?
JANET: shorp kha. nee roop arai kha?
SUPORN: roop wat khrap.
JANET: khun seuh roop nee meuarai kha?
SUPORN: seuh arthit thee laeo khrap. suk san wan kert khrap.
JANET: khorpkhun mark kha. khorng khwan nar rak chang loei na kha.

SUPORN: *Here's a present for you.*
JANET: *Thank you very much. You're very kind. What is it?*
SUPORN: *I'm not telling you. Open it and see.*
JANET: *Oh, it's a picture. It's very pretty (lit. This picture is very pretty).*
SUPORN: *Do you like it?*
JANET: *Yes. What is it?*
SUPORN: *It's a picture of a temple.*
JANET: *When did you buy it?*
SUPORN: *Last week. Happy birthday.*
JANET: *Thank you very much. The present is really lovely.*

Vocabulary

hâi	for, to give	**chang (loei)**	really, very
khŏrng khwǎn	present	**mêuarài**	when?
chai dee	kind (*lit.* good heart)	**thêe laéo**	last, ago
		sùk	happy
bòrk	to say, tell	**kèrt**	birth
pèrt	to open	**sùk san wan kèrt!**	Happy birthday!
rôop	picture		

Language points

Past time expressions

As we saw in Lesson 8, past time is indicated not by a change in the verb form but by time adverbials such as 'last night' 'two years ago'. A common way of indicating past time is with the expression **...** **thee laeo.**

phom pai Chieng Mai *arthit/* **deuan/pee** *thee laeo.*	I *went* to Chieng Mai *last week*/month/year.
phom pai Chieng Mai sorng *pee thee laeo.*	I went to Chieng Mai two *years* ago.
seuh rot sarm *wan thee laeo.*	I *bought* the car three *days ago*.

Questions about the past

The most common question forms referring to past time are:

khun pai thanarkhan reuplao?	Did you go to the bank (or not)?
khun pai thanarkharn shai mai?	You went to the bank, didn't you? (i.e. you expect the answer 'yes')
khun pai thanarkharn reuh?	You went to the bank, didn't you? (you think the answer will probably be 'yes')

Notice the negative forms:

khun mai dai pai thanarkhan reuh?	You didn't go to the bank, then?
khun mai dai pai thanarkharn shai mai?	

Questions with meuarai

As with most other question words **meuarai** comes at the end of the question. It can be used to refer to past or future time:

khun pai rohng phayarbarn *meuarai?*	*When* did you go to the hospital?
khun ca pai rohng phayarbarn *meuarai?*	*When* will you go to the hospital?

hai *('for')*

> **seuh nangseuh *hai* pheuan.** I bought a book *for* my friend *or* I bought my friend a book.

hai is often used on its own to mean 'for you':

> **phom cha seuh nangseuh *hai*.** I'll buy a book *for you.*

Giving

hai is also used as a verb to mean 'give'. The normal word order is for the direct object to precede the indirect:

> **khao *hai* khorng khwan shan.** He gave me a present.

Language and culture notes

Compounds with chai

In the dialogue you saw the expression **chai dee** ('good heart') meaning 'kind'. There are a number of very common expressions using **chai**:

dee chai	happy
sia chai	to be sorry
chai rorn	hot tempered
chai yen	calm, even tempered

Many Thai people pride themselves on their **chai yen** and on facing life coolly and calmly. **Farang** are often criticized for their **chai rorn**. Losing one's temper with officials, raising one's voice, showing impatience or answering someone rudely are all evidence of **chai rorn**. To keep smiling and outwardly calm when faced with pressure or irritations are evidence of **chai yen**.

Varieties of pronunciation

The way people pronounce words varies according to the part of the country they come from: people from Bangkok have a different pronunciation from someone who hails from Songkhla in the south and both would differ from an inhabitant of Chieng Mai, for example. In Bangkok, for example, the **khw** sound is often pronounced 'f' so **khorng khwan** becomes **khorng fan**. When there is a cluster of two consonants at the beginning of a word the second consonant is often omitted: **khrap** becomes **khap**, **plar** becomes **par**.

The sound *r* (as in **arai** or **aroi**) is often pronounced *l* so you will hear **alai** or **aloi**.

Vocabulary

meuawarnnee phom seuh nangseuh. seuh nangseuh phim duey. seuh parkkar seuh khorng len hai lookshai phom. phom dai narlikar chark khun phor.

mêuawarneé	yesterday	**pàrkkar**	pen
nángsěuh phim	newspaper	**khǒrng lên**	toy
nángsěuh	book	**dâi**	to receive, get, earn
narlikar	watch, clock		

fon tok. phom mai mee rom.

rôm	umbrella

Exercise 1

You haven't seen your friend for a while but you've heard of several things he's been doing. How would you ask him when he:

1 bought a car
2 got married
3 went to America
4 saw a mutual friend
5 had something to eat
6 went to visit his father in Japan
7 sold his house

Exercise 2

Answer the questions you asked in Exercise 1, choosing between last year, last month, last week and yesterday.

Exercise 3

Your friend is really out of touch. Tell her that you did these things several days, weeks, months or years ago.

1 khun cha khai rot khun meuarai?
2 khun cha seuh barn meuarai?
3 khun taeng ngarn laeo reu yang?
4 khun khit war cha pai amerikar reuplao?
5 khun pai rohng phayarbarn laeo reu yang?
6 khun khit war cha seuh rarn aharn meuarai?

Exercise 4

You've been doing your Christmas shopping and your friend wants
to know what you have bought and for whom. Match each gift with
a recipient and tell him or her what you plan.

watch	your wife/husband
cigarettes	your daughter
a book	your son
a pen	your mother
an umbrella	your father
a fridge	your friend's daughter
a plane	your friend's mother
a toy	your friend

Exercise 5

It was your birthday last week and you got numerous presents. Use
the lists in Exercise 4 to tell your friend what you received from
whom.

Exercise 6

You've just had a very successful party where everyone gave someone a present. Describe who gave and received what.

Exercise 7

Complete this dialogue:

A: shorp _____ khun kha. seuh mai shai mai kha?
B: shai kha.
A: _____ thee nai kha?
B: _____ .
A: seuh meuarai kha?
B: sorng _____ kha.

A: _____ ?
B: har phan bart kha.

Exercise 8

Write a brief description of the career of this businessman.
Example: **sip see pee thee laeo seuh rarn aharn yai.**

1980	bought a big restaurant
1982	sold the restaurant and bought a hotel
1983	sold the hotel and went to America
1984	bought a boat and an aeroplane
1989	sold the boat and the aeroplane, bought two hotels, three restaurants and two houses
1991	had to sell the hotels, the restaurants and his small house when his bank collapsed
1993	bought a small restaurant

Dialogue ▣

Janet tells Suporn about her shopping trip

SUPORN: pai nai mar khrap?
JANET: pai seuh khorng mar.
SUPORN: seuh arai mar khrap?
JANET: seuh nangseuh hai pheuan sorng lem. laeo ko seuh seua kap kaprong mar.
SUPORN: see arai khrap?
JANET: see dam kha. suey mai?
SUPORN: suey chang loei khrap.
JANET: shan shorp mark. lae seuh krapao duey.
SUPORN: doo noi see khrap.
JANET: nee kha. tham chark nang. dee mai kha?
SUPORN: dee khrap. doo khaeng raeng dee khrap. phaeng mai khrap?
JANET: phaeng nitnoi kha. har roi bart.

SUPORN: *Where have you been?*
JANET: *I've been shopping.*
SUPORN: *What did you buy?*
JANET: *I bought two books for a friend. And I bought a blouse and a skirt.*

SUPORN: *What colour?*
JANET: *Black. Do you like it?*
SUPORN: *Yes. It's very pretty.*
JANET: *I like it a lot. And I bought a bag as well.*
SUPORN: *Show me.*
JANET: *Here. It's made of leather. Do you think it's good?*
SUPORN: *Yes, it's good. It looks nice and strong. Was it expensive?*
JANET: *A little. Five hundred bart.*

Vocabulary

lêm	(classifier for books)	**dam**	black
sêua	blouse, shirt	**krapǎo**	bag
kraprohng	skirt	**khǎeng raeng**	strong
sǎe	colour	**nǎng**	leather

Language points

Classifiers

Here are some more classifiers which you will need to use with
words you have learned so far:

khan	vehicles	**rot sarm** *khan*
lem	books	**nangseuh sorng** *lem*
shabap	newspapers	**nangseuh phim sarm** *shabap*
darm	pens	**parkkar see** *darm*
tua	clothing	**kraprohng sorng** *tua*
bai	bag, wallet	**krapao sorng** *bai*
khoo ('pair')	shoes	**rorng thao kee** *khoo*
an	umbrella	**rom sorng** *an*

an is used for a variety of objects and can also be used when you
don't want to be specific:

seuh sorng an.	I bought two of them.

Notice that the main noun and the classifier/numeral are separated
in sentences like the following:

khun hai karng keng sarmee khun kee tua?	How may (pairs of) trousers did you give your husband?

Imperatives with see

We saw in Lesson 7 that you can use the verb alone to give directions. A more polite way of telling someone to do something is to add **see**. (An even more polite way is to use **shern** as we saw in Lesson 8.)

kin see!	Eat it!
hai ngern phom see khrap.	Give me the money.

The imperative is often softened with **noi**:

doo noi see khrap.	Show me.

hai *('to lose')*

We have already seen in this lesson that **hai** with a falling tone means 'to give'. With a rising tone it means 'to lose':

narlikar phom hǎi.	I've lost my watch.

You will practise these tone differences later in this lesson.

Colours

sěe khǎo	white
sěe nám ngern	blue
sěe khǐeo	green
sěe daeng	red
sěe nám tarn	brown
sěe lěuang	yellow

Vocabulary

krapao satarng phom hai.

krapǎo satarng	wallet

phom seuh seua phar mar. seuh karng keng, seua nork, rorng thao laeo ko rorng thao.

sěua phâr	clothing, clothes
karng keng	trousers
sěua nôrk	jacket
rorng tháo	shoe

Exercise 9

You are stuck in a traffic jam in Bangkok and counting the number of vehicles in front of you. Answer your friend's questions.

1 mee rot kee khan?
2 mee rot mortersai kee khan?
3 mee rot me kee khan?
4 mee rot taeksee kee khan?
5 mee rot tua kee khan?

Exercise 10

You've been on a spending spree. Answer your friend's questions:

1 seuh seua nork kee tua?
2 seuh seua kee tua?
3 seuh kraprohng kee tua?
4 seuh karng keng kee tua?
5 seuh krapao kee bai?
6 seuh rorng thao kee khoo?

Exercise 11

You are planning an expedition for a small group. Your friend has been helping you with the arrangements. Ask her how many of the following she has or has bought:

1 books
2 newspapers
3 cars
4 motorcycles
5 pens
6 jackets

Exercise 12

Answer the questions:

1 thee London rot taeksee see arai?
2 thee London rot me see arai?
3 thee sanarm yar khun yar see arai?
4 barn khorng khun see arai?
5 rot khorng khun see arai?

6 seua khorng khun see arai?
7 rorng thao khorng khun see arai?

Exercise 13

Ask your friend to give you something in these situations:

1 You're going out and you think it might rain.
2 You want to see what time it is.
3 You want to see what's on at the cinema.
4 You want something to occupy you on a long bus ride.
5 You haven't had a smoke all day.
6 You're going shopping and need some money.
7 You want to write a letter to a friend.

Exercise 14

Complete this conversation:

A: khun seuh arai barng khrap?
B: seuh _____ sorng tua. khun shorp see _____ reuh see
     _____ ?
A: _____ see khieo khrap. phaeng mai khrap?
B: _____

Exercise 15

John has lost something and reports it to the hotel. Find out:

1 what he lost
2 what it was like
3 where and when he lost it

JOHN: krapao satarng khorng phom hai khrap.
B: krapao satarng khun pen yangngai kha?
JOHN: bai lek, see nam tarn. kao laeo duey khrap.
B: hai meuarai kha?
JOHN: hai meua warnnee khrap.
B: hai thee nai kha?
JOHN: thee hong narm khrap.

Exercise 16

Now rewrite the conversation in Exercise 15 about another object.

Vocabulary building

1
Here are some common compound words made up of words you already know. See if you can guess (or remember) the meaning of the compound.

1 **narm som**
2 **too thohrasap**
3 **phoot len**
4 **thee kert**
5 **krapao satarng**
6 **khon khai khorng**
7 **khon khai aharn**
8 **khon dern thanon**
9 **khon mar har**
10 **khon rak**
11 **nangseuh arn len** (**arn** = 'read')

2
Write as many examples as you know of compound words containing: **khorng**, **rohng**, **horng**.

3
We saw above a number of compounds containing **chai**. See if you can find the appropriate one to complete these sentences:

1 khao hai narlikar phom. khao _____ mark.
2 faen phom klap barn phrungnee. phom _____ mark.
3 rot khao hai. khao kroht mark. khao _____.
4 rot khao hai. khao bork war 'mai pen rai'. khao _____ mark.
5 rot khorng khun hai reuh? shan _____ duey.

Tone practice [CO]

Practise the tones in these words:

**tháo nárm láeo shár pám námman bòrk pèrt sùk
kèrt klàp sěe nám ngern sěe khǐeo sěe daeng
sěe nám tarn sěe lěuang**

Compare the tones in the different meanings of **hai**:
hâi   hǎi   hâî

khao hai narlikar phom

narlikar phom hai
seuh narlikar hai pheuan
khao cha seuh narlikar hai

Exercise 17

1 What would you say when you receive a present wrapped in expensive looking paper?
2 How would ask your friend how many books he gave his wife?
3 Your friend asks you what to give you as a wedding present. Tell her to give you two shirts/blouses.
4 Your friend has bought two jackets. Tell him you like the blue one but not the green one.

Reading and writing

Vowels and consonants

ใจ   เสีย

chai   sia

The numerals

๐ ๒ ๓ ๔ ๕ ๖ ๗ ๘ ๙ ๑๐
1   2   3   4   5   6   7   8   9   10

The numerals after ten are written exactly as in English, by putting the individual figures together. 321, for example, is

๓๒๑

Exercise 18

1 Write these words in transliteration:

ใจเย็น เลี้ยวขวา คนเดียว   ไปเที่ยว

ลูกสาวฉันเรียนหนังสือ

2 What did your friend buy and what did he receive?

คุณพ่อให้เงินผม   ผมซื้อของเล่นให้ลูกชายผม
แม่ให้ร่มผม   ซื้อรองเท้ากางเกงซื้อเสื้อด้วย

Exercise 19

Fill in this form. Use Thai numerals where numbers are called for.

เกิดวันที่ วัน__ เดือน__ ปี__   อายุ_____
ชื่อ_____มาจาก _____ เกิดที่_____
ที่อยู่_____ แต่งงานแล้ว__   ยังไม่แต่งงาน__

Dialogue 🔘

Malee meets Janet, who looks upset. Janet tells her about a misfortune that has befallen her

MALEE: pen arai kha?
JANET: krapao khorng shan hai kha.
MALEE: reuh? krapao pen yangngai kha?
JANET: tham chark nang. see dam. suey mark kha. tham thee itarlee.
MALEE: phaeng mai kha?
JANET: phaeng mark kha. faen shan hai sarm pee thee laeo.
MALEE: nar sia dai na kha.
JANET: mee waen thee khao hai duey. mee waen tar, parkkar, mee nangseuh, mee kraprohng thee seuh meuawarnnee.
MALEE: krapao yai ching ching na kha.
JANET: mee khorng len duey na kha. shan pai seuh khorng mar. seuh khorng len hai looksao shan.
MALEE: krapao see dam reuh kha?
JANET: shai kha.
MALEE: kraprohng see arai kha?
JANET: see leuang kha
MALEE: nangseuh sheuh arai kha?

JANET: sheuh 'barn lae rot' kha. tharm thammai kha?

MALEE: khun hen phooying khon nan mai? mee krapao see dam bai yai, mee kraprohng see leuang, mee nangseuh 'barn lae rot' duey.

JANET: chingching reuh kha! pai har khao duey kan mai!

Comprehension

1 What has Janet lost?
2 What details does she give of it?
3 What happens about it?

10 welar warng

Free time

In this lesson you will learn how to:

- talk about what you do habitually
- refer to times in the future
- make polite responses
- say what you have to do
- say what is possible or not allowed
- ask someone to do you a favour
- tell the time

Dialogue 🔢

Ken meets Malee again and she tells him about her family and their lifestyles

KEN: khun tham ngarn reuplao khrap?

MALEE: mai dai tham kha. pen mae barn. pai seuh khorng. tham kapkhao. tham khwarm sa-art barn. doo theewee. tham ngarn barn thuk wan. nar beua.

KEN: lookshai khun yoo barn mai khrap?

MALEE: mai yoo kha.

KEN: nar sia dai. mai dai cher khao.

MALEE: khao rian nangseuh thee amerikar.
cha klap krungthep eek sorng pee.

KEN: khao pai narn chang loei. khun khit theung khao mai khrap?

MALEE: khit theung kha.

KEN: sarmee khorng khun tham ngarn nak mark shai mai khrap?

MALEE: shai kha. tham ngarn wan la sip see shuamohng. tham ngarn thuk wan yut wan arthit. wan arthit len korp. pai doo nang. meuankan thuk arthit thang pee. khun Ken len korp reuplao kha?

KEN: len meuankan tae mai boi. mai mee welar warng.

KEN: *Do you work?*

MALEE: *No, I'm a housewife. I go shopping, cook, clean the house, watch TV. Doing housework every day is very boring.*

KEN: *Is your son at home?*

MALEE: *No.*

KEN: *That's a pity. You don't see him then.*

MALEE: *He's studying in America. He will come back to Bangkok in two years.*

KEN: *He's gone for a long time then. Do you miss him?*

MALEE: *Yes, I do.*

KEN: *Your husband works very hard, doesn't he?*

MALEE: *Yes. He works fourteen hours a day. He works every day and (just) has Sunday off. On Sunday he plays golf and goes to the cinema. The same every week, all the year. Do you play golf?*

KEN: *I do, but not often. I don't have the time.*

Vocabulary

tham kàpkhâo	to cook, do the cooking	**měuankan**	the same
thee wee	TV	**tháng**	all
rian nángsěuh	study	**kórp**	golf
eèk sǒrng pee	in two years	**bòi**	often
wan arthít	Sunday	**welar**	time
thúk	every	**wârng**	free, not busy

Language points

Days of the week

wan arthit	Sunday
wan chan	Monday
wan angkarn	Tuesday
wan phút	Wednesday
wan pháréuhàt	Thursday
wan sùk	Friday
wan sǎo	Saturday

Expressing frequency

len korp wan la neung khráng	I play golf once a day.
len korp arthit la sorng khrang.	I play golf twice a week.
len korp thuk wan/arthit/ deuan/pee.	I play golf every day/week/ month/year.
wan arthit khun tham arai?	What do you do on Sunday?
pròkkatì len korp.	I usually play golf.
len korp bòi bòi.	I often play golf.
len korp saměr/barng thee/ barng khráng barng khrao.	I play golf always/sometimes/ occasionally.

Future time reference

In Lesson 8 we practised two patterns of past time expressions. In this lesson we practise similar patterns for referring to the future.

cha pai meuang thai *pee/ deuan/arthit/nâr*	I'm going to Thailand next year/ month/week.

cha pai krungthep eek sarm *wan/arthit/deuan/pee.*	I'm going to Bangkok in three days/weeks/months/years.

Present time

You will have noticed that the same form of the verb can be used to say what someone does habitually (e.g. play golf) as well as to describe what someone is doing now (e.g. studying in America). You will learn one way of indicating an action in progress in Lesson 12.

rian nangseuh

The verb **rian** does not occur without an object complement; if there is no other complement, **nangseuh** is used.

Language and culture notes

Responses

We use a number of phrases in English to show interest, concern or pleasure in response to what someone has said. There are similar phrases in Thai, such as **nar sia dai**, but they tend to be used less than in English. A very common way of showing your concern etc. in Thai is to ask a question about what has been said or comment on it where in English we might say 'That's nice' or 'I'm sorry to hear that'. In the dialogue, for example, Ken responds to what Malee says by saying **mai dai cher khao** and **khun khit theung khao mai khrap**? You should practise questions and comments like this as they will make you sound a lot more interested in the conversation.

Showing you're concerned or sorry

narlikar phom hai	**nar sia dai**
	hai meuarai?

If you want to show you are really sorry (as opposed to just sounding polite) you could use **sia chai**:

phom mai sabai.	I'm not well.
shan sia chai duey (thee khun mai sabai)	I'm sorry (that you are not well)

Showing pleasure

shan pai amerikar.	I'm going to America.
dee see khrap!	That's great.
dee mark.	Good.
khun shohk dee mark.	You are lucky.
dee chai duey kha.	I am happy.

Showing you're interested

shan pai amerikar.	I'm going to America.
reuh kha?	Are you?
chingching reuh?	Really?

You will remember from Lesson 1 that you can respond to thanks or apologies by using **mai pen rai**.

Vocabulary

Janet len tenit. shorp wai narm. shorp dern len. shorp doo keelar thee thee wee. arp narm wan la sorng khrang.

tenít	tennis	**keelar**	sport
waî nárm	swimming	**àrp nárm**	(to have a) shower
pai dern lên	to go walking, for a walk		

Steve shorp kin lao. shorp len phai. len dontree thuk wan. seuh karset mark mark.

kin lâo	to drink spirits	**dontree**	music
lên phâi	to play cards	**karset**	cassette

Exercise 1

This is how Steve spends his week. Say that you do the same things the following day.

1 wan sao khao len korp.
2 wan suk khao len tenit.
3 wan arthit khao pai talart.
4 wan phareuhat khao pai wainarm.
5 wan phut khao tham kapkhao.
6 wan angkarn khao doo theewee.
7 wan chan khao rian nangseuh.

Exercise 2

Steve loves travelling and is a fanatic for all sorts of games but he does enjoy the occasional cigarette and drink. Answer these questions about him:

1 khao len korp boi mai?
2 khao wai narm boi mai?
3 khao pai thieo boi mai?
4 khao soop booree boi mai?
5 khao kin lao boi mai?
6 khao doo theewee boi mai?
7 khao arn nangseuh boi mai?
8 khao len phai boi mai?

Now answer the same questions about Suporn, who is a bit of a couch potato and drinks and smokes heavily.

Exercise 3

1 You are an ambitious business person who has plans to buy and sell all sorts of things. Say what you plan to do and when you intend to do it.
2 You are a keen traveller and have made plans for your next few holidays. Say where you intend to go, when, and what you will do there.

Exercise 4

Read the descriptions of these two people and make a note of what they have in common and how they differ.

A rian nangseuh thee krungthep. shorp keelar. pai wai narm arthit la sarm khrang. mai shorp tham kapkhao. pai rarn aharn thuk wan. shorp aharn cheen. doo theewee barng khrang barng khrao. doo keelar. shorp dontree farang. shorp pai seuh khorng. seuh seua phar lae ko karset.

B yoo thee Chieng Mai. mai tham ngarn. shorp tham kapkhao cheen. pai rarn aharn deuan la sorng sarm khrang. shorp len dontree thai. mai shorp len keelar tae shorp doo keelar thee theewee. shorp seuh khorng. seuh khorng len lae seua phar hai look sao khao.

Exercise 5

Decide on an appropriate response to these statements:

1 meuawarnnee krapao satarng phom hai.
2 arthit nee shan mee wan yut.
3 shan seuh rot mai mar.
4 khorthoht khrap thee mai dai seuh khorng khwan hai khun.
5 shan seuh kraprohng mar. doo see kha!
6 khun mae hai seua shan. phaeng tae mai shorp.
7 look sao shan klap barn phrungnee.
8 look sao shan pai amerikar sarm pee thee laeo.

Exercise 6

Find a statement which might produce these responses.

1 pai thammai?
2 cha pai meuarai?
3 ching ching reuh?
4 nar sia dai.
5 chork dee na khrap.
6 len boi mai?

Exercise 7

Arrange these utterances in order to make a conversation (note that the same speaker may say more than one utterance before the other speaker comes in).

shorp khrap.
look sao shan ko shorp kha.
len meuankan tae barng khrang barng khrao thaonan.
khun shorp dontree mai kha?
khao len dontree thuk wan.
khun len dontree reuplao kha?
mai mee welar warng.

Dialogue 🔊

Janet has found somewhere to live and asks Suporn for help

JANE: khun Suporn.
SUPORN: khrap.
JANET: wan phareuhat khun warng mai kha?
SUPORN: wan phareuhat reuh khrap? khit war warng khrap. khun
tharm thammai khrap?
JANET: shan torng yai barn. khun shuey shan dai mai kha?
SUPORN: dai khrap. torng pai kee mohng?
JANET: kee mohng ko dai kha.
SUPORN: torn shao reuh torn bai khrap?
JANET: torn nai ko dai kha.
SUPORN: tok long. phom cha pai rap khun torn paet mohng shao na
khrap.
JANET: mai torng mar shao rok kha! torn kao mohng ko dai. yar
leuhm na kha!

JANET: *Suporn.*
SUPORN: *Yes?*
JANET: *Are you free on Thursday?*
SUPORN: *Thursday? I think I'm free. Why?*
JANET: *I have to move house. Can you help me?*
SUPORN: *OK. What time do you have to go?*
JANET: *It doesn't matter.*
SUPORN: *Morning or afternoon?*
JANET: *Either.*
SUPORN: *OK. I'll fetch you at eight o'clock.*
JANET: *There's no need to come early. Nine o'clock will be all
right. Don't forget!*

Vocabulary

tôrng	must, have to	**kô dâi**	(note the various equivalents in this dialogue)
yái	to move, transfer		
yái bârn	to move house		
shûey	to help	**kèe mohng**	What time?
dâi	can, possible	**ráp**	to fetch, receive
tòk long	OK	**sháo**	early
torn sháo	morning	**leuhm**	to forget
torn bài	afternoon		

Language points

Expressing necessity

torng can be used to say that you must, must not or need not do
something:

phrungnee *torng* pai rohng phayarbarn.	I *have to* go to hospital tomorrow.
khun *torng* mai kin lao	You *must not* drink alcohol.
mai *torng* pai rohng phayarbarn.	I *don't have* to go to hospital.

A more common way of saying what you must not do (i.e. what is
forbidden) is **harm**:

***harm* soop buree**	You *must not* smoke (smoking is forbidden).

You will see this used in notices to indicate that something is not
allowed but it is also used in everyday speech where it can correspond to 'don't' or 'you mustn't'.

Expressing possibility

dai is used at the end of the sentence to indicate that something is
possible or that you are able to do it.

phom shuey khun *dai*.	I *can* help you.

Since **dai** is considered to be the main verb, **mai** is placed just before
it in negative statements:

pai seuh khorng *mai dai*.	I can't go shopping.
torng yoo thee barn.	I have to stay at home.

Similarly in short responses, it is **dai** that is used, not the other verb:

shuey phom *dai* mai khrap?	*Can* you help me?
dai kha.	Yes.
mai dai kha.	No.

dai is also used to say whether something is suitable or all right:

pai khon dieo *dai* mai kha?	*Is it OK* if I go on my own?

As in the example in the dialogue, you can use it to ask someone to do you a favour:

khun shuey shan dai mai kha? Can you help me?

Morning, noon and night

In English we are clear about when morning stops and afternoon begins but less so about the dividing lines between afternoon, evening and night. In Thai the day is divided as follows:

torn shao	1 a.m. to 12
thiang	12 (midday)
torn bai	12 to 5 p.m
torn yen	5 p.m. to 6 p.m.
torn meuht	6 p.m. onwards
thiang kheuhn	12 (midnight)

Telling the time

Traditionally Thai divides the clock not into twelve-hour blocks but into six-hour blocks. A twelve-hour system is, however, commonly used up to midday. After 6 p.m., however, you must be careful as you start counting again at one:

tee neung ... tee har	Up to 5 a.m.
hok mohng shao ... sip et mohng shao	6 a.m. to 11 a.m.
bai mohng ... bai see mohng	1 p.m. to 4 p.m.
har mohng yen ... hok mohng yen	5 p.m. to 6 p.m.
neung thum ... har thum	7 p.m. to 11 p.m.

Early and late

Thai distinguishes between early or late in the day and ahead of or behind schedule:

khao mar reo.	He came early (i.e. ahead of schedule).
khao mar sháo mark.	He came early (in the morning).
khao mar shár.	He came late (behind schedule).
khao mar săi	He came late (in the morning).
khao mar dèuhk	He came late (at night).

Language and culture notes

ko dai

The phrase **ko dai** is one of the ways of showing how easy-going you are. As you saw in the dialogue, you can use it to indicate that something will do (i.e. is good enough): **mai torng mar shao rok kha! torn kao mohng ko dai**. Used on its own it can mean something like 'That'll be all right':

wannee pai thieo mai dai. pai phrungnee mai?	I can't go out today. Shall we go tomorrow?
ko dai.	That'll be OK.

It can also suggest, however, that although you would be prepared to go along with something, it wouldn't be your first choice. This makes it a convenient way of saying 'no' without saying 'no'.

yennee pai rohng nang mai khrap?	Shall we go to the cinema tonight?
ko dai kha.	OK (but I'd rather not).

We will practise this construction in Lesson 13.

Vocabulary

rarn pert paet mohng shao. pit bai sorng mohng.

pèrt	to open
pìt	to close

mee phonlamai yarng euhn mai khrap?

yàrng euhn	any other

phom yeuhm har roi bart noi dai mai khrap?
khor yeuhm har roi bart noi dai mai khrap?

yeuhm	to lend, borrow

Exercise 8

Note the excuse B gives for not accepting A's suggestion.

A: pai kin khao duey kan mai?
B: mai dai khrap. torng pai har mor.

Use the same way of giving an excuse to avoid doing what is suggested.

1 pai len korp duey kan mai?
2 pai doo nang duey kan mai?
3 pai kin karfae duey kan mai?
4 pai dern len duey kan mai?
5 pai seuh khorng duey kan mai?

Exercise 9

khorthoht thee mar shar khrap. mai mee rot me. torng pai taek-see. rot tit. khap reo mai dai.

1 What are A's excuses for arriving late?
2 See how many excuses you can give for arriving late.

Exercise 10

Complete this dialogue:

A: _____ khun warng mai?
B: khorthoht kha _____ .
A: thammai khrap?
B: _____ rian nangseuh kha.
A: wan arthit _____?
B: _____ . torng _____ .

Exercise 11

Your friend looks overworked and has generally been leading an unhealthy lifestyle. See how many things you can tell her to do or not to do.

Exercise 12

Your friend is going overseas to study and asks you for advice. Tell her whether these things are necessary or not.

1 torng rian nangseuh thuk wan reuh?
2 torng pai har mor korn reuh?
3 torng seuh seua phar mai shai mai?
4 torng seuh rot mai reuh?
5 torng pai sanarmbin torn shao shai mai?
6 torng ao ngern mark mark reuh?

Exercise 13

You want to ask your friend to do you some favours. How would you ask him to:

1 help you buy some clothes
2 give you some money
3 lend you a pen
4 lend you his car
5 buy a book for you
6 lend you a cassette

Exercise 14

How would you refuse someone permission to do these things:

1 soop buree dai mai kha?
2 chort thee nee dai mai khrap?
3 pai tharng nee dai mai khrap?
4 chort trong kharm satharnthoot dai mai kha?
5 lieo kwar dai mai khrap?
6 dern trong pai dai mai kha?

Exercise 15

Your friend regards you as an information bureau. Tell her the opening and closing times of the following establishments

1	**tharnkharn amerikan**	9 a.m.	3 p.m.
2	**rarn aharn cheen**	11 a.m.	10 p.m.
3	**rarn aharn thai**	10 a.m.	11 p.m.
4	**rarn aharn farangset**	midday	midnight
5	**rohng rian St James**	7 a.m.	4 p.m.

Exercise 16

A: phom cha pai rap khun torn paet mohng shao na khrap.
B: torn sip mohng ko dai

Your friend is very eager to pick you up. Tell him that a time two hours later than he suggests will be OK.

1 phom cha pai rap khun torn tee sarm.
2 phom cha pai rap khun torn tee har.

3 phom cha pai rap khun torn chet mohng shao.
4 phom cha pai rap khun torn sip et mohng shao.
5 phom cha pai rap khun torn bai see mohng.
6 phom cha pai rap khun torn hok mohng yen.

Exercise 17

Use the cues to complete this conversation:

wan phareuhat torn shao khun warng mai kha?
1 Say you're not free in the morning but you are in the afternoon. Ask why.
shan torng pai rap pheuan thee sanarmbin. pai duey kan dai mai kha?
2 Say that's lucky as you are going to the airport too.
dee see kha. khun pai kee mohng?
3 Say you have to go at 7 a.m. Ask if that's OK.
ko dai kha.
4 Tell her you'll pick her up at 6 a.m.

Exercise 18

1 How would you tell your friend about someone who has a very boring life, always doing the same things at the same time?
2 You believe someone is keen on sports. How would you check this and find out how often she goes swimming?
3 You have to go to the airport to meet a friend. How would you explain this to someone and ask him to lend you his car? Tell him it is not necessary for him to come with you but your friend has to go to the hospital at 3 p.m. and must not be late.

Vocabulary building

A
We have seen that **warng** can mean 'free' or 'not busy'. Its precise meaning often depends on the context. How would you translate the phrases containing it in these sentences?

1 Manat pen khon warng ngarn.
2 phrungnee pai har pheuan mai dai. shan mai warng.
3 horng narm mai warng khrap.
4 mai mee khon yoo barn phom. barn warng.
5 welar warng phom shorp doo keelar.

6 shan mai hiu kha. kin khorngwarng thaonan.
7 yark tham ngarn thee nee. mee ngarn warng mai?

B

The word **sia** can also mean different things according to the context including 'lose', 'waste', 'spend', 'not working'. What is the meaning of the phrases contained in these contexts?

1 meuawarnnee phom seuh narlikar. phaeng mark tae sia laeo. phom sia ngern mark. nar sia dai!
2 khun mai sabai reuh? phom sia chai duey.
3 khao pen khon mai dee. sia sheuh.
4 phom pai har khao tae khao mai yoo. sia welar mark.
5 khao chai rorn. hua sia.

Tone practice

Practise the tones in these words and expressions to do with time:

> **torn sháo   torn bài   torn meûht   thîang   thîang kheuhn
> torn tee sǎrm   torn tee hâr   torn chèt mohng sháo
> torn sìp èt mohng sháo   torn bài sèe mohng
> torn hòk mohng yen**

Reading and writing

Final consonants

Syllables end only in the sounds *ng*, *n*, *m*, *y*, *w*, *k*, *t* and *p*. They can be written, however, with a consonant which otherwise has a different sound. So the sound of some consonants is different in final position from its sound in initial position:

	Initial	Final
บ	b	p
ด	d	t
ล	l	n
จ	ch	t
ช	kh	t
ส	s	t
ร	r	n

Silent consonants

When a final consonant is not pronounced it has the sign ˇ over it:

อาทิตย์

(The sign sometimes cancels out the last two consonants.)
   Here are some more consonants you will need for the days of the week:

ธ   วันพุธ   ฤ   วันพฤหัส   ศ   วันศุกร์

   th   reu   s

Exercise 19

1 Write these words in transliteration:

ตำรวจ อาหาร วันอังคาร   วันอาทิตย์

วันจันทร์   เบียร์   หนังสือพิมพ์

2 Look at these extracts from Manop's diary. Find out what he did
   on each day.

วันอาทิตย์   อ่านหนังสืออ่านเล่น

วันจันทร์ ไปทำงาน

วันอังคาร   ไปเดินเล่น

วันพุธ   เล่นไพ่กับเพื่อน

วันพฤหัส   เล่นดนตรี

วันศุกร์ ไปว่ายน้ำ

วันเสาร์   รับเพื่อนที่สนามบิน

3 Find out the opening and closing times of this shop.

วันจันทร์ เปิด 8 โมงเช้า ปิด 5 โมงเย็น
วันศุกร์ เปิด 9 โมงเช้า ปิด 6 โมงเย็น
วันเสาร์ เปิด 10 โมงเช้า ปิด 4 โมงเย็น
วันอาทิตย์ ปิด

Writing

Write a brief diary for a week.

Dialogue 📼

Steve goes to see the doctor for a check-up

MOR: khun tham ngarn nak mark shai mai khrap?
STEVE: shai khrap.
MOR: tham ngarn wan la kee shuamohng khrap?
STEVE: sip reuh sip et shuamohng khrap.
MOR: tham ngarn nak mark na khrap. khun deuhm lao reuplao khrap?
STEVE: deuhm nitnoi khrap.
MOR: arthit la kee khuat?
STEVE: arthit la sorng khuat khrap.
MOR: khun soop buree wan la kee tua?
STEVE: pramarn yee sip reuh sarm sip tua khrap.
MOR: khun len keelar arai barng?
STEVE: len korp khrap.
MOR: len boi mai khrap?
STEVE: mai boi khrap. pee la sorng sarm khrang thaonan.
MOR: khun len keelar yarng euhn duey reuplao khrap?
STEVE: len phai thuk wan khrap.
MOR: len phai mai shai keelar khrap. welar warng tham arai khrap?
STEVE: pai doo nang khrap.
MOR: khun shorp kin khao reuplao khrap?
STEVE: shorp khrap. faen phom tham kapkhao aroi mark khrap. khun khit war phom torng len keelar yarng euhn shai mai khrap?

MOR: shai khrap. torng pai wai narm, len tenit reuh yarng euhn
lae khun torng mar har phom eek sorng arthit. harm kin
lao. harm soop buree.

STEVE: phom mai shorp len keelar khrap.

MOR: pai dern len ko dai khrap. harm len phai duey na khrap.

Comprehension

1 Note down the details Steve gives of his lifestyle.
2 What advice does the doctor give him?

11 karn rian

It's a learning experience

In this lesson you will learn how to:

- talk about languages
- say what you know how to do
- refer to something you have been doing and are still doing
- make some more requests

Dialogue 🔘

Malee compliments Ken on his Thai and asks him how he learned it

MALEE: khun Ken phoot pharsar thai keng na kha
KEN: khorpkhun khrap. phoot dai nitnoi, mai mark khrap.
MALEE: phoot khlorng kha.
KEN: phoot dai tae kham ngai ngai khrap.
MALEE: khian dai mai kha?
KEN: mai khoi dai khrap.
MALEE: arn pen mai kha?
KEN: arn dai barng kham khrap.
MALEE: khun Ken rian pharsar thai kap khroo shai mai kha?
KEN: khorthoht khrap. mai khao chai khrap. phoot shar
shar noi dai mai khrap?
MALEE: rian pharsar thai kap khroo reuh rian duey tua eng kha?
KEN: rian duey tua eng khrap. yark mark khrap.
MALEE: keng mark kha!

MALEE *You speak Thai very well, Ken.*
KEN: *Thank you. I speak a little, not very much.*
MALEE: *You speak fluently.*
KEN: *I just know how to say the easy words.*
MALEE: *Can you write it?*
KEN: *Hardly at all.*
MALEE: *Can you read it?*
KEN: *I can read some words.*
MALEE: *Have you studied it with a teacher?*
KEN: *I'm sorry. I didn't understand. Can you speak slowly?*
MALEE: *Have you studied it with a teacher or on your own?*
KEN: *I studied it on my own. It's very difficult.*
MALEE: *You're very good at it!*

Vocabulary

phôot	to speak	**ngâi (ngâi)**	easy
pharsǎr	language	**khǐan**	to write
pen	can, know how	**mâi khôi**	hardly at all
	to do something	**barng**	some
khlôrng	fluently	**dûey tua eng**	on one's own
kham	word	**yârk**	difficult

Language points

Saying what you know how to do

In Lesson 9 you learned the use of **dai** to refer to something you are able to do. The other common way of expressing what you are able to do is **pen**. Like **dai**, **pen** is used at the end of the sentence and is regarded as the main verb in negative statements and short responses:

khao khap rot *pen*.	He *can* drive a car.
khao khap rot mai *pen*.	He *can't* drive a car.
khun khap rot *pen* mai?	*Can* you drive a car?
***pen* khrap.**	Yes.
mai *pen*.	No.

Unlike **dai**, **pen** refers specifically to what you have learned to do. **dai** can be used for any kind of ability:

phom pai sanarmbin mai *dai* (not *pen*)	I *can't go* to the airport.
phom phoot pharsar thai *pen* (or *dai*)	I *can* speak Thai.

Sometimes you need to differentiate between the two meanings:

phom khap rot pen tae wannee khap mai dai.	I know how to drive a car but I can't drive today. (e.g. because I'm ill)

Requests

We saw in Lesson 9 that you can use **dai** to ask someone to do something for you:

khun shuey phom dai mai khrap?   Can you help me?

You can also use it to ask someone's permission or agreement to do something:

soop buree dai mai khrap?   Do you mind if I smoke?

In affirmative requests adjectives and adverbs (such as **dee**, **shar**) are often repeated:

tham dee dee.   Do it properly.

As we saw in Lesson 9, **noi** is used to soften the request and make it sound more polite.

In negative requests you often add **nak** ('so', 'so much') as well as the filler word **na**:

yar phoot reo nak nakhrap.   Don't speak so fast.

Language and culture notes

Knowledge of Thai

You will find that any attempts to use Thai, however modest or flawed, will be warmly appreciated and you can expect to hear plenty of compliments such as **phoot pharsar thai keng khrap!**

Vocabulary

khun phim deet dai mai? dai kha. shai kormpiuter dai mai? dai kha. shorp thai roop mai? shorp kha.

phim dèet	to type	**shái**	to use
kormpiutêr	computer	**thài roôp**	(to take a) photograph

Exercise 1

How would you ask someone if they can speak:

1 Japanese
2 English
3 French
4 Thai
5 Chinese

How would you find out if they can read and write the same languages?

Exercise 2

How would you describe these people?

1 Ken: a good linguist, has learned several languages
2 Steve: a very bad linguist; can manage only a few words in one
3 Janet: quite a good linguist, has picked up a few languages but only the spoken form
4 James: a very bookish student who enjoys Oriental languages but has never tried to speak them

Exercise 3

Ask a follow-up question with **pen**:

1 phom cha seuh rot.
2 phom cha pai shai thale.
3 phom cha pai sanarm korp.
4 shan cha pai yeepun.
5 phom shorp dontree thai.
6 phom cha seuh khreuang khrua.
7 phrungnee khao cha seuh kormpiuter.

Exercise 4

You are very keen on getting a job but you don't meet any of the requirements. Tell someone that although you can't do the following there is something almost as useful you can do.

1 khap rot me
2 phoot pharsar cheen
3 tham kapkhao farangset
4 shai kormpiuter
5 len dontree thai
6 khian pharsar yeepun

Exercise 5

Criticize these people by saying they are no good at what they do. (Remember that in Lesson 4 we saw that **nak** indicates someone whose job is to do something.)

1 Tawat pen khon khap rot taeksee.
2 Saowalak pen khroo.
3 Saowanee pen mae barn.
4 Suporn pen nak keelar
5 Manat pen nak dontree
6 Steve rian pharsar thai.
7 Janet rian arn pharsar cheen
8 Don pen nak nangseuh phim.
9 John pen nak thai roop

Exercise 6

How would you compliment someone on their:

1 driving
2 spoken English
3 written English
4 cooking
5 musical ability
6 swimming
7 photographs

Exercise 7

Suggest (in English) why your friend is unable to do these things:

1 wannee phom khap rot mai dai.
2 khap rot mai pen.
3 wannee phoot phasar angkrit mai dai.
4 shan wai narm mai pen.
5 wannee wai narm mai dai.
6 khorthoht, kha, wannee len dontree mai dai.
7 wannee thai roop mai dai.

Exercise 8

Ask if it's OK to do these things:

1 smoke in the hospital
2 speak English
3 take a photograph
4 have a coffee
5 go to see the house
6 sit here
7 read the newspaper

Exercise 9

Rewrite the dialogue in this part between Janet and Suporn. Janet compliments Suporn on his English. Suporn replies modestly and tells her he is learning it because he is going to work in England. He has a teacher and studies six hours a day.

Dialogue ▱

Malee explains why she can't speak English

MALEE: rian pharsar thai mar narn laeo reu yang kha?
KEN: pramarn hok deuan thaonan khrap. lae khun la khrap? phoot pharsar angkrit dai mai khrap?
MALEE: mai dai kha. rian thee rohng rian tae leuhm laeo.
KEN: khun khoei pai angkrit mai khrap?
MALEE: mai khoei kha. mai khoei pai tarng prathet kha. mai mee ohkart kha.
KEN: khun khit war cha pai sak wan neung mai khrap?
MALEE: wang war yang ngan kha.

MALEE: *Have you been learning Thai long?*
KEN: *Only about six months. What about you? Can you speak English?*
MALEE: *No, I can't. I studied it at school but I've forgotten it.*
KEN: *Have you ever been to England?*
MALEE: *Never. I've never lived abroad. I didn't have the opportunity.*
KEN: *Do you think you will go one day?*
MALEE *I hope so.*

Vocabulary

mar narn laéo	to have been doing something for a long time
khoei	to have done something
ohkàrt	chance, opportunity
tàrng prathêt	abroad
sak wan nèung	one day
wǎng	to hope
wǎng wâr yang ngán	I hope so

Language points

Talking about what you have been doing

When the verb phrase **mar narn laeo** is added to a sentence it indicates that the action referred to has been going on for a long time and is still going on:

> **phom wai narm thuk wan mar narn laeo.**
> I have been swimming every day *for a long time now.*

You will probably find question forms with **narn** more useful:

> **khun rian pharsar thai *narn* laeo reu yang?**
> Have you been learning Thai *for long?*

> **khun rian pharsar thai mar *narn* thaorai laeo?**
> *How long* have you been learning Thai?

Asking about past experiences

> **khun khoei pai angkrit mai?** Have you ever been to England?
> **khoei.** Yes.
> **mai khoei.** Never.
> **phom mai khoei rian pharsar farangset.** I've never studied French.

Like 'never', **mai khoei** can also be used for present time. So **mai kin karfae** can mean 'I never drink coffee' or 'I have never drunk coffee'.

Talking about the past

In affirmative statements **khoei** means 'used to':

> **sip pee thee laeo phom *khoei* pen khroo.**
> Ten years ago I *used to* be a teacher.

Vocabulary

torn nee shan tham ngarn thee rarn aharn thai. pen khon serp. neuai mark. meua korn rian banshee. phoot pharsar yerraman. mai khao chai pharsar angkrit.

torn née	now, at the moment	**banshee**	accounts
khon sèrp	waiter, waitress	**yerraman**	German
nèuai	tired	**khăo chai**	to understand
mêua kòrn	before now		

dieo nee phom yoo khon dieo. mai mee khrorpkhrua. phom yar laeo.

diĕo née	now, at the moment
khrôrpkhrua	family

yàr   divorced

 khon thai shorp khui kan.

khui   chat

Exercise 10

1 You're planning your next holiday. Ask your friend if he has ever been to the countries you're interested in visiting.
2 There are several languages you are interested in trying. Ask your friend if he has ever studied any of them.
3 You're also thinking of something new to do in your spare time. Ask him if he has ever done what you are considering.

Exercise 11

Unfortunately your friend has never done anything interesting. Tell someone how boring she is by listing all the things she has never done.

Exercise 12

Complete these statements by saying what used to be the case:

1 torn nee khao pen khroo ———.
2 torn nee shan mai shorp deuhm lao tae ———.
3 torn nee yoo thee London ———.
4 torn nee khao rian pharsar cheen ———.
5 torn nee khao doo thee wee thuk wan ———.
6 torn nee phom mai mee ngern ———.

Exercise 13

1 You used to have an exciting life but you've fallen on hard times. Describe your past.
2 Things used to be tough for you before you finally came good. Tell your grandchildren all about your early days.

Exercise 14

How many questions can you ask these people using **mar narn laeo reu yang**?

1 You meet a young Thai man on a golf course in England. He tells you he's studying music in London.
2 You meet a Thai lady from Bangkok who teaches English in Chieng Mai. She tells you she's studying Chinese and plays tennis every day.

Exercise 15

Now see how many questions you can ask them using **mar narn thaorai**.

Exercise 16

Your friend is about to embark on a tour of six countries. Ask him how long he is going to spend in each one.

Exercise 17

1 You are a reformed character. How would you tell someone that you used to do these things but have given them up:

1 drive very fast
2 smoke a lot
3 drink a lot
4 spend a lot of money
5 play cards every day
6 watch television eight hours a day

Exercise 18

Decide which of the statements are true and which are false according to this conversation.

A: khun rian pharsar yeepun mar narn laeo reu yang kha?
B: pramarn kao deuan thaonan khrap.
A: khun arn lae khian pharsar yeepun dai mai kha?
B: mai khoi dai khrap. khian dai barng kham khrap.
A: rian pharsar yeepun duey tua eng shai mai kha?
B: mai shai khrap. rian thee rohng rian pharsar tarng prathet.
A: yark mai kha?
B: khit war ngai khrap.
A: khun khoei pai thieo yeepun mai kha?
B: khoei khrap. pai sarm pee thee laeo. wang war cha klap pai eek hok deuan.

1 khao rian pharsar cheen kao deuan thee laeo.
2 khao rian pharsar yeepun kao pee thee laeo.
3 khao khian pharsar yeepun nitnoi tae mai keng.
4 khao rian pharsar yeepun kap khroo
5 khao khit war rian pharsar yeepun yark mark.
6 khao khoei pai yeepun.
7 khao pai thura thee yeepun sarm pee thee laeo.
8 khao pai yeepun hok deuan thee laeo.
9 khao wang war cha klap pai yeepun

Exercise 19

1 You have gone for a job as a cook in a restaurant serving mainly Chinese food. Tell the manager you can cook French food.
2 You want to find out how long your friend has been learning to play Chinese music.
3 You have been to visit a friend you have not seen for a year or two. You find that she has changed considerably. Describe the changes.

Vocabulary building

A
Find the odd one out in these groups of words:

1 phoot pharsar khlorng kham khoei khao chai
2 welar bai thai roop shuamohng deuan narlikar
3 keelar dontree wai narm dern len len phai phoot len
4 karng keng rorng thao kraprohng sia
5 waen rom nang krapao charn

B
Match the words that are opposite or complementary in meaning.
Note: **cham dai** = 'remember'.

ngai	**phanrayar**
pit	**phorm**
cham dai	**yark**
reo	**soong**
laeo	**pert**
phrungnee	**leuhm**
sarmee	**meuawarnne**
tia	**shar**
uwan	**yang mai**

Tone practice 🔳

Practise the tones in these words and phrases:

    phôot   pharsăr   khlôrng   kham   khĭan   mar narn laéo   yârk
    khâo chai   phim dèet   tàrng prathêt   wăng wâr yangngán

Reading and writing

Consonants

ษ อังกฤษ ภ   ภาษา ญ

initial	s	ph	y
final	t		n

Note that the pronunciation of ฤ here is *ri* not *reu*.

Consonant clusters

We have already seen that Thai sometimes inserts an unwritten vowel sound between two consonants. There are, however, a number of common consonant clusters. The combinations possible are:

        kr   khr   tr   pr   phr
        kl   khl   pl   phl
        kw   khw

ไกล ใคร ตรง ปลา

Exercise 20

1 Write these words in transliteration (be careful – there are one or two tricky ones):

กลับ ขวา ใกล้ น่าเกลียด สกปรก

ผลไม้ ของขวัญ กระไปรง   คลอง

ต่างประเทศ ครอบครัว

2 What are the meanings of these signs?

ห้ามสูบบุหรี่   ห้ามเข้า ห้ามถ่ายรูป

ห้ามจอกรถ   ห้ามผ่าน

3 Translate these job advertisements. Vocabulary: **rapsamak** (recruit), **samak** ('apply'), **prasopkarn** experience

รับสมัคร   เลขานุการ พูดภาษาอังกฤษ

เวลาทำงาน 8 โมงเช้า · 6   โมงเย็น

ต้องมีประสพการณ์ เงินเดือน 2000   บาท

สมัครที่นี่ รับสมัคร คนครัวทำอาหารจีน

โทรศัพท์ 2583913   อาทิตย์ละ 500 บาท

4 Translate these extracts from job applications:

ตอนนี้เป็นแม่บ้านเคยเป็นเลขานุการ

พูดภาษาจีนได้ พิมพ์ดีดได้ ใช้คอมพิวเตอร์ได้

ตอนนี้ทำงานที่กรุงเทพเป็นนักธุรกิจ

เคยเป็นตำารวจ

สิบห้าปีที่แล้วอยู่ที่ลอนดอนเรียนหนังสือ

Exercise 21

1 You are a very fussy landlord. Write some signs forbidding certain things to be put up in your house.

2 Fill in this form in Thai:

Languages you speak _____ _____

(English, Chinese)   (English, Thai)

Occupation _____ _____

(you are a businessperson)   (you're a teacher of
                              English)

Employment record _____ _____

(thirteen years ago you were a doctor)   (eight years ago you
                                          worked in London
                                          teaching Thai)

Dialogue

*Steve is interviewing someone for a job in his company. He is look-
ing for someone with a good knowledge of English, and preferably
another language, office experience (especially accounts) and an
interest in people*

STEVE: khun khoei pen lekharnukarn reuplao khrap?

TANA: mai khoei kha. khoei pen khon serp.

STEVE: tham ngarn thee rarn aharn pen yangngai barng khrap?

TANA: beua kha. mai shorp. neuai mark.

STEVE: tham ngarn thee opfit ko neuai meuankan.

TANA: shai kha. khoei tham ngarn thee opfit. sip see pee thee laeo
kha. shorp kha.

STEVE: thammai shorp khrap?

TANA: dai cher kap khon mark thuk wan. shorp khui kap khon
thee tham ngarn duey kan.

STEVE: khun khoei rian banshee reuplao?

TANA: mai khoei kha. mai mee ohkart rian kha.

STEVE: khun mee khrorpkhrua laeo reu yang?

TANA: mee kha tae dieo nee shan yoo khon dieo.

STEVE: thammai la khrap? sarmee ka look look khorng khun yoo
thee Chieng Mai reuh khrap?

TANA: shan yar laeo kha. look shan yoo kap khun mae .

STEVE: khun khoei pai tarng prathet mai khrap?

TANA: khoei pai kha. yoo thee amerikar, laeo ko yoo thee yerraman.

STEVE: phoot pharsar angkrit dai reuplao?

TANA: dai kha. shan yoo thee amerikar har pee, phoot khlorng.

STEVE: arn lae khian dai mai khrap?

TANA: arn dai kha khian dai tae mai keng.

STEVE: khun khao chai nang amerikan mai khrap?

TANA: khao chai nitnoi kha phro phoot reo mark.

STEVE: lae pharsar yerraman phoot dai mai khrap?

TANA: meua korn phoot dai kha tae dieo nee leuhm laeo kha.

STEVE: arn dai mai khrap?

TANA: mai khoi dai kha.

STEVE: torn nee khun tham ngarn thee pam namman shai mai khrap?

TANA: shai kha.

STEVE: pam namman yoo thee nai?

TANA: yoo trong kharm satharnthoot yerraman kha.

STEVE: khun tham ngarn thee nan mar narn thaorai laeo?

TANA: sorng deuan laeo kha. mai nar son chai kha. shan wang war khun cha hai shan tham ngarn thee nee na kha.

Comprehension

1 How suitable is the candidate?
2 What does Steve know about her before the interview?
3 What details does she give of her family situation?

12 khwarm torng karn

You can't always get what you want

In this lesson you will learn how to:

- say what you want to do
- explain why you can't do something
- use some more ways of saying goodbye to someone
- say that something is excessive or insufficient

Dialogue 🔘

Ken asks Saowanee why she doesn't work and points out that she may not be as unfortunate as she thinks

KEN: khun Saowanee khrap.

SAOWANEE: kha.

KEN: thammai khun yoo barn khrap? khee kiat tham ngarn reu khrap?

SAOWANEE: khorthoht kha. mai khao chai. mai khwarm war arai kha?

KEN: thammai khun mai pai tham ngarn khrap?

SAOWANEE: phro war mai mee ngarn tham kha.

KEN: yark tham ngarn mai khrap?

SAOWANEE: yark tham, tae tham ngarn mai dai kha. shan mai keng. phoot pharsar angkrit mai dai. phim deet mai pen. khap rot mai pen. sorn nangseuh mai pen. khit war shan kae kern pai!

KEN: yang mai kae rok khrap. khun shohk dee thee mai torng tham ngarn. phom yark pai thieo, yark arn nangseuh tae mee welar mai phor. tham ngarn nak kern pai.

SAOWANEE: shan sia chai duey kha.

KEN: *Soawanee.*

SAOWANEE: *Yes?*

KEN: *Why do you stay at home? Are you (too) lazy to work?*

SAOWANEE: *I'm sorry, I don't understand. What do you mean?*

KEN: *Why don't you go to work?*

SAOWANEE: *Because I haven't got a job!*

KEN: *Do you want to work?*

SAOWANEE: *Of course I want to, but I can't. I don't have a skill. I can't speak English. I can't type. I can't drive a car. I can't teach. I think I'm too old.*

KEN: *You're not old! And you're lucky not to work. I want to go places, read books but I don't have enough time. I work too hard.*

SAOWANEE: *I'm sorry for you.*

Vocabulary

khêe kìat	lazy	**(mârk) kern pai**	too
măi khwarm	to mean	**phor**	enough
phró wâr	because	**mâi phor**	not enough
yàrk	want	**sŏrn**	teach

Language points

Expressing wants

yark or **yark cha** are used to say you want or don't want to do something:

yark **pai wai narm.**	*I want* to go swimming.
yark cha **klap barn.**	*I want* to go home.
khao mai *yark* **mar.**	*He doesn't want* to come.

yark cha often corresponds to 'would like to':

yark cha **shuey khun.**	*I would like to* help you.

Unlike 'want', **yark** and **yark cha** are not used without a verb:

yark **dai narlikar.**	*I want* a watch.

As an alternative, you can use the verb **torng karn**:

khun phor shan cha hai khorng khwan shan. yark dai narlikar.	My father is going to give me a present. I want a watch.
khun *torng karn* **arai?**	What *do you want*?

Explaining

mar shar phro war rot tit.	I was late because the traffic was bad.

With **phro**, **war** can be omitted: **mar shar phro rot tit.** The clause with **phro** or **phro war** can also come before the clause you are explaining. You would translate 'Because it was raining, I returned home late' by: **phro war fon tok klap barn shar.**

Saying that something is too much or not enough

pharsar cheen yark kern pai. Chinese is too difficult.

kern pai follows the adjective it qualifies.

We have seen that **mark**, **mark mark** and **nitnoi** are also used to qualify uncountable nouns:

mee ngern nitnoi. I have a little money.

mark kern pai can be used with nouns in the same way:

khao mee ngern mark kern pai. He has too much money.

The contrasting idea is expressed by **mai phor**:

khao mee ngern mai phor. He does not have enough money.

Notice that **mai phor** follows the noun it relates to.

Vocabulary

The weather

arkart yae. fon tok. narm thuam. mai mee rom. wannee arkart nao. mee lom duey.

arkàrt	weather	**nárm thûam**	(there are) floods
yâe	terrible	**lom**	wind

fon tok nak. phom torng karn rom.

Note: **torng karn** can also mean 'need'.

Exercise 1

Explain why you want or don't want to do these things by saying what you like or don't like about them.

1 thammai mai torngkarn pai rohng nang?
2 thammai torngkarn pai rarn aharn farangset?
3 thammai mai torngkarn pai amerikar?
4 thammai torngkarn seuh karset nee?
5 thammai torngkarn seuh rot khan nee?
6 thammai mai torngkarn pai shai tale?

Exercise 2

Complete these statements by saying either that you want to do something or that you can't.

1 yark pai kin khao tae —————.
2 yark khap rot khorng khao tae —————.
3 ————— tae tham kapkhao thai mai dai.
4 yark arn nangseuh phim cheen tae —————.
5 ————— tae phoot pharsar thai mai dai.
6 ————— tae wai narm mai pen.

Exercise 3

You are going on a group tour to Thailand and the Thai organiser has asked you to write down six things that you want to do there.

Exercise 4

Your friend is rather surprised at some of your decisions. Explain why you want or don't want to do the following using **mark kern pai**, or 'not enough'.

1 thammai mai yark seuh barn lang nan?
2 thammai mai shorp ngarn nee?
3 thammai mai yark rian pharsar yeepun?
4 thammai mai seuh rot khan nee?
5 thammai mai yark pai tham ngarn thee London?
6 thammai mai yark pai rarn aharn farangset?

Exercise 5

Continue these statements using **torng karn**:

1 khun mae shan cha seuh khorng khwan hai shan.
2 yark seuh khorng khwan hai khun.
3 khit war fon cha tok.
4 phom mar shar samer.
5 nao mark.
6 pai tham ngarn rot me shar mark.

Exercise 6

A: beua.
B: yark tham arai?
A: yark doo thee wee.

Complete these dialogues following this model.

Dialogue 1
A: hiu.
B:
C:

Dialogue 2
A: hiu narm.
B:
C:

Dialogue 3
A: pai seuh khorng.
B:
A:

Dialogue 4
A: yark rian nangseuh.
B:
A:

Dialogue 5
A: yark cha pen khroo.
B:
A:

Dialogue 6
A: yark khai khorng.
B:
A:

Exercise 7

Complete these sentences giving the weather or your ill health as a reason for what has happened. Use **phro** or **phro war**.

1 mai yark yoo thee London . . .
2 mar shar . . .
3 mai dai pai len korp . . .

4 khreuang bin mar shar ...
5 mai dai pai tham ngarn ...
6 mai shorp krungthep ...

Exercise 8

B is describing her holiday in England. Make a note of her complaints.

A: pai nai mar khrap?
B: pai angkrit mar khrap.
A: pen yangngai barng khrap?
B: yae mark khrap. arkart mai dee. fon tok thuk wan khrap. phan-rayar phom leuhm rom khrap. nao mark duey. phom dee chai thee klap mar krungthep!

Dialogue

Ken prepares to leave the party

KEN: khorthoht khrap phom pai korn na khrap. songsai fon cha tok.
SAOWANNEE: yoo korn see kha. ngarn kamlang sanuk kha.
KEN: khorthoht khrap. phom torng reep phro war mee nat yen nee.
SAOWANNEE: yindee thee dai roochak khun kha.
KEN: meuan kan khrap. wang war rao cha dai phop kan eek na khrap.
SAOWANNEE: nae norn kha.
KEN: lar korn na khrap.
SAOWANNEE: sawatdee kha. shohk dee na kha.

KEN: *I'm sorry, I must go now. I think it's going to rain.*
SAOWANNEE: *Stay a little longer, won't you? The party's just getting fun.*
KEN: *I'm sorry. I must hurry as I've got an appointment tonight.*
SAOWANNEE: *I enjoyed meeting you.*
KEN: *Me too. I hope we'll meet again sometime.*
SAOWANNEE: *Maybe.*
KEN: *Goodbye.*
SAOWANNEE: *Goodbye.*

Vocabulary

kòrn	first, before (sometimes indicates that an action is of short duration)
lar	to say goodbye
sǒngsǎi	to think (deduce)
rêep	to hurry
nát	appointment
phóp	to meet

Language points

Expressing hopes

You have already come across constructions with **khit war** ('I think that'). Sentences with **wang war** are formed in the same way:

wang war **khao cha mar.**	*I hope* he will come.

Notice that with **khit** and **wang** you can't drop **war** in the way we drop 'that' in English.

With **wang** there is also no equivalent of the construction 'I hope to come'. In Thai you have to say:

phom *wang war* **cha phop khun.**	*I hope* I will meet you.

Notice these two common responses:

wang war **yang ngan.**	*I hope* so.
wang war **khong mai.**	*I hope* not.

songsai

songsai is similar in meaning to **khit** but suggests that you have deduced something to be the case.

songsai **mai mee ngern.**	*I suspect* he hasn't any money. (perhaps he is wearing shabby clothes)

Unlike **khit** it is not followed by **war**.

Describing an action in progress

nang kamlang sanuk.	The film's just getting interesting.
phom kamlang khian nangseuh.	I'm in the process of writing a book.

Notice that **kamlang** can be used with some adjectives to mean 'become', for example:

barn kamlang suey.	The house is beginning to look pretty. (for example, you are just finishing decorating it)

You will remember that it is perfectly possible to talk about an action that is in progress without using **kamlang**:

phom khian nangseuh.	I'm writing a book.

kamlang is simply a way of making the meaning more explicit. Another way of indicating an action in progress is by the use of **yoo**:

khao tham ngarn *yoo.*	He *is* working.

Referring to an action that is imminent

Another use of **kamlang** is with **cha** to indicate an action that is about to happen:

phom *kamlang cha* **pai sanarmbin.**	*I'm just* off to the airport.

Language and culture notes

Saying goodbye

As we saw in Lesson 1, if it is clear that you are leaving you can just say **sawatdee khrap** or **kha**. There are a number of ways of announcing that you are leaving:

shan pai korn na kha. lar korn na kha.	I'm going now. Goodbye.
phom lar korn na khrap. mee thura.	I have to say goodbye now. I've some business to do.
pai la na.	I'm going now.

lar is used to say goodbye to someone when it is not just a casual farewell. For example, you might not know them that well and you are not sure if you will see them again. Or perhaps you are leaving for a long time. You would not use **lar** if you are just popping out for a few minutes and will see someone again shortly. One other peculiarity of **lar**: it is only used by the person leaving.

There are also a number of ways of expressing the hope that you will see someone again (which, as in English, you may or may not mean):

laeo phop kan mai na khrap.	See you again.
cher kan phrungnee.	See you tomorrow.
pai har phom barng see khrap.	Come and see me sometime.

Vocabulary

A: phrungnee cha sorp. wang war cha pharn.
B: shan sorp laeo. sorp tok.

sòrp	(to take an) exam
(sòrp) phàrn	to pass
sòrp tòk	to fail

phom cha thohrasap har khun phrungnee. yark phoot reuang karn rian. mee panhar reuang kormpiuter.

Notice that 'to telephone someone' is **thohrasap har**.

rêuang	about
karn	to do with
panhăr	problem

shan mai shorp muey thai. shorp futborn.

muey	boxing
fútborn	football

Exercise 9

You are having difficulty getting away from a party. Explain you have to leave giving the following reasons:

1 you want to see the boxing on TV
2 you have a problem with your car
3 you have an appointment at the airport
4 you have a problem with your telephone

5 you have to take an exam
6 you have to go and play music with a friend
7 your wife/husband is not well

Exercise 10

How would you say goodbye to someone you will see:

1 the same evening
2 tomorrow afternoon
3 next week
4 in three days' time
5 in six months' time
6 sometime (but you're not sure)

Exercise 11 ▐▌

Respond to the speaker with either **wang war yang ngan** or **wang war khong mai**:

1 khun torng pai rohng phayarbarn shai mai?
2 khit war shan cha sorp tok.
3 phrungnee shan cha hai ngern khun.
4 khit war narlikar phom hai.
5 khit war thai roop suey mark.
6 khit war narm tuam.
7 songsai fon cha tok.

Exercise 12

Say what you hope will happen in these situations:

1 You've heard that a friend might be coming to see you and that he has a pleasant surprise for you.
2 You hear that your boss has got some good news for you.
3 From the tone of your wife's/husband's voice you think you are going to get some bad news.
4 Your son has just started on a very expensive computer course which leads to a tough examination.
5 Your friend has borrowed your new car and is late coming back.

Exercise 13

You share a flat with six other people who are all busy. Someone comes to see them. Tell him what they are all doing.

Exercise 14

Your friend comes across you in these situations. Tell him where you are going or what you're on the point of doing:

1 you are clutching a fistful of **bart**
2 you have an air ticket sticking out of your pocket
3 you are carrying a set of golf clubs
4 you are carrying a violin case
5 you are holding a bottle of wine and a bunch of flowers
6 you have a French grammar book in your hand
7 you look pale and nervous and you're holding a copy of the Highway Code

Exercise 15

What do you say in these situations:

1 You come across a friend who is looking very nervous. You know he's been taking driving lessons.
2 You have just returned from a few days' holiday. The weather was terrible. Someone in your office makes a snide remark about your having long holidays in the sun.
3 You've just won some money and you are telling your friend how you are going to spend it.

Vocabulary building

1 Words in context
The following words are all to do with time and appointments:

reep   nat   phop   shar   reo   har   sai

Use each one once to complete the following sentences:
1 mee welar mark. mai torng . . .
2 khun warng mai? mai warng kha. mee . . .
3 torng reep. khit war cha pai . . .
4 rot mai tit. khit war mar . . .
5 A: mar . . . .khun Suporn.

B: khorthoht kha mai yoo.
6 phom mar shar. mai dai . . . khao.
7 sip mohng laeo. thammai mar tham ngarn . . .?

Exercise 16

2 We saw in the dialogue at the beginning of Lesson 10 the compound **khwarm sa-art**. On its own **sa-art** means 'clean'; **khwarm** is often used to indicate an abstract concept (state of being clean). See if you can deduce the meaning of these compounds:

1 khwarm khit
2 khwarm ching
3 khwarm torng karn
4 khwarm rak
5 khwarm reo
6 khwarm mai
7 khwarm wang
8 khwarm suk

Exercise 17

3 We also saw that **karn** means 'something to do with' or 'matters of'. This can be used with other words to make a noun compound. For example, **karn meuang** means 'politics'. Match the Thai words on the left with their English equivalent:

karn khar	experiment
karn ngern	politician
karn chark pai	finance
karn shern	agreement
karn dern tharng	excursion
nak karn meuang	invitation
karn tok long	trade, business
karn thot rorng	departure
karn pai thieo	travel

Tone practice

Practise the tones in these words and phrases:

khêe kiàt   mǎi khwarm   phró wâr   tôrng karn   nárm thûam
  sǒngsǎi   yindee thêe dâi róochàk   réep   nát

Reading and writing

Vowels

When the symbol ะ is used in connection with another vowel symbol it shortens the vowel sound: เ_าะ

เพราะ   เกาะ
phro   ko

Exercise 18

1 Write these words in transliteration:

อากาศ น้ำท่วม   ปัญหา   มวย ฟุตบอลล์   มีชื่อ

2 Translate this message:

มีปัญหาเรื่องเครื่องบินเพราะว่า   อากาศไม่ดี

3 Translate this postcard which a friend has received:

ฉันพักอยู่โรงแรมที่สวยมาก

อากาศเริ่มหนาวฝนตกทุกวัน

ฉันไปซื้อของใช้เงินมาก

ไม่เคยไปชายทะเล

คิดถึงคุณ   โชคดีค้ะ

Write a postcard to someone describing your holiday.

Dialogue 🔘

Steve works for a publishing company and is doing some work with Suporn. Steve has been trying to contact Suporn, so he is pleased when he runs into him in the street

STEVE: sawatdee khrap khun Suporn. khun cha pai nai khrap? phom yark phop khun mar narn laeo.

SUPORN: khorthoht khrap. mee thura mark. mee sorp arthit thee laeo.

STEVE: karn sorp pen yangngai barng khrap?

SUPORN: sorp mai pharn khrap.

STEVE: phom sia chai duey na khrap. khun cha pai nai khrap?

SUPORN: kamlang cha pai doo apartmen. yark seuh apartmen thee thanon Sukhumvit.

STEVE: dee khrap. phom yark phoot kap khun reuang nangseuh khrap.

SUPORN: nangseuh arai khrap?

STEVE: nangseuh thee khun kamlang khian khrap. nangseuh reuang muey.

SUPORN: shai khrap.

STEVE: set laeo reu yang khrap?

SUPORN: yang mai set. arthit thee laeo yark phop khun Khaosai. pen nak muey mee sheuh. tae yang mai dai phop.

STEVE: thammai khrap?

SUPORN: phom pai shar kern pai khrap.

STEVE: thammai mar shar khrap?

SUPORN: fon tok nak phom klap barn pai ao rom. narm tuam thee barn phom. khap rot pai mai dai. torng pai rot me rot tit mark.

STEVE: thammai mai pai taeksee khrap?

SUPORN: mee ngern mai phor. yark pai thanarkharn tae mee welar mai phor.

STEVE: deuan thee laeo khun ko phoot baep nee. phom khit war mai yark khian nangseuh.

SUPORN: yark mark khrap tae torn nee mee panhar mark mark phom lar korn na khrap. torng pai dieo nee laeo khrap korn thee cha sai eek. rot me mar laeo. phom cha thohrasap har khun arthit nar.

STEVE: dieo korn see khrap . . .

Vocabulary

khao pen nak dontree mee sheuh.

mee shêuh   famous

A: set laeo reu yang?
B: yang mai set.

sèt ready

    shan mai shorp muey.
    khun phoot baep nee samer.

bàep née   in this fashion

Comprehension

1 Why did Steve want to see Suporn?
2 Why has Suporn not been in contact with Steve?
3 What explanations does Suporn give for the delays?

13 karn pai thieo

Decisions, decisions

In this lesson you will learn how to:

- compare things and note their advantages and disadvantages
- say that something is possible
- ask for advice

Dialogue 📼

Ken is planning a trip at the weekend but he can't make up his mind how to travel

MANAT: sao arthit nee cha pai nai reuplao khrap?
KEN: khit war cha pai Chieng Rai. khun khoei pai mai khrap ?
MANAT: pai mokkarar pee thee laeo khrap.
KEN: pen yangngai barng khrap?
MANAT: pen meuang lek lek tae mee phu khao suey khrap.
KEN: pai yangngai dee khrap?
MANAT: pai rot tua reuh pai khreuang bin ko dai khrap.
KEN: pai yangngai dee kwar kan khrap?
MANAT: pai khreuang bin reo kwar khrap. pai rot tua thook kwar khreuang bin khrap.
KEN: phom khit war mee ngern mai phor pai khreuang bin.

MANAT: *Are you going anywhere this weekend?*
KEN: *I'm thinking of going to Chieng Rai. Have you ever been there?*
MANAT: *I went last January.*
KEN: *What's it like?*
MANAT: *It's a very small town but the hills are pretty.*
KEN: *How should I go? (lit. going how is good?)*
MANAT: *You can go either by bus or by plane.*
KEN: *Which is better?*
MANAT: *The plane is quicker. The bus is cheaper than the plane, though.*
KEN: *I don't think I have enough money to go by plane.*

Vocabulary

sǎo arthít	weekend	**phu khǎo**	mountain, hill
mokkarar	January	**kwàr**	more
meuang	town	**thòok**	cheap

Language points

Comparing qualities of things

To indicate that something is superior in some respect you use **kwar** after the adjective or adverb:

pharsar angkrit *yark kwar* **pharsar thai.**	English is *more difficult* than Thai.
khao phoot pharsar thai *dee kwar* **phom.**	He speaks Thai *better* than me.

Notice how you say something is inferior in some respect:

pharsar angkrit *mai yark kwar* **pharsar thai.**	English is *not as difficult* as Thai.

Asking how things compare

Notice that when you mention two or more things you want to compare you use **kan** (together):

pai rot tua reuh khreuang bin dee kwar kan?	Which is better – the plane or the coach?

You can also use **ka** (short for **kap**) instead of **reuh**:

Steve ka Ken khrai keng kwar kan?	Who is better (more clever), Steve or Ken?

Comparing what you do

When you are comparing verbs or verb phrases you use **mark kwar** rather than **kwar**:

phom shorp aharn cheen, *mark kwar* **aharn farangset.**	I like Chinese food *more than* French food.
phom shorp aharn farangset noi kwar aharn cheen.	I don't like French food *as much as* Chinese food.

Degree of difference

Notice the word order when you want to show the extent to which something is superior or inferior:

Ayuthaya suey kwar Khon Kaen mark.	Ayuthaya is much prettier than Khon Kaen.

Saying things are the same

parkkar rarkhar meuankap narlikar **parkkar lae narlikar rarkhar meuankan.**	The price of the pen is the same as that of the watch.

Asking for an opinion or advice

dee is often used in questions to ask for advice or opinions:

pai nai *dee*? Where *should I* go?

Short answers are often given using **see kha** or **see khrap**:

pai Ayuthaya *see kha*. (*You should*) go to Ayuthaya.

Notice the difference between asking what someone's opinion is and asking what they are thinking:

khun khit war pen yangngai?	What do you think about this? (i.e.
khun war yangngai?	What's your opinion?)
khun kamlang khit arai?	What are you thinking about?

Avoiding giving your opinion

We saw in Lesson 10 that **ko dai** can indicate that something will do. It can be used in the following combinations:

rao cha pai nai?	Where shall we go?
pai nai ko dai.	Anywhere (wherever you like)
rao cha kin arai?	What shall we eat?
kin arai ko dai.	Anything.
rao cha klap barn meuarai?	When shall we go home?
meuarai ko dai.	Whenever you like.
rao cha shern khrai dee?	Who shall we invite?
shern khrai ko dai.	Whoever you like.

It is often used to suggest that either of the alternatives mentioned or understood is acceptable:

phom cha pai barn khun welar nai dee?	What time shall I go to your house?
welar nai ko dai.	Any time will do.
rao cha kin rarn aharn nai kan dee?	Which restaurant shall we eat in?
rarn nai ko dai.	Any one will do.

Vocabulary

The months

Be warned – the words for the months of the year are difficult. You may find it easier to learn them gradually, whenever there is a particular month you want to refer to. As you saw in the dialogue you can refer to them without the final syllable. However, there are no other short cuts for learning them! We have already seen that 'January' is **deuan mokkarar**.

deuan kumpharphan	February
deuan meenarkhom	March
deuan mesăryon	April
deuan phreútsapharkhom	May
deuan míthunaryon	June
deuan korrákadarkhom	July
deuan sínghărkhom	August
deuan kanyaryon	September
deuan tularkhom	October
deuan phreútsachìkaryon	November
deuan thanwarkhom	December

rohng raem phaeng tae saduak.

sadùak   comfortable

Exercise 1

From the description of the two hotels tick the one which rates higher on each of the criteria mentioned.

	Cost	Size	Comfort	Distance	Food: cost	Food: quality
Orbis						
Rama						

rohng raem Orbis yai kwar rohng raem Rama phaeng kwar duey. rohng raem Orbis saduak kwar rohng raem Rama tae klai kwa duey. thee rohng raem Rama aharn aroi kwar thee rohng raem Orbis lae phaeng kwar.

Exercise 2

Look at the data on these three athletes and answer the questions.

	Time (minutes)	Height	Weight (kilos)	Age
A	17	5 ft 9 in	73	19
B	16	5 ft 8 in	68	21
C	21	6 ft 1 in	65	23

1 A ka B khrai keng kwar kan?
2 A ka C khrai soong kwar kan?
3 B ka C khrai nak kwar kan?
4 C ka A khrai kae kwar kan?
5 C ka A khrai soong kwar kan?
6 A ka C khrai keng kwar kan?

Exercise 3

Look at the test results of these students. How would you compare:

1 A and B
2 B and C
3 A and C

	pharsar phoot	yeepun arn	khian	pharsar phoot	angkrit arn	khian
A	75	55	35	10	25	35
B	20	45	45	85	50	40
C	60	30	10	60	55	30

Exercise 4

You are trying to decide where to go for a holiday and how to travel. Use this table first to compare packages in three different places. You then decide to make your own travel arrangements and compare the options for one of the places.

Place	Price	Hours	Comfort	Attractions	Size	Distance
A				****	*	100 km
B				**	**	50 km
C				*	*	550 km
Method						
Train	1000	9	**			
Bus	350	13	*			
Plane	4500	1	*****			

Exercise 5

1 Complete this dialogue:

A: shorp kraprohng tua nai mark kwar kha? tua see dam reuh tua see daeng?

B: ——————————.

A: thammai kha?

B: ——————————.

Now rewrite the conversation to talk about cars/jackets/houses/books/films.

Exercise 6

1 Tell someone which months of the year in England are usually cold, very cold and hot (relatively speaking!).
2 You are considering going to Thailand in one of six months. How would you ask someone what the weather is like in each of these months?

Exercise 7

You would like to take a holiday somewhere but you have no idea where or when to go or how to travel. How would you ask someone for advice?

Exercise 8

You are very easy-going. Answer these questions by saying you really don't mind.

1 khun yark rian arai?
2 khun yark pai yangngai?
3 khun yark kin khao meuarai?
4 khun yark len arai?
5 khun yark yoo rohng raem nai?
6 khun mar har khrai?

Exercise 9

How many different ways can you find of asking questions in these situations?

1 You want to know if someone knows Chieng Rai.
2 You want to know what they think of a hotel you're considering staying at.
3 You want to know which of two fridges your friend recommends.
4 You want to know if someone is busy next week.
5 You want to know how long someone has lived in London.

Dialogue 🔲

Ken meets Manat's friend Suthaep who is interested in his travel plans and gives him some advice

SUTHAEP: khun pai Chieng Rai reuh? pai yangngai khrap?
KEN: yang mai nae. khun khit war pai rot tua reuh pai khreuang bin dee kwar kan khrap?
SUTHAEP: phom war khap rot pai dee thee sut khrap.
KEN: phom mai mee rot khrap.
SUTHAEP: shao rot pai see khrap. khar shao rot khong wan la 200 bart.
KEN: nar son chai meuankan na khrap. torng shai bai khap khee thai reuplao khrap?
SUTHAEP: shai bai khap khee sarkon ko dai khrap. khun khuan cha thohrasap chorng rot korn phro war sao arthit mee nak torng thieo mark.

SUTHAEP: *So you're going to Chieng Rai? How are you going?*
KEN: *I'm not sure. Which do you think is better – to go by bus or by plane?*
SUTHAEP: *I think it's best to go by car.*
KEN: *I don't have a car.*

SUTHAEP: *You can hire one. It will probably cost you about 200 bart a day to hire one.*

KEN: *That's interesting. Do I need a Thai driving licence?*

SUTHAEP: *No, an international one will do. You should telephone first to book it as there are a lot of tourists at the weekend.*

Vocabulary

nâê	to be sure	**bai khàp khèe**	driving licence
wâr	to think that	**sǎrkon**	international
thêe sùt	the most	**khuan cha**	should
khong	probably	**chorng**	to book (reserve)
shâo	to hire	**nák thôrng thîeo**	tourist

Language points

Superlatives

To use an adjective or adverb in the superlative form, use **thee sut** after the word it qualifies:

khreuang bin *reo thee sut*.　　The plane is *the quickest*.

Saying something is probable

khong or **khong cha** indicate that something is probable or likely:

khao *khong cha* **mar.**　　He will *probably* come.

Note the position of **khong cha**, before the main verb.

khao khong cha mai mar.　　He will probably not come.

Saying somebody should do something

khuan cha is used in the same position in the sentence as **khong cha**:

khun *khuan cha* **klap barn reo.**　　You *should* go home early.

khun *mai khuan* kin kung.　　You *shouldn't* eat prawns.

khong cha and **khuan cha** tend to refer to a specific occasion. **khong** and **khuan** alone refer to what is generally likely or desirable.

Vocabulary

phom pai thieo shai tale pheua phakporn. shorp ngiap sangop.

pheua	for	**ngîap**	quiet
phákpòrn	rest	**sangop**	peaceful

Exercise 10

From this description of three people, which one would you choose to:

1 be a cook
2 help you move some furniture
3 be a Chinese–English interpreter
4 be your English-speaking driver
5 go on holiday with you
6 give life assurance to

Manop phoot pharsar angkrit keng kwar Suporn tae Suchart phoot keng thee sut. Suporn khaeng raeng kwar Manop tae Suchart khaeng raeng thee sut. Suchart phoot pharsar cheen dee kwar Manop tae Suporn phoot dee thee sut. Suchart khap rot reo kwar Suporn tae Suporn khap keng kwar Suchart. Manop khap keng thee sut. Manop shorp len korp mark kwar Suporn. Suporn shorp dern len mark kwar Manop. Suchart shorp dern len mark thee sut. Suchart soop buree mark kwar Suporn tae Manop soop buree mark thee sut. Suporn kin lao mark kwar Manop tae Suchart kin lao mark thee sut. Suporn shorp tham kapkhao farangset tae Suchart tham kapkhao keng thee sut.

Exercise 11

Look again at the table in Exercise 2. Say which athlete scores highest in each respect.

Now look at the table in Exercise 4. Say which place or means of transport scores highest in each respect.

Exercise 12

You are planning a holiday to an area where you have both mountains and beaches as well as old temples and restaurants to visit. Say what you will probably do.

Exercise 13

Your friend is coming on holiday to Britain. Tell him six things he should or should not do.

Exercise 14

Complete this dialogue:

A: pai Ayuthaya yangngai ——— khrap?
B: khun ——— cha pai rot fai. saduak ———
A: rot tua ——————- barng khrap?
B: yae mark kha. ——— cha narn mark.
A: sia welar narn thaorai khrap?
B: ———- cha sia welar see ——— kha.

Exercise 15

Complete the dialogue.

Ask if your friend is going anywhere tomorrow.
yang mai nae kha. barng thee pai Oxford reuh barng thee pai Cambridge. khun khoei pai Cambridge mai kha?
Say you haven't been to Cambridge but you know Oxford.
khit war Cambridge suey.
Tell her you think Oxford is prettier than Cambridge and more fun.
Oxford ngiap sangop shai mai?
Tell her it's not really quiet but there are more tourists in Cambridge and it's smaller.

Exercise 16

1 Your sister has three boyfriends. How would you compare their different attributes and how well they can do things?
2 How would you ask your friend if he has ever been to London in February?
3 How would you tell your friend that you are probably going to Thailand next month and ask him if there is anything you should buy?
4 Your friend asks you if she should buy the red skirt or the green one. How would you tell her that either would be OK?

Tone practice

Practise the tones in these words:

   shâo   **nák thôrng thîeo**   **phu khǎo**   **phák phòrn**

Now compare the tones in these words:

lom	rôm	klai	klâi	sháo	shâo
yàr	yàr	khâo	kháo	sái	sài
yài	yái	hǎi	hâi		

Vocabulary building

The words on the left all refer to classes of objects. Match them to a word on the right which belongs to the class.

arkart	moo
keelar	kluey
khorngwarn	muey
meuang	daeng
khreuang deuhm	too yen
aharn	farangset
neua	parkkar
phonlamai	bia
see	phonlamai
khreuang khrua	lom
khreuang khian	khao

Reading and writing

Exercise 17

1 You are interested in hiring a car. Translate this advertisement:

รถให้เช่า   ค่าเช่าวันละ 200 บาทต้องการใบขับขี่สากล

2 You are looking for a house to rent. Translate this advertisement:

บ้านให้เช่า เดือนละ ๕๐๐๐ บาทมีห้องนอนสามห้อง

มีโทรศัพท์ มีแอร์ มีที่จอดรถด้วย

ใกล้สถานทูตอังกฤษ

3 Your friend has received another postcard (see Lesson 12). Translate it for him.

ฉันมาอยู่ที่นี่สามเดือนแล้ว

อากาศยังแย่ฉันพักผ่อนทุกวันเบื่อแล้ว

นักท่องเที่ยวชอบเงียบสงบ

แต่ฉันคิดว่าไม่สนุก

ฉันไม่ชอบอาหารฝรั่งคิดถึงบ้าน

Exercise 18

1 Write an advertisement for a flat you wish to let. อพาร์ทเมนท์
2 Write another postcard telling your Thai friend what an enjoyable holiday you are having.

Dialogue

Steve decides to arrange a holiday and goes to see Tana who works in a travel agency

TANA: mee arai hai shuey mai kha?
STEVE: khrap. phom torng karn pai thieo phro war phom tham

ngarn nak mar mark laeo. phom torng karn pai thee nai ko dai thee suey pheua phakphorn. khun war pai nai dee khrap?

TANA: shan khit war khun pai shai tale dee thee sut kha. khuan cha pai Phuket, Ko Samui reuh Ko Samit ko dai kha.

STEVE: khun khit war thee nai dee thee sut khrap?

TANA: khit war Ko Samui dee thee sut kha phro war ngiap sangop kha. mai yai mark kha.

STEVE: khun khit war Ko Samit pen yangngai barng khrap?

TANA: Ko Samit lek kwar Ko Samui. mee nak torng thieo noi kwar kha. shan khit war khun cha beua thee nan mark kha. thee Ko Samui mee phukhao, mee rarn aharn mark kwar lae khun shao rot mortersai khap dai kha.

STEVE: thee nai klai kwar kan khrap?

TANA: Ko Samui kha.

STEVE: khar tua Ko Samui phaeng kwar Ko Samit shai mai khrap?

TANA: shai kha.

STEVE: rohng raem thee Ko Samui phaeng kwar Ko Samit mai khrap?

TANA: rarkhar meuankan kha.

STEVE: thee Ko Samit shai tale suey kwar thee Ko Samui mai khrap?

TANA: shai kha. tae pai Ko Samit sia welar narn kwar Ko Samui phro war mai mee khreuang bin. khun torng nang rot tua pai sarm shuamohng lae nang reua eek see sip narthee.

STEVE: lae Ko Samui sia welar narn thaorai khrap?

TANA: pai khreuang bin sarm sip narthee thaonan kha. saduak kwar mark.

STEVE: lae khun khit war Phuket pen yangngai barng khrap?

TANA: Phuket ko suey kha. yai mark thee sut duey. mee bar, disko lae rarn aharn mark kwar Ko Samui tae rohng raem phaeng thee sut.

STEVE: shai tale thee Phuket suey mai khrap?

TANA: barng thee ko suey barng thee ko sokkaprok kha.

STEVE: khun khit war arkart thee nai dee thee sut khrap?

TANA: khit war ko meuankan kha.

STEVE: deuan nee fon cha tok mai khrap?

TANA: khit war mai kha.

STEVE: phom khor khit doo korn na khrap. lae phrungnee cha mar mai. khorpkhun mark khrap.

TANA: mai pen rai kha.

Comprehension

How does the travel agent compare the three places she suggests? What are their advantages and disadvantages? What information does she give about the weather?

14 karn nat phop reuang thurakit 1

Looking for Suporn again

In this lesson you will learn how to:

- use another way of expressing probability
- say what you know or don't know
- report what has been said or asked
- use 'when' and 'since' time clauses

Dialogue 📼

Ken makes another attempt to see Suporn and discuss business with him

RECEPTIONIST: mar har khrai kha?
KEN: mar har khun Suporn khrap.
RECEPTIONIST: (*to a colleague*) khun sarp mai kha war khun Suporn yoo reuplao?
COLLEAGUE: mai yoo khrap.
KEN: khao cha klap meuarai sarp mai khrap?
COLLEAGUE: mai sarp khrap. mai sarp war khao pai nai.
RECEPTIONIST: art ca klap korn thiang kha.
ror korn see kha.
KEN: khit war mai khrap. laeo cha mar mai.

RECEPTIONIST: *Whom do you want to see? (lit. whom have you come to see?)*
KEN: *I'd like to see Suporn.*
RECEPTIONIST: *(to a colleague) Do you know if Suporn is in?*
COLLEAGUE: *No, he's not here.*
KEN: *Do you know when he'll be back?*
COLLEAGUE: *I don't know. I don't know where he went.*
RECEPTIONIST: *He'll probably be back before midday. Would you like to wait a little?*
KEN: *I think not. I'll come back again.*

Vocabulary

art	probably
ror	wait

Language points

Expressing probability

We saw in Lesson 13 one way of expressing probability with **khong cha**. **art cha** is used with a similar meaning:

art cha **mar shar.**   I'll *probably* be late.

Asking what someone knows

We saw in Lesson 4 how to say 'I think that ...'. You will remember that we must use **war** ('that') after **khit**:

> *khit war* **cha mar** *I think* he'll come

We also use **war** after **sarp** where in English we would only use a question word or 'if' or 'whether':

> **mai** *sarp war* **khao pai** I don't know *when* he is going.
> **meuarai.**
>
> **mai** *sarp war* **khao pai** I don't know *whether* he is going.
> **reuplao.**

Notice that the subordinate clause ('if he came', 'when he will come back', etc.) always contains a question word. You can use the same question marker as you would in a straightforward question. The same constructions are used with questions:

> **khun sarp mai war khao** Do you know where he went?
> **pai nai?**

Vocabulary

1 wannee mai warng. torng pai rarn khai yar. pai tat phom duey. torng tham weesar. yen nee pai sa wainarm

yar	medicine	**sà wâinárm**	swimming pool
rárn khǎi yar	chemist's	**weesar**	visa
tàt phǒm	to get one's hair cut		

Note: we have already used one word for 'to meet' (**cher**). **cher** suggests a chance meeting ('I came across ...'); **phop** suggests an arranged meeting.

Notice the construction **rarn khai yar** ('shop sell medicine'): you will practise later in the lesson using it to say the names of other types of shops.

2 torng pai satharnee rot fai. rot fai ork chet mohng shao. theung bai sorng mohng. shai welar narn tae saduak.

sathǎrnee	station	**thĕung**	to arrive
òrk	to leave	**shái welar**	to take time

Exercise 1

What could you say to elicit these responses?

1 sarp mai war khao cha klap meuarai?
2 mai sarp war khao pai nai.
3 mai sap war khao pai meuarai.
4 sarp mai war khao pai thammai?
5 mai sarp war khao pai yangngai.
6 khun sarp mai war khao len korp wannee reuplao?
7 mai sarp war khao seuh rot reuplao.

Exercise 2

> torng karn seuh yar. khun sarp mai war rarn khai yar yoo thee nai?

Ask a follow-up question as in the example (see the note above about kinds of shops).

1 torng karn seuh nangseuh
2 torng karn tat phom
3 torng karn tham weesar angkrit
4 torng karn pai rot fai
5 torng karn pai wai narm
6 torng karn seuh rorng thao
7 torng karn seuh karng keng

Exercise 3

You are the head of a school and you hear that some VIPs intend to visit it (you have no more details than that). Your deputy took the call: how would you find out from her what she knows about the visit?

Exercise 4

You are talking to a friend who has recently met someone you have lost contact with. Here are some things which used to be true about your acquaintance. Find out if your friend knows whether they still apply.

1 khao khoei len keelar thuk wan
2 khao khoei len phai thuk wan

3 khao khoei shorp dern len
4 khao khoei sorn pharsar angkrit
5 khao khoei len dontree
6 khao khoei soop buree mark mark

Exercise 5

Your friend is fairly predictable and you know what his likely movements are tomorrow. Answer these questions about him.

1 khao cha pai nai?
2 khao cha pai meuarai?
3 khao cha pai yangngai?
4 khao cha phop khrai?
5 khao cha tham arai?
6 khao cha klap barn meuarai?

Exercise 6

Your friend is being persistent and asking you a lot of questions about someone you know very little about. Answer her questions saying you don't know.

1 khao shorp len phai reuplao?
2 khao pai sa wainarm meuawarnnee reuplao?
3 khao pai talart seuh rom reuplao?
4 khao pai rot taeksee reuplao?
5 khao cha klap opfit korn thiang reuplao?
6 khao phoot pharsar yeepun dai mai?

Exercise 7

Complete this dialogue:

A: khun sarp ———— khrap ———— Suporn yoo thee nai?
B: pai satharnee rotfai laeo kha.
A: ———— satharnee rotfai yoo ————?
B: mai sarp kha.
A: ———— sarp ———— khao ork ————
B: pai har thum kha.
A: phom phop khao dai meuarai?
B: shan mai ———— cha klap ————.

Exercise 8

Arrange these sentences in order to make a coherent dialogue.

B: yang mai nae. khit war sia welar see shuamohng.

B: har thum khrap.

B: khan nan khrap.

A: khorpkhun khrap. khun sarp mai war ork meuarai?

A: khun sarp mai khrap war sia welar narn thaorai?

A: korthot khrap rot tua pai Chieng Mai khan nai sarp mai khrap?

Exercise 9

Answer (in English) these questions about the conversation:

1 What does the travel agent recommend?
2 What details does she give?
3 What is the disadvantage of the alternative and what does she know about it?
4 Why does she have so little information on it?

A: shan cha pai Singapore yangngai dee kha?

B: pai Thai International dee thee sut kha. mee khreuang bin thuk wan. ork paet mohng shao theung Singapore pramarn thiang kha.

A: khun sarp mai kha war chort thee Kuala Lumpur reuplao?

B: mai sarp kha. khit war mai chort.

A: khun sarp mai war mee rot fai pai Singapore reuplao kha?

B: khit war mee kha tae shai welar narn. ork chark krungthep wan phareuhat. mai sarp war theung Singapore meuarai. shai welar pramarn sorng reuh sarm wan.

A: rot fai dee reuplao kha?

B: mai sarp kha. khit war mai saduak. mai sarp war khar tua thaorai.

A: thammai khun mai sarp war rotfai dee reuplao kha?

B: phro war nak thorng thieo shorp pai khreuang bin mark kwar kha. mee khon nitnoi pai rotfai thaonan kha.

Dialogue

Ken returns to the office and sees the same receptionist

KEN: khun Suporn klap mar laeo reu yang khrap?
RECEPTIONIST: klap mar laeo kha.
KEN: khor phop khao dai mai khrap?
RECEPTIONIST: khorthoht kha. khao ork pai eek laeo kha.
KEN: tangtae mar krungthep phom yark phop khao. khun bork khao reuplao khrap war phom mar har?
RECEPTIONIST: bork kha.
KEN: khun tharm khao reuplao war khao cha klap mar meuarai?
RECEPTIONIST: tharm kha tae khao mai sarp kha. mee thura duan mark. mee panhar reuang kormpiuter.
KEN: khun bork khao war phom cha mar phrungnee dai mai khrap?
RECEPTIONIST: meua khao klap opfit mar leao cha bok hai kha. shan nae chai khao cha yoo opfit phrungnee kha.

KEN: *Has Suporn come back yet?*
RECEPTIONIST: *Yes . . .*
KEN: *Can I see him?*
RECEPTIONIST: *I'm sorry. He went out again.*
KEN: *I've been wanting to see him ever since I came to Bangkok. Did you tell him I called?*
RECEPTIONIST: *Yes.*
KEN: *Did you ask him when he'll be back?*
RECEPTIONIST: *He didn't know. He has some urgent business. There is a problem with the computer.*
KEN: *Can you tell him that I will come back tomorrow?*
RECEPTIONIST: *When he comes back to the office I'll tell him. I'm sure he'll be in his office tomorrow.*

Vocabulary

dùan	urgent
nâe chai	sure

Language points

Verb compounds

We have already seen **pai** and **mar** used in combination with other words:

pai tham ngarn **mar thieo** **pai dern len**

pai and **mar** can be used following another verb to indicate direction away from or towards the speaker (see the comprehension passage for Lesson 12):

phom klap *pai* **barn.**	I'm *going back* home.
khao klap *mar* **barn.**	He's *coming back* home.
phom khap rot pai mai dai.	I couldn't go by car.
khao khap rot mar mai dai.	He can't come by car.
khao ork *pai* **laeo.**	He's *left* already. (i.e. gone)
khao ork *mar* **laeo.**	He's *left* (*to come here*) already.
khao khao *pai* **laeo.**	He *went in*.
khao khao *mar* **laeo.**	He *came in*.
phom dern *mar* **opfit.**	I *came to* the office on foot.
phom dern *pai* **opfit.**	I *went to* the office on foot.

Reporting speech

We can use verbs like **bork** ('tell') and **tharm** ('ask') in the same constructions as we saw with **sarp** in the first part of this lesson.

phom bork khao war phom cha pai wainarm.	I told him that I was going swimming.
phom bork khao war phom pai meuarai.	I told him when I was going.
phom tharm khao war khao pai thee nai.	I asked him where he was going.
phom tharm khao war khao pai reuplao.	I asked him whether he went.

Referring to a starting point

tangtae can be used where in English we would use either 'since' or 'ever since'. You can use it either with a definite time expression (e.g. 'last year') or with a clause ('since I came to Bangkok'):

phom yoo thee rohng raem Hilton *tangtae* **arthit thee laeo.**	I have stayed in the Hilton *since* last week.
phom yoo thee rohng raem Hilton *tangtae* **mar krungthep.**	I have stayed in the Hilton *since* I came to Bangkok.

Statements with 'when'

We have seen that in questions the equivalent of 'when' is **meuarai**. In statements **meua** is used. **meua** can refer to past, present or future time; it can also refer either to a point of time (e.g. 'when I saw him') or a period (e.g. 'while I was at university').

meua **khao mar phom cha bork.**	*When* he comes I'll tell him.
meua **shan yoo thee London tham ngarn thee rarn aharn thai.**	*When* I was in London I worked in a Thai restaurant.

Vocabulary

phom chop maharwitthayarlai pee thee laeo. torn nee tham ngarn thee borrisat IMB.

chòp	to finish, complete
mahǎrwítthayarlai	university
borrisàt	company

phom mai warng. mee prashum.

prashum	meeting

khao khap rot reo kern pai. mee ubat het. yoo nai khuk.

ubàt hèt	accident
nai	in
khúk	prison

phom mai phoot kap khao mar narn laeo. tit tor mai dai.

tìt tòr	to get in touch with

Exercise 10

Your friend has just bought something interesting. You meet her brother in the street. Find out if he asked her the details of what his sister bought (where and when she bought it, how much she paid, etc.)

Exercise 11

Your friend can't keep a secret to save his life. He had promised not to tell someone anything about Suporn or his movements. Find out what he told him.

Exercise 12

You're acting as Suporn's personal assistant. Pass on these messages to him in English.

1 phom Suchart phoot khrap. shuey bork khun Suporn war wannee pai len korp mai dai.
2 shan sheuh Saowalak. shuey bork khun Suporn war cha thohras- ap mar phrungnee.
3 shan Malee phoot kha. shuey tharm khun Suporn war cha mar barn shan wan sao nar dai mai kha.
4 phom Manat phoot khrap. shuey tharm khun Suporn war sorp thee nai khrap?
5 phom thohrasap chark satharnthoot cheen. shuey bork khun Suporn war mee nat kap Mr Wang phrungnee sip et mohng shao dai mai khrap?
6 shan Sunnee phoot kha. shuey tharm khun Suporn war rot fai ork kee mohng.

Exercise 13

Arrange these sentences in order to make a coherent conversation.

khun tharm khao war shan phop khao phrungnee dai mai kha?
bork war khong cha mar wan chan nar kha
mai yoo kha. pai satharnthoot cheen.
khao bork war phrungnee mai mar thamngarn kha.
khao bork mai war mar tham ngarn meuarai?
khun Suporn yoo mai kha?

Exercise 14

Your friend is curious about what you plan to do. Tell her when you intend to do these things (using **meua**).

1 khun cha thai roop eek mai?
2 khun cha seuh rot mai reuplao?
3 khun cha dai ngarn mai reuplao?
4 khun cha dai bai khap khee reuplao?
5 khun cha shao rot reuplao?
6 khun cha taeng ngarn reuplao?

Exercise 15

You are hiring a new member of staff and are looking at details of one of the applicants. Answer the questions about him.

rian nangseuh thee rohng rian Sayarm	yoo thee rohng phayarbarn 4 deuan
rian nangseuh thee maharwitthayarlai	rian thai roop pai thieo amerikar
tham ngarn thee thanarkhan amerikan	taeng ngarn
pai thieo yeepun	mee ubat het
tham ngarn thee satharnthoot angkrit	pai khuk

1 pai rohng phayarbarn meuarai?
2 rian thai roop meuarai?
3 pai thieo amerikar meuarai?
4 taeng ngarn meuarai?
5 mee ubat het meuarai?
6 yoo nai khuk meuarai?

Exercise 16

You are looking at some more applications for the job. Answer these questions about them using **tangtae**.

Applicant 1
rian chop
yoo thee meuang farangset

Applicant 2
chop maharwitthayarlai
tham ngarn thee satharnee rotfai

Applicant 3
pai amerikar
rian kompiuter

Applicant 4
ork chark borrisat ILC
sorn banshee

Applicant 5
klap krungthep
yar rarng

Applicant 6
taeng ngarn
pen khon khrua

Applicant 1	yoo thee meuang farangset mar narn thaorai laeo?
Applicant 2	tham ngarn thee satharnee rotfai mar narn thaorai laeo?
Applicant 3	rian kompiuter mar narn thaorai laeo?
Applicant 4	song banshee mar narn thaorai laeo?
Applicant 5	yar rarng mar narn thaorai laeo?
Applicant 6	pen khon khrua mar narn thaorai laeo?

Exercise 17 ▢▢

Answer these questions about the conversation. Malee is interviewing Sunantha who has applied for a job in her office. What is her current job? How long has she worked there? What subjects has she studied? Where and when has she studied English?

M: torn nee khun tham ngarn thee borrisat MPA shai mai kha?
S: shai kha. pen lekharnukarn.
M: tham ngarn thee nan mar narn thaorai laeo kha?
S: tangtae chop maharwitthayarlai kha.
M: khun rian arai mar kha?
S: rian kompiuter lae pharsar yeepun kha.
M: phoot pharasar angkrit dai mai kha?
S: dai kha.
M: rian mar meuarai kha?
S: rian meua yoo thee amerikar kha.

Exercise 18

1 Your boss thinks you know all about someone who has applied for a job in your office. How would you tell him that you have no idea where, what or how long she studied or what she has been doing since she left university?

2 A very odd-looking person has just called at your office. Your receptionist, who spoke to him, is not very communicative. How would you find out from her what was said and what she knows about the caller?

3 You are planning a journey from Bangkok to Kuala Lumpur. What questions would you ask the travel agent?

4 You were due to meet Suporn this afternoon at the Oriental Hotel. Your train from Ayuthaya is late because of flooding and you want to postpone the meeting until tomorrow. You also want to ask Suporn if he will have dinner with you tomorrow evening. He is not in his office but his secretary asks if she can give him a message. What would you tell her?

Vocabulary building

1 Match the words on the left with a word which has a similar meaning on the right:

phop	bork
art	khuap
khit	kae
nao	cher
kin	khong
faen	num
pen	sarmee
sanuk	khon dieo
sao	dai
pee	nar son chai
kao	songsai
phoot	yen
duey tua eng	deuhm

2 What verb would you use to translate the verbs in these sentences?

1 Did you walk here?
2 Did you walk there?

3 Has he come back home?
4 Did he go back home?
5 He drove there.
6 We drove here.

Tone practice

Practise the tones in these words:

mahǎrwítthayarlai	khúk	borrisàt	ubàt hèt	sà wâinárm
tàt phǒm	rárn khǎi yar	sathǎrnee	thěung	thěung laéo

Reading

Exercise 19

1 Where would you find these notices?

สระว่ายน้ำ   ร้านขายยา   ร้านขายหนังสือ

ร้านขายรองเท้า   ร้านขายเสื้อผ้า   ร้านตัดผม

มหาวิทยาลัย   ร้านอาหารญี่ปุ่น   สถานทูตอเมริกา

ห้องน้ำผู้หญิง   ห้องน้ำผู้ชาย   ตู้โทรศัพท์

สถานีรถไฟ   สนามมวย

2 Your flatmate has left you these notes. Translate them.

ต้องไปบริษัทขายเครื่องครัวมีธุระด่วน

คุณโทรศัพท์บอกที่ทำงานก่อนเที่ยง

มีปัญหาเรื่องตั๋วเครื่องบิน

คุณพ่อคุณถึงสถานีรถไฟ ๙ โมงเช้า

มาจากเชียงใหม่คุณไปรับได้รึเปล่า

Dialogue 🔲

Ken meets Suthaep, who has been in touch with Suporn

KEN: khun dai phop khun Suporn meua wannee reuplao khrap?

SUTHAEP: phop khrap.

KEN: khao bork arai khun khrap?

SUTHAEP: khao bork war khun khuan cha pai phop khao.

KEN: khun tharm khao war khao shuey phom dai reuplao khrap?

SUTHAEP: tharm khrap. khao mai nae chai. torng karn phoot kap khun korn.

KEN: khun sarp mai war khao cha klap amerikar meuarai?

SUTHAEP: mai sarp, khrap. khao mai dai bork war klap amerikar reuplao.

KEN: khun tharm khao mai war thammai mai tit tor phom?

SUTHAEP: tharm khrap. khao bork war tangtae klap chark amerikar mee thura mark. lae arthit thee laeo khao mee ubat het reuang rot.

KEN: khao pen arai reuplao khrap?

SUTHAEP: khit war mai pen arai khrap. khao mee panhar thee barn khao duey.

KEN: panhar arai khrap?

SUTHAEP: phom mai dai tharm khrap. khun Suporn mee panhar samer. khoei mee panhar reuang phooying. tangtae taeng ngarn mee panhar reuang ngern.

KEN: khun nae chai mai war khao cha shuey phom dai khrap?

SUTHAEP: nae norn khrap. Suporn chai dee mark lae pen khon keng thee sut thee phom roochak. phom nae chai war khao cha shuey khun dai.

KEN: khun tharm khao reuplao khrap war khao cha phop phom phrungnee dai mai?

SUTHAEP: khao cha pai len korp torn shao lae bork war torn bai mee prashum.

KEN: khun tharm khao mai war khao warng meuarai?

SUTHAEP: khao cha pai har khun phor khun mae khao wan angkarn nar sorng reuh sarm wan. meua khao klap mar khun ko phop khao thee opfit dai khrap.

KEN: phom wang war yangngan khrap. phom cha yoo thee krungthep eek neung arthit thaonan.

Comprehension

1 Why has Suporn not been in touch with Ken?
2 Why is there a delay before he can see Ken?

15 karn nat phop reuang thurakit 2

Getting down to business

Dialogue 📼

Ken is getting no closer in his efforts to track down Suporn but he does make some progress ...

KEN:	phom sheuh Ken Stevens khrap khor phoot kap khun Suporn noi dai mai khrap?
RECEPTIONIST:	khun Suporn mai mar tham ngarn kha. mai sabai kha.
KEN:	khun sarp mai war khao cha mar meuarai?
RECEPTIONIST:	art cha mar phrungnee kha.
KEN:	thar khao mar phrungnee khun shuey bork khao war phom cha pai har khao sip mohng shao dai mai khrap?
RECEPTIONIST:	dai kha. mee reuang arai kha? barng thee khon thee thamngarn thee opfit art cha shuey khun dai kha.
KEN:	reuang sin khar song ork pai angkrit khrap.
RECEPTIONIST:	shan khit war khun Manop khong shuey khun dai kha.

KEN:	*Hello. It's Ken Stevens here. Can I speak to Suporn, please?*
RECEPTIONIST:	*Suporn is not in today. He's ill.*
KEN:	*Do you know when he will be back?*
RECEPTIONIST:	*He'll probably be in tomorrow.*
KEN:	*If he comes tomorrow can you tell him that I will come and see him at 10 a.m.?*
RECEPTIONIST:	*Certainly. What is it about? Perhaps somebody (else) in the office can help you?*
KEN:	*It's about exporting goods to England.*
RECEPTIONIST:	*I think Manop might be able to help you.*

Vocabulary

thâr	if	**sòng**	to send
reûang	on the subject of	**sĭn khár òrk**	export(s)
barng thee	maybe	**sĭn khár sòng òrk pai**	export(s) to
sĭn khár	goods		

Language points

Conditionals

> **thar khao mar phrungnee**   If he comes tomorrow I'll tell him.
> **phom bork khao.**

As in English, the conditional clause can also come after the main clause: **phom cha bork khao thar khao mar phrungnee**.

There are other more complicated ways of expressing conditionals which we will not attempt to cover in this book.

Verb compounds

We saw in the dialogue another use of **pai** to indicate direction away from the speaker:

> **sin khar song ork** *pai* **angkrit** export *to* England

The verbs 'export' and 'import' are expressed by combining verbs:

> *song ork* **khreuang khrua**   *export* kitchen appliances
> *nam khao* **khreuang khrua**   *import* kitchen appliances

The verbs **chop** which we saw in the last lesson and **set** which we saw in Lesson 12 can also be used in verb compounds:

> **khao thamngarn set laeo.**   He has finished working.
> **rao doo nang mai chop.**   We didn't see the film to the end.

Vocabulary

1

phom yark phoot kap khun reuang sin khar khao. yark nam khao borarn watthu. khun sarp mai war torng karn bai anuyart reuplao?

sǐn khár khâo	import	**bai ànúyârt**	permit
borarn wátthù	antique		

2

phrungnee phom pai tarng prathet. torng karn nangseuh dern tharng.

nángsěuh dern tharng   passport

3

    phom pai praisanee song chotmai.

praisanee	post office
chòtmǎi	letter

Exercise 1

You want to talk to the following people about the following topics. Answer the receptionist's questions.

Akorn	permit
Suporn	exports
Manop	imports
Malee	importing antiques
Ena	exporting antiques
Manat	driving licence
Saowanee	the accident at the university
Saowalak	your passport

1 khun Akorn mai yoo kha. mee reuang arai?
2 khun Suporn mai yoo kha. mee reuang arai?
3 khun Manop mai yoo kha. mee reuang arai?
4 khun Malee mai yoo kha. mee reuang arai?
5 khun Ena mai yoo kha. mee reuang arai?
6 khun Manat mai yoo kha. mee reuang arai?
7 khun Saowanee mai yoo kha. mee reuang arai?
8 khun Saowalak mai yoo kha. mee reuang arai?

Exercise 2

Match what you can do in the left-hand column (A) with the condition for doing them on the right (B).

khun pai krungthep phrungnee dai	khun mee nangseuh dern tarng prathet
khun pai praisanee song chotmai dai	khun mee bai khap khee sarkon
khun pai tharng prathet dai	khun mee bai anuyart
khun dai ngarn dee dai	khun arn nangseuh mark
khun sorp pharn dai	khun phoot pharsar angkrit pen
khun khap rot dai	khun mee tua laeo
khun song ork borarn watthu dai	khun khian chotmai laeo

1 Say that you can do A if you have B.
2 Say that you can't do A if you do not have B.

Exercise 3

Someone wants to see you. This is your schedule:

Tuesday	at the university
Thursday	Chieng Mai
Friday	the MCA Company
the weekend	Khon Kaen
next week	London
next month	Paris

Tell him where you will be if he comes when he suggests.
Example:

A: barng thee phom cha mar wan chan.
B: thar khun mar wan chan phom yoo thee barn.

Exercise 4

You have another friend who wants you to do some errands for her.
You don't mind as long as you are passing (**pharn**) the appropriate
places. How would you respond to her requests?

1 seuh nangseuh hai shan dai mai kha?
2 seuh tua rotfai hai shan dai mai kha?
3 khun pai ao weesar yeepun hai shan dai mai kha?
4 khun seuh yar hai shan dai mai kha?
5 khun seuh tua khreuang bin hai shan dai mai kha?
6 khun song chotmai hai shan dai mai kha?

Exercise 5

Your friend wants you to do some favours for him. You are willing
to do them as long as he does something similar for you in return.
How would you respond to his requests?

1 khun sorn pharsar angkrit phom dai mai khrap?
2 khun hai phom yeuhm nangseuh lem nan dai mai khrap?
3 khun shuey phom khian nangseuh reuang muey dai mai khrap?
4 khun shuey phom tham khwarm sa-art barn dai mai khrap?
5 khun pai rap pheuan phom thee sanarmbin dai mai khrap?

6 khor yeuhm rom khun noi dai mai khrap?
7 song chotmai hai phom dai mai khrap?

Exercise 6

You are trying to arrange a meeting. Complete the following dialogue.

sawatdee kha.
1 Ask to speak to Manat.
khun Manat mai yoo kha.
2 Ask if someone else can help.
mee reuang arai kha?
3 Tell her what it's about.
phrungnee khun Manat warng kha. mar thee nee sip mohng shao dai mai kha?
4 Say you can't as you're going away on holiday.
khun yark phop khao meuarai kha?
5 Say when you can see him.
dai kha. shan cha bork khao hai.
6 Ask if Manat has received your letter.
khit war mai kha.

Exercise 7

You are answering the phone in your office. Complete the following dialogue:

shan Saowanee Rodchue kha. khor phoot kap khun Steve noi dai mai kha?
1 Explain that Steve has been ill all week.
khun sarp mai war khao cha mar meuarai?
2 Say you're not sure. His wife told you he should be back next week.
khun bork khao war shan thohrasap khao wan chan torn shao dai mai kha?
3 Say that if his wife telephones you'll pass the message on. Ask what it's about.
mee panhar kormpiuter. wang war khao cha shuey shan dai arthit nee.
4 Explain that you have a problem with the computers in your office and there's nobody free this week.

Dialogue 🔘

Ken explains to Manop what he is trying to do

MANOP: phom shuey arai khun dai mai khrap?
KEN: yark phoot kap khun Suporn reuang sin khar song ork pai angkrit.
MANOP: khun torng karn cha song arai pai barng khrap?
KEN: phom son chai cha song borarn watthu. khit war khao cha shuey phom dai khrap.
MANOP: khun torng karn sarp arai barng khrap?
KEN: torng karn sarp war mee sin khar arai thee harm song ork barng.
MANOP: harm song phra thang kao lae mai khrap. thar khun torng karn song ork borarn watthu khun torng mee bai anuyart korn khrap.
KEN: phom torng tham bai anuyart yangngai khrap?
MANOP: mai sarp khrap. khun torng tharm khun Suporn khrap.

MANOP: *Can I help you?*
KEN: *I want to talk to Suporn about exporting goods to England.*
MANOP: *What are you thinking of importing?*
KEN: *I'm interested in importing antiques and I think he can help me.*
MANOP: *What do you need to know?*
KEN: *I want to know if there are things I cannot take out of the country.*
MANOP: *You cannot take out Buddha figures old or new. If you want to export antiques you need a permit.*
KEN: *How do I get a permit?*
MANOP: *I'm not sure. You'll have to talk to Suporn about that.*

Vocabulary

phrá   Buddha figure, monk

Language points

Verb compounds

ork can also be used after another verb to indicate that the action was or was not brought to a conclusion. The resulting verb compound often corresponds to a verb plus adverbial in English. For example, **khit ork** means 'to work something out':

yark mark. phom *khit* **mai** *ork*	It's very difficult, *I can't work it out*.
phom arn mai ork	I can't read it (and make sense of it).

Notice that in the negative **mai** is placed before **ork** not before the main verb.

Vocabulary

A: shan torng karn seuh khreuang thorng khreuang ngern lae phar mai. khun nae nam shan dai mai kha? khit war meua seuh khreuang thorng torng rawang mark.

B: seuh thee nee ko laeo kan. phar mai chark phak isarn dee thee sut nai lohk.

khrêuang thorng	gold
khrêuang ngern	silver

Note: you can also say **thorng** and **ngern** without **khreuang**:

phâr măi	silk
naé nam	to advise, advice
rawang	to be careful
kô laéo kan	(used to show preference for a course of action)
phak isarn	the north-east of Thailand
lôhk	world

khao mai roo reuang!

róo	to know
róo rêuang	to understand

So far we have used **sarp**, the formal word, to mean 'to know'. **roo** is the informal word.

Exercise 8

How would you tell someone you are interested in:

1 silver/gold/antiques/silk/music/boxing/sports/prisons
2 exporting antiques/importing silk/buying gold/selling silver

Exercise 9

Make as many sentences as you can from this table:

phar mai			
ngern		meuang thai	
thorng		itarlee	dee thee sut nai lohk
futborn	chark	amerika	
seua pha		angkrit	
rorng thao			
dontree			

Exercise 10

From the conversation explain in English what Janet bought, what the starting price was and how much she paid for them.

JANET: kraprohng see daeng rarkhar thaorai kha?
S: har roi bart kha.
JANET: khit war phaeng kha. lae kraprohng see khao rarkhar thao-rai kha?
S: see roi bart kha.
JANET: thar shan seu kraprohng sorng tua rarkhar thaorai kha?
S: chet roi har sip bart ko laeo kan
JANET: khun khit war chet roi bart dai mai kha?
S: dai kha.

Exercise 11

You are trying to buy some watches. Complete this dialogue (the classifier for 'watch' is **reuan**).

1 Ask the price.
   reuan la sorng roi har sip bart kha.
2 Say that you find that expensive.
   mai phaeng rok kha.
3 Ask how much they would be if you buy five.
   reuan la sorng roi bart.
4 Ask if she would accept one hundred and fifty bart.
   thar khun seu narlikar sip reuan shan khit war rarkhar roi chet sip har bart.
5 Say that you will take ten for that price.

Exercise 12

Look back at previous lessons and write a description of:

1 Suporn
2 Ken's stay in Thailand

Exercise 13

Suporn visits London in six months' time and contacts Ken to ask him about the success of his business venture. Write a dialogue between them.

Exercise 14

You are a business person who imports clothes and you go to the Thai Embassy for a visa. The official asks you what you intend to do in Thailand, whether you have business there, how long you will stay, whether you have friends there and have been there before. He also asks what your profession is and whether you are interested in temples and antiques as many foreign tourists are. He adds that Thai beaches are the best in the world. Write the dialogue.

Vocabulary building

fang	to listen
siang	noise

Match the Thai expressions on the left with the appropriate meaning of **ork** on the right (above are two additional words which you will need to work out some of the expressions).

arn ork khian dai	to be able to tell just by looking, ascertain
ork nangseuh	pronounce, vote
doo ork	to be literate
tharng ork	to understand a language when spoken
ork siang	to publish a book
fang pharsar angkrit mai ork	exit

Tone practice

Practise the tones in these words and expressions:

> sĭn khár khâo   phâr măi   sĭn khár òrk   náe nam
> bai ànúyârt   kô laéo kan   chòtmǎi   borarn wátthù

Reading

The tone sign +

This changes the tone of a syllable to a rising tone.

ตั๋ว

Notice that the sign ฯ means that a word has been abbreviated:

กรุงเทพ ฯ

(**krungthep** is the abbreviation for the much longer Thai name of Bangkok.)
The sign ๆ means that a word is repeated.

Vocabulary

karunar	please	**thort**	to take off
antarai	danger, dangerous		

Exercise 15

1   Translate these signs:

อันตราย ระวัง กรุณาถอดรองเท้า

ขอบคุณครับ อย่าลืมปิดไฟ อย่าลืมปิดแก๊ส

ด่วนมาก หนังสือเดินทาง

2   Martin has been to Thailand and has started up a small import business. He receives this letter from his Thai girlfriend who has promised to send him some goods. Translate the letter for him.

สวัสดีค๊ะ คุณสบายดีไหมค๊ะ ฉันคิดถึงคุณมาก
ตั้งแต่คุณกลับไปแล้วฉันต้องทำงานหนักมากเลยไม่มี
วันหยุด ฉันทำหนังสือเดินทางแล้ว
พรุ่งนี้ไปสถานทูตอังกฤษ เรื่องวีซ่า
คงจะชื้อตัวอาทิตย์หน้า ฉันรอรับจดหมายจากคุณอยู่
กว่าจดหมาย ของฉันจะไปถึงคุณ
ฉันคงได้รับจดหมาย ของคุณแล้วแน่เลย
หวังว่าของเล่นที่ชื้อจากกรุงเทพ ๆ
คงขายได้แล้วและขอให้ได้กำไรมาก ๆ นะ
ฉันชื้อของเล่นอีกแต่ตอนนี้แพงกว่า ฉันจะส่งให้
คุณวันศุกร์ และจะโทรศัพท์ วันเสาร์ โชคดีนะค๊ะ
ลาก่อนค๊ะ

Dialogue 🔲

Ken finally gets to have his business meeting with Suporn and asks for his advice on importing goods from Thailand

KEN: sawatdee khrap khun Suporn. phom yark phop khun mar narn laeo khrap.

SUPORN: khorthoht duey khrap. phom mee ngarn yung mark khrap. phom cha shuey arai khun dai barng khrap?

KEN: phom pen pheuan Anthony. khao bork war khun cha nae nam phom dai khrap. phom yark nam sin khar khao prathet angkrit khrap. phom mee borrisat lek lek thee London. sin khar khao chark lai lai prathet tae yang mai dai tham thurakit thee meuang thai.

SUPORN: khun khit war dee reuh khrap?

KEN: phom wang war yangngan.

SUPORN: sin khar arai thee khun torng karn nam khao pai angkrit khrap?

KEN: yang mai nae loei khrap. art cha song khreuang ngern thorng phar mai reuh borarn watthu.

SUPORN: borarn watthu torng rawang mark khrap. harm song borarn watthu thar mai mee bai anuyart. prokkati farang shorp phra tae harm nam ork chark prathet thai. lae mee borarn watthu mai ching mark. phom khit war khun art cha mee panhar mark mark.

KEN: lae khun khit war song ork khreuang ngern reuh thorng dee mai khrap?

SUPORN: khit war mai dee khrap phro war mee khon song ork mark.

KEN: lae phar mai la khrap?

SUPORN: phom khit war song ork phar mai dee thee sut phro war mai phaeng mark. khun cha khai dai kamrai dee phro phar mai rakkhar thook. phar mai thee dee thee sut tham chark phak isarn.

KEN: khun seuh phar mai hai phom dai mai khrap?

SUPORN: dai khrap. phom cha seuh seua, seua nork lae seua khorng yarng euhn thee tham chark phar mai hai khun dai. khun roo mai khrap war phar mai khorng thai suey thee sut nai lohk.

KEN: roo nitnoi khrap. thar phom seuh seua neung roi tua, rarkhar thaorai khrap?

SUPORN: tua la har sip bart khrap.

KEN: phom khit war phaeng phro torng sia khar song ork. torng khart thun nae norn loei khrap. khun khit war sarm sip har bart dai mai khrap?

SUPORN: thar khun seuh har roi tua phom khit war rarkhar see sip bart khrap.

KEN: tok long khrap.

SUPORN: meuarai khun torng karn khrap?

KEN: leo thee sut thar pen pai dai khrap.

SUPORN: khun khit war dee mai, phom cha pai phak isarn wan sao nar khun cha pai kap phom reuplao ? pai doo war khao tham phar mai yangngai.

KEN: phom yark pai khrap tae phom torng klap angkrit phrungnee laeo.

SUPORN: nar sia dai na khrap. phom wang war khun cha mar meuang thai eek.

KEN: phom ko wang war yangngan khrap. phom khit war rao khong tham thurakit duey kan dai dee khrap.

Vocabulary

phom mee ngarn yung. yark nam sin khar ork pai angkrit. thar seuh thook kamrai dee. thar seuh phaeng khart thun. mai dee loei.

yûng	difficult, complicated	nam òrk	to take out, away
nam	to take, bring	loei	at all (with a negative)
kamrai	profit	khart thun	loss

Comprehension

1 What does Suporn think of the four possibilities Ken mentions?
2 What do they agree on?

Reference grammar

1 **Sentence patterns**
2 **Nouns and noun phrases**
3 **Verbs**
4 **Adverbials**

1   Sentence patterns

Affirmative statements

khun Malee yoo.   Malee is here.

Negative sentences

khun Malee *mai* mar   Malee is *not* coming.

You make a sentence negative by adding **mai** immediately before the main verb.

Yes/no questions

There are several ways of asking questions in Thai. Their meanings differ according to the context. The simplest form of question is to use **mai** at the end of a statement:

khun Malee yoo *mai*?   Is Malee here?

Short answers to questions with mai

Question	*Yes answer*	*No answer*
khun Malee tham ngarn mai?	**tham.**	**mai tham.**

The question form shai mai

yoo thee barn *shai mai*?   *Is* she at home?

The question form **shai mai** serves to check what you think to be true. Notice that you use the same marker to confirm a negative statement:

khao mai yoo thee barn shai *mai*?   He's not at home, *is he*?

Short answers to shai mai *questions*

Question	*Yes answer*	*No answer*
khun pai London shai mai?	**shai, khrap.**	**mai shai, kha.**

The use of pen *('to be')*

When the predicate contains a noun you use the verb 'to be': **pen**:

khao *pen* khon thai.   He *is* Thai.

Negative statements with mai shai

If you want to make a sentence with **pen** negative you use **mai shai** instead of **pen**:

phom *mai shai* khon angkrit. I'm *not* English.

Questions and answers with reuh

The use of **reuh** is very similar to **shai mai**. It suggests you want to check whether something is the case.

khun Ken pai London *reuh*?	Ken is going to London, *is he*?
khrap/kha.	Yes.
mai shai.	No.

Like **shai mai** you can use it in negative questions:

khun mai pai opfit *reuh*?   You're not going to the office, *then*?

Implications of questions with mai

A question like **pai talart mai** can suggest that you are asking about the other person's intention. In **pai duey kan mai** the implication is that you are making a suggestion.

Questions with reuplao

The literal meaning of **reuplao** is 'are you ... or not?'. Although not as firm as the literal English equivalent, it is a more insistent way of asking a question. (**reuplao** is the question word normally used when you are asking about the past.) Notice how you give a short answer to a question with **reuplao**:

khun pai *reuplao*?	*Are you* going?
pai khrap.	Yes
mai pai khrap.	No.

Questions with laeo reu yang

The question words **laeo reu yang** (lit. 'already' or 'not yet') are used rather like **reuplao** to ask whether something has been done. Like **reuplao** it is a fairly insistent way of asking a question.

khun kin khao *laeo reu yang*? Have you eaten *yet*?

Questions with thammai

pai *thammai*?	*Why* are you going? (i.e. What are you going for?)

thammai can be used (like the question word 'why') either when you want an explanation or when you want to know the purpose of something. When it is used at the end of the sentence, it usually asks for the purpose of something. (what ... for?). To ask for an explanation, you normally use **thammai** at the beginning of the sentence.

Questions with nai

pai *nai*?	*Where* are you going?

Notice that the question word **nai**, like most other question words in Thai, comes at the end of the sentence. You can also use **thee nai** instead of **nai**:

khun Saowalak yoo *thee nai*? *Where* is Saowalak?

Questions with arai

arai normally has the same position in the sentence as the noun it refers to (this is usually at the end of the question):

khun kin *arai*?	*What* are you drinking?
kin karfae.	I'm drinking coffee.

Questions with khrai

Like **arai**, **khrai** has the same position in the question as the word it refers to:

barn lang nan khorng *khrai*?   *Whose* is that house?
***khrai* yoo thee barn lang nan?**   *Who* lives in that house?

Questions with meua rai

As with most other question words, **meua rai** comes at the end of the question. It can be used to refer to past or future time:

khun pai rohng phayarbarn   *When* did you go to the hospital?
   meua rai?
khun ca pai rohng phayar-   *When* will you go to the hospital?
   barn *meua rai*?

The negative particle plao

plao can be used in answer to all types of questions to show strong disagreement or correct firmly what someone has said.

khun pen khon angkrit reuh? *plao* kha!

Notice how you answer negative questions:

mai **pai reuh?**	You're *not* going *then*?
Confirming	*Denying*
khrap (No, I'm not going.)	**plao** (On the contrary, I am going.)

Negatives with mai dai

mai dai is often used instead of **mai** to negate action verbs, verbs of motion, **pen** and **shue**.

pai thanarkharn reuplao?   Did you go to the bank?
***mai dai* pai.**   *No, I didn't go.*

It is often used to refer to past time and in present situations which are contrary to expectations:

khao *mai dai* sheuh Steve.   He's *not* called Steve.
nar sia dai *mai dai* tham   It's a pity you *don't* work in
   ngarn thee Langsit.   Langsit.

Expressing contrast

    horng khrua lek tae sa-art.   The kitchen is small but clean.

Relative clauses with thee

thee corresponds to 'who', 'which' or 'where':

phooying *thee* phoot kap Steve suey.	The girl *who* is talking to Steve is pretty.
phooying *thee* khun roochak suey.	The girl you know is pretty.
barn thee khun seuh suey.	The house you bought is nice.
barn *thee* yoo klai rohng phayarbarn suey.	The house *which* is near the hospital is nice.
rohng rian thee khao pai dee.	The school he goes to is good.

Explaining

    mar shar phro war rot tit.   I was late because the traffic was bad.

With **phro**, **war** can be omitted:

    mar shar phro rot tit

The clause with **phro** or **phro war** can also come before the clause you are explaining. You would translate 'Because it was raining, I returned home late' by: **phro war fon tok klap barn shar.**

Comparing qualities of things

To indicate that something is superior in some respect you use **kwar** after the adjective or adverb:

pharsar angkrit yark *kwar* pharsar thai.	English is *more* difficult than Thai.
khao phoot pharsar thai dee *kwar* phom.	He speaks Thai *better* than me.

Notice how you say something is inferior in some respect:

pharsar angkrit *mai* yark *kwar* pharsar thai.	English *is not as* difficult as Thai.

Asking how things compare

Notice that when you mention two or more things you want to compare you use **kan** ('together'):

pai rot tua reuh khreuang bin dee kwar kan? Which is better – the plane or the coach?

You can also use **ka** (short for **kap**) instead of **reuh**:

Steve *ka* Ken khrai keng kwar kan? Who is better (more clever), Steve *or* Ken?

Comparing what you do

When you are comparing verbs or verb phrases you use **mark kwar** rather than **kwar**:

phom shorp aharn cheen *mark kwar* aharn farangset. I like Chinese food *more than* French food.
phom shorp aharn farangset noi *kwar* aharn cheen. I don't like French food *as much as* Chinese food.

Degree of difference

Notice the word order when you want to show the extent to which something is superior or inferior:

Ayuthaya suey kwar Khon Kaen mark. Ayuthaya is much prettier than Khon Kaen.

Saying things are the same

parkkar rarkhar meuankap narlikar The price of the pen is the same as that of the watch.
parkkar lae narlikar rarkhar meuankan.

Superlatives

To use an adjective or adverb in the superlative form, use **thee sut** after the word it qualifies:

khreuang bin *reo thee sut*. The plane is *the quickest*.

Asking what someone knows

We use **war** after **sarp** where in English we would use only a question word or 'if' or 'whether':

> **mai** *sarp war* **khao pai meua**   I don't know *when* he is going.
> **rai.**
> **mai** *sarp war* **khao pai**   I don't know *whether* he is going.
> **reuplao.**

Notice that the subordinate clause ('if he came', 'when he will come back', etc.) always contains a question word. You can use the same question marker as you would in a straightforward question. The same constructions are used with questions:

> **khun sarp mai war khao**   Do you know where he went?
> **pai thee nai?**

Reporting speech

We can use verbs like **bork** ('to tell') and **tharm** ('to ask') in the same constructions as with **sarp**:

> **phom** *bork* **khao war phom**   I *told* him that I was going swim-
> **cha pai wainarm.**   ming.
> **phom** *bork* **khao war phom**   I *told* him when I was going.
> **pai meuarai.**
> **phom** *tharm* **khao war khao**   I *asked* him where he was going.
> **pai thee nai.**
> **phom** *tharm* **khao war khao**   I *asked* him whether he went.
> **pai reuplao**

Statements with 'when'

In questions the equivalent of 'when' is **meuarai**. In statements **meua** is used. **meua** can refer to past, present or future time; it can also refer either to a point of time (e.g. 'when I saw him') or a period (e.g. 'while I was at university').

> *meua* **khao mar phom cha**   *When* he comes I'll tell him.
> **bork.**
> *meua* **shan yoo thee London**   *When* I was in London I worked in
> **tham ngarn thee rarn**   a Thai restaurant.
> **aharn thai.**

Conditionals

thar **khao mar phrungnee phom cha bork khao.**	*If* he comes tomorrow I'll tell him.

As in English, the conditional clause can also come after the main clause: **phom cha bork khao thar khao mar phrungnee.**

Imperatives

You can make an imperative sentence by using the main verb alone:

pai!	Go away!
mar thee nee.	Come here.

This is fine in a neutral situation like giving directions (or with children, close friends, etc.) but would not work if you want to ask someone politely to do something.

Negative imperatives

Imperatives can be made negative by adding **yar**:

yar **mar thee nee.**	*Don't* come here.

Again, you would not use this form alone to ask someone politely not to do something.

Imperatives with see

A more polite way of telling someone to do something is to add **see**. An even more polite way is to use **shern**:

kin see.	Eat it!
shern **nang kha.**	*Please* sit down.

Directions

As in English you can give directions by using the normal affirmative form:

khun dern pharn rohng phayarbarn.	You walk past the hospital.

Direct and indirect objects with 'to give'

The normal word order is for the direct object to precede the indirect:

khao hai khorng khwan shan. He gave me a present.

2 Nouns and noun phrases

Absence of pronouns

The use of the personal pronouns in Thai is optional – you use them normally if what you say would otherwise be ambiguous.

Articles

Thai does not use articles, so the noun **barn**, for example, can mean 'house', 'a house' or 'the house'.

There is no need to use words like 'some' or 'any':

mai mee look.   I don't have any children.

Personal pronouns

phom	I (male speaker)
shan	I (female speaker)
khun	you (male or female, singular or plural)
khao	he, she, they
rao	we

People often use names when in English we would use 'I' or 'you'. Malee talking to Ken might say **Malee yoo thee barn**, for example. She might also say **Ken** or **khun Ken** instead of 'you'.

The classifier khon

Thai has a special way of referring to one or more persons (or things). Instead of saying, as in English 'I have two children', Thai puts this as follows:

I have	children	two	persons
mee	**look**	**sorng**	**khon**
	Noun	*number*	*classifier*

The word **khon** in this case is known as a classifier because there are different words for different sorts of nouns.

In English we use a similar way of counting uncountable nouns. For example we usually say two bottles or glasses of milk rather than two milks. Thai uses the same system for all nouns. You can use the classifier **khon** for all people except monks and royalty.

Classifiers for objects

You use a different classifier with different types of objects. The classifiers are used:

to indicate plurals:

mee barn sorng lang   There are two houses.

to specify what you are talking about:

barn lang nai?   Which house?

to refer back to a noun you have mentioned:

lang nan.   That one. (i.e. that house)

Here are some more of the classifiers:

khan	vehicles	**rot sarm khan**
lem	books	**nangseuh sorng lem**
shabap	newspapers	**nangseuh phim sarm shabap**
darm	pens	**parkkar see darm**
tua	clothing	**kraprohng sorng tua**
bai	bag, wallet	**krapao sorng bai**
bai	fruit	**saparot sarm bai**
reuan	watch	**narlikar sorng reuan**

A classifier which is used for a variety of objects and can also be used when you don't want to be specific is **an**:

seuh sorng an   I bought two of them

Demonstratives

nee (near the speaker):

tamruat khon *nee*   *this* policeman

nan (away from the speaker):

tamruat khon *nan*   *that* policeman

nohn (further away but within view):

> **tamruat khon *nohn***   *that* policeman *over there*

kee *('how many')*

Notice the word order in questions asking how many:

> **mee look *kee* khon?**   you have children *how many* people?

Since **kee** is automatically referring to a number of people or things you always use it with the appropriate classifier.

Possessives

Sometimes possession is indicated without any overt marker:

> **khun phor shan**   my father (*lit.* father me)
> **khun mae Suchart**   Suchart's mother (*lit.* mother Suchart)

A more explicit way is to use the word **khorng** ('belonging to'):

> **ngern *khorng* phom**   *my* money

khorng is optional unless the noun you are referring to is omitted:

> **ngern khorng khrai?**   Whose is the money?
> **khorng phom.**   Mine.

Noun compounds

A large number of noun compounds are formed in Thai by adding a verb or verbs to a base noun:

> **horng norn**   (room for sleeping)
> **horng nang len**   (room for sitting and playing)

Classifers with compounds

With some compound nouns the classifier is the same as the base word in the compound:

> **horng norn**   bedroom
> **mee horng norn sarm horng.**   There are three bedrooms.

Adjectives of nationalities

Notice that the Thai equivalent of 'He is American' is 'He is person American' (**pem khon amerikan**).

Adjectives follow the noun they modify:

khon thai	a Thai
khon amerikan	an American

Use of adjectives

phom ruey.	I am rich.

Notice that you do not use the verb 'to be' with adjectives: the adjectives can actually be used like verbs, so that **ruey** can mean 'rich' or 'to be rich'. Singular and plural forms of adjectives are exactly the same. In questions and negatives the adjectives function exactly like verbs:

khun *ruey* mai?	Are you *rich*?
shan mai *ruey*.	I'm not *rich*.

Adjectives of nationality follow the noun they modify. Other adjectives are used in the same way:

khao pen khon *ruey*.	He's a *rich* man.

Anything, anyone and anywhere

When **arai** is used with another question marker such as **mai**, it means 'anything':

deuhm *arai*?	*What* are you drinking?
deuhm *arai mai*?	Are you drinking *anything*?

With a negative marker it means 'nothing':

mai *mee arai*.	There's *nothing*.

khrai and **nai** are used in the same way:

mai mee khrai.	There isn't anybody.
pai har khrai mai?	Are you going to see anybody?
pai nai mai?	Are you going anywhere?
mai pai nai.	I'm not going anywhere.

The use of ... ko dai *to mean 'anywhere', 'anything', etc.*

ko dai often suggests that any of the things suggested or talked about will do. It can be used in the following combinations:

rao cha pai nai?	Where shall we go?
pai nai *ko dai.*	*Anywhere* (wherever you like)
rao cha kin arai?	What shall we eat?
kin arai *ko dai.*	*Anything.*
rao cha klap barn meua rai?	When shall we go home?
meua rai *ko dai.*	*Whenever* you like.
rao cha shern khrai dee?	Who shall we invite?
shern khrai *ko dai.*	*Whoever* you like.

It is often used to suggest that either of the alternatives mentioned or understood are acceptable:

phom cha pai barn khun welar nai dee?	What time shall I go to your house?
welar nai *ko dai*	*Any time* will do.
rao cha kin rarn aharn nai kan dee?	Which restaurant shall we eat in?
rarn nai *ko dai.*	*Any one* will do.

Uncountable nouns

In English we often use a word like 'piece of' or 'glass of' to refer to one or more units of an uncountable noun. Thai uses equivalent words in the same way:

khor bia sorng khuat.	Two bottles of beer, please.
khor khao sorng charn.	Two plates (portions) of rice please.

Asking about types or numbers of things

We use **arai** when we are referring to one thing:

khun seuh *arai?*	*What* are you buying? (assumes you are buying one particular thing)
khun seuh *arai* **barng?**	*What* are you buying? (assumes you may be buying several things)

We use the same construction to ask for a list of what is available:

mee phak arai barng?	What vegetables are there?

Expressing quantity

Words indicating quantity are used with the appropriate classifier:

mee khon *lai* **khon.**	There are *several/many* people.
mee khon *barng* **khon.**	There are *some* people.
mee khon *noi* **khon.**	There are *few* people
mee barn *lai* **lang.**	There are *several/many* houses.
mee barn *barng* **lang.**	There are *some* houses.
mee barn *noi* **lang.**	There are *few* houses.

3 Verbs

Verb forms

There are no verb endings to show tense or aspect in Thai. There are a number of time words which can be used to make your meaning explicit.

mar *after a main verb*

mar used after the main verb corresponds to the present perfect in English:

pai nai *mar?*	Where *have* you *been*?
pai seuh khorng *mar.*	*I've been* shopping.

Just as in English this is used to refer to the indefinite past and you do not use definite time expressions in conjunction with **mar** in this sense. **mar** is often omitted from the answers when the time reference is clear from the context:

pai nai *mar?*	Where *have* you *been*?
pai thieo.	*I've been* out.

Future with cha

In many cases you do not need any explicit marker of past, present or future time in Thai. There are, however, one or two markers which you can use to make the reference more obvious. The question **pai nai** can refer to past, present or future time. If you want to make it clear you are referring to the future, you should use **cha pai nai**. **cha** comes immediately before the main verb.

Talking about what you have been doing

When the verb phrase **mar narn laeo** is added to a sentence it indicates that the action referred to has been going on for a long time and is still going on:

phom wai narm thuk wan *mar narn laeo.*	I have been swimming every day *for a long time now.*

You will probably find question forms with **narn** more useful:

khun rian pharsar thai narn laeo reu yang?	Have you been learning Thai for long?
khun rian pharsar thai mar narn thaorai laeo?	How long have you been learning Thai?

Asking about past experiences

khun khoei pai angkrit mai?	Have you ever been to England?
khoei	Yes.
mai khoei	Never.
phom mai khoei rian pharsar farangset.	I've never studied French.

Like 'never', **mai khoei** can also be used for present time. So **mai kin karfae** can mean 'I never drink coffee' or 'I have never drunk coffee'.

Talking about the past

In affirmative statements **khoei** means 'used to':

sip pee thee laeo phom khoei pen khroo.	Ten years ago I used to be a teacher.

Questions about the past

The most common question forms referring to past time are:

khun pai thanarkhan *reuplao*?	*Did you go* to the bank (or not)?
khun pai thanarkharn *shai mai*?	You went to the bank *didn't you*? (i.e. you expect the answer 'yes')
khun pai thanarkharn *reuh*?	You went to the bank *didn't you*? (you think the answer will probably be 'yes')

Notice the negative forms:

> **khun mai dai pai thanarkhan reuh?** You didn't go to the bank then?
>
> **khun mai dai pai thanarkharn shai mai?** You didn't go to the bank, *did you?*

Describing an action in progress

You will have noticed that the same form of the verb can be used to say what someone does habitually (e.g. play golf) as well as to describe what someone is doing now (e.g. studying in America). To make clear that something is in progress we use **kamlang**:

> **nang *kamlang* sanuk.** The film's *just getting* interesting.
>
> **phom *kamlang* khian nangseuh.** I'm *in the process of* writing a book.

Notice that **kamlang** can be used with some adjectives to mean 'become', for example:

> **barn *kamlang* suey.** The house *is beginning* to look pretty. (for example, you are just finishing decorating it)

It is perfectly possible to talk about an action that is in progress without using **kamlang**:

> **phom khian nangseuh.** I'm writing a book.

kamlang is simply a way of making the meaning more explicit.

Referring to an action that is imminent

Another use of **kamlang** is with **cha** to indicate an action that is about to happen:

> **phom *kamlang cha* pai sanarmbin.** *I'm just off* to the airport.

Indicating possession (mee)

mee can mean 'to have' when referring to relationships:

> **mai *mee* look.** I don't *have* children.

It also means 'have' in the sense of possession:

> **khun** *mee* **barn mai?**   Do you *have* a house?

You can also use it to mean 'there is' or 'there are':

> *mee* **rohng raem mai?**   *Is there* a hotel?
> **mai** *mee* **khon.**   *There's* nobody here.

Expressing likes and dislikes

shorp ('to like') can be followed by a noun or a verb phrase:

> *shorp* **aharn farangset.**   I *like* French food.
> *shorp* **pai talart.**   I *like* going to the market.

mai shorp is used in the same way:

> *mai shorp* **aharn cheen.**   *I don't like* Chinese food.

To say how much you like something you can use **nitnoi** or **mark**:

> *shorp* **aharn thai mai?**   Do you *like* Thai food?
> **shorp** *mark*.   I like it *a lot*.
> **shorp** *nitnoi*.   I like it *a little*.

Expressing necessity

torng can be used to say that you must, must not or need not do something:

> **prungnee** *torng* **pai rohng phayarbarn.**   I *have to* go to hospital tomorrow.
> **khun** *torng* **mai kin lao.**   You *must* not drink alcohol.
> **mai** *torng* **pai rohng phayarbarn.**   I don't *have to* go to hospital.

A more common way of saying what you must not do (i.e. what is forbidden) is **harm**:

> *harm* **soop buree.**   You *must not* smoke. (smoking is forbidden)

You will see this used in notices to indicate that something is not allowed but it is also used in everyday speech where it can correspond to 'don't' or 'you mustn't'.

Expressing possibility

dai is used at the end of the sentence to indicate that something is possible or that you are able to do it.

> **phom shuey khun** *dai.*   I *can* help you.

Since **dai** is considered to be the main verb, **mai** is placed just before it in negative statements:

> **pai seuh khorng** *mai dai.*   I *can't* go shopping.
> *torng* **yoo thee barn.**   I *have to* stay at home.

Similarly in short responses, it is **dai** that is used not the other verb:

> **shuey phom** *dai* **mai khrap?**   *Can* you help me?
> *dai* **kha.**   Yes.
> **mai** *dai* **kha.**   No.

dai is also used to say whether something is suitable or all right:

> **pai khon dieo** *dai* **mai kha?**   *Is it OK* if I go on my own?

You can also use it to ask someone to do you a favour.

Saying what you know how to do

pen can be used to indicate what you can do, that is, what you know how to do. Like **dai**, **pen** is used at the end of the sentence and is regarded as the main verb in negative statements and short responses:

> **khao khap rot** *pen.*   He *can* drive a car.
> **khao khap rot** *mai pen.*   He *can't* drive a car.
> **khun khap rot** *pen* **mai?**   *Can* you drive a car?
> *pen* **khrap.**   Yes.
> **mai** *pen.*   No.

Unlike **dai**, **pen** refers specifically to what you have learned to do. **dai** can be used for any kind of ability:

> **phom pai sanarmbin** *mai*   I *can't* go to the airport.
>   *dai* (not **pen**)
> **phom phoot pharsar thai**   I *can* speak Thai.
>   *pen* (or **dai**)

Sometimes you need to differentiate between the two meanings:

phom khap rot *pen* tae wannee khap *mai dai*	I *know how* to drive a car but I *can't* drive today. (e.g. because I'm ill)

Requesting something

khor (*lit*. 'I request') is often used to ask for or order something.

***khor* bia khrap.**	A beer, *please.*

You can also use **dai** to ask someone to do something for you:

khun shuey phom dai mai khrap?	*Can you* help me?

dai can also be used to ask someone's permission or agreement to do something:

soop buree *dai* mai khrap?	*Do you mind* if I smoke?

In affirmative requests adjectives and adverbs (such as **dee**, **char**) are often repeated:

tham dee dee.	Do it properly.

noi is used to soften the request and make it sound more polite. In negative requests you often add **nak** ('so', 'so much') as well as the filler word **na**:

yar phoot reo nak na khrap.	Don't speak so fast.

Expressing wants

yark or **yark cha** are used to say you want or don't want to do something:

***yark* pai wainarm.**	I *want to* go swimming.
***yark cha* klap barn.**	I *want to* go home.
khao mai *yark* mar.	He *doesn't want to* come.

yark cha often corresponds to 'would like to':

***yark cha* shuey khun.**	I *would like to* help you.

Unlike 'want', **yark** and **yark cha** are not used without a verb:

***yark* dai narlikar.**	I *want* a watch.

As an alternative, you can use the verb **torng karn**:

khun phor shan cha hai khorng khwan shan. *yark* **dai narlikar.**	My father is going to give me a present. I *want* a watch.
khun *torng karn* **arai?**	What *do you want*?

Expressing hopes

You have already come across constructions with **khit war** ('I think that'). Sentences with **wang war** are formed in the same way:

wang war **khao cha mar.**	*I hope* he will come.

Notice that with **khit** and **wang** you can't drop **war** in the way we drop 'that' in English.

With **wang** there is also no equivalent of the construction 'I hope to come'. In Thai you have to say:

phom wang war cha phop khun.	I hope I will meet you.

Notice these two common responses:

wang war **yang ngan.**	*I hope* so.
wang war **khong mai.**	*I hope* not.

Saying something is probable

khong or **khong cha** indicate that something is probable or likely:

khao *khong cha* **mar.**	He will *probably* come.

Note the position of **khong cha**, before the main verb.

khao *khong cha* **mai mar.**	He will *probably* not come.

khong without **cha** is used when you don't want to refer specifically to the future.

art cha is used with a similar meaning to **khong cha**:

art cha **mar char.**	I'll *probably* be late.

Saying somebody should do something

khuan cha is used in the same position in the sentence as **khong cha**:

khun *khuan cha* **klap barn reo.**	You *should* go home early.
khun *mai khuan* **kin kung.**	You *shouldn't* eat prawns.

khong cha and **khuan cha** tend to refer to a specific occasion. **khong** and **khuan** alone refer to what is generally likely or desirable.

Verb compounds

We can use two verbs together without any linking words:

pai tham ngarn	to go to work
mar tham ngarn	to come to work
pai kin khao	to go and eat

You will find this very common in Thai. Sometimes a number of verbs are used together in this way to convey the meaning of one English verb.

pai and **mar** can be used with another verb to indicate direction away from or towards the speaker:

phom klap *pai* barn	I'm *going back* home.
khao klap *mar* barn	He's *coming back* home.
phom khap rot *pai* mai dai.	I *couldn't go* by car.
khao khap rot *mar* mai dai.	He *can't come* by car.
khao ork *pai* laeo.	He's left already (i.e. *gone*)
khao ork *mar* laeo.	He's left (to *come here*) already.
khao *khao pai* laeo.	He *went in.*
khao *khao mar* laeo.	He *came in.*
phom *dern mar* opfit.	I *came* to the office on foot.
phom *dern pai* opfit.	I *went* to the office on foot.

ork is used after another verb to indicate that the action was or was not brought to a conclusion. The resulting verb compound often corresponds to a verb plus adverbial in English. For example, **khit ork** means 'to work something out':

yark mark. phom *khit* mai *ork*.	It's very difficult, I can't *work it out.*
phom arn mai ork.	I can't read it (*and make sense of it*).

Notice that in the negative **mai** is placed before **ork** not before the main verb.

The verbs **chop** and **set** can also be used in verb compounds:

khao tham ngarn set laeo.	He has finished working.
rao doo nang mai chop.	We didn't see the film to the end.

4 Adverbials

Prepositions

You will have noticed that you do not need a preposition with **pai** to mean 'to':

pai London.	I'm going to London.

In informal speech **thee** can also be omitted:

yoo barn.	She's at home.

Saying where something is

ngern yoo thee nai?	Where's the money?
yoo thee *nee.*	It's *here.*
yoo thee *nan.*	It's *there.*
yoo thee *nohn.*	It's *over there.*

Adverbials of location and direction

sai	(to the) left
kwar	(to the) right
tarng sai/kwar	on the left/right
pharn	after
korn	before
trong pai	straight on
trong kharm	opposite

Saying where you are from (mar chark + town or country)

shan *mar chark* **London.**	I am *from* London.
khun *mar chark* **thee nay.**	Where are you *from*?

'from' and 'to'

seuh *chark* **Suporn.**	I bought it *from* Suporn.
khai *hai* **Suporn.**	I sold it *to* Suporn.

hai *(for)*

seuh nangseuh *hai* phuen.	I bought a book *for* my friend. *or* I bought my friend a book.

Expressing frequency

len korp wan la neung khrang.	I play golf once a day.
len korp arthit la sorng khrang.	I play golf twice a week.
len korp thuk wan/arthit/deuan/ pee.	I play golf every day/week/ month/year.
wan arthit khun tham arai?	What do you do on Sunday?
prokkati len korp	I usually play golf.
len korp boi boi/samer/barng thee/barng khrang barng khrao.	I play golf often/always/some-times/occasionally.

Future time reference

cha pai meuang thai pee/ deuan/arthit nar.	I'm going to Thailand next year/ month/week.
cha pai krungthep eek sarm wan/arthit/deuan/pee.	I'm going to Bangkok in three days/weeks/months/years.

Past time expressions

Past time is indicated not by a change in the verb form but by time adverbials such as 'last night', 'two years ago'. A common way of indicating past time is with the expression . . . **thee laeo**.

phom pai Chieng Mai arthit/deuan/pee korn.	I went to Chieng Mai last week/ month/year.
phom pai Chieng Mai sorng pee thee laeo.	I went to Chieng Mai two years ago.
seuh rot sarm wan thee laeo.	I bought the car three days ago.

Referring to a starting point

tangtae can be used where in English we would either use 'since' or 'ever since'. You can use it either with a definite time expression (e.g. 'last year') or with a clause ('since I came to Bangkok'):

phom yoo thee rohng raem Hilton *tangtae* **arthit korn.**	I have stayed in the Hilton *since* last week.
phom yoo thee rohng raem Hilton *tangtae* **mar krungthep.**	I have stayed in the Hilton *since* I came to Bangkok.

yang *('still' or 'not yet')*

yang **yoo thee krungthep.**	He *still* lives in Bangkok.
yang mai **klap barn.**	He hasn't come home *yet*.

laeo *('already')*

kin *laeo*.	I have had something to eat/drink *already*.

laeo indicates an action that has already taken place. In English we can do this through the verb form alone (e.g. 'John has gone'). Since Thai does not have verb forms which indicate tense or aspect, **laeo** is sometimes used where we would not need to add 'already':

Steve mar laeo.	Steve has come.

Saying that something is too much or not enough

pharsar cheen yark kern pai.	Chinese is too difficult.

kern pai follows the adjective it qualifies.

We have seen that **mark**, **mark mark** and **nitnoi** are also used to qualify uncountable nouns:

mee ngern *nitnoi*	I have *a little* money.

mark kern pai can be used with nouns in the same way:

khao mee ngern mark kern pai.	He has too much money.

The contrasting idea is expressed by **mai phor**:

khao mee ngern mai phor.	He does not have enough money.

Notice that **mai phor** follows the noun it relates to.

Key to the exercises

Lesson 1

Exercise 1

khun Ken yoo mai khrap?
khun Malee yoo mai khrap?
khun Ena yoo mai khrap?
khun Sakorn yoo mai khrap?
khun Steve yoo mai khrap?
khun Saowalak yoo mai khrap?

Exercise 2

mai yoo kha.
yoo kha.
mai yoo kha.
mai yoo kha.
yoo kha.
yoo kha.

Exercise 3

1 yoo khrap. **2** mar khrap. **3** mai tham ngarn khrap. **4** yoo khrap.
5 mai mar khrap. **6** mai mar khrap.

Exercise 4

1 sawatdee kha.   sawatdee khrap.
2 khun malee mai yoo khrap.   khorpkhun khrap.
3 khorpkhun khrap.   mai pen rai.
4 khun Ena yoo mai kha?   yoo, khrap.
5 khun Ken yoo mai kha?   mai yoo kha.

Exercise 5

1 khun Sawat yoo mai khrap? **2** khun Steve mar tham ngarn mai?
3 khun Ken mar mai? **4** khun Sakorn mar tham ngarn mai? **5** khun
Malee mar mai?

Exercise 6 (suggested answer)

MARY: sawatdee kha. A: sawatdee khrap. MARY: khorthoht kha. khun
Suchart yoo mai kha? A: yoo khrap. MARY: khorpkhun khrap. A: mai pen
rai khrap.

Exercise 7

1 A: khun A yoo mai khrap? B: mai yoo kha. yoo thee London. A: khun
B yoo mai khrap? B: mai yoo kha. yoo thee Chieng Mai. A: khun C yoo mai
khrap? B: mai yoo kha. yoo thee krungthep.
2 A: khun A yoo mai kha? B: mai yoo khrap. pai opfit. A: khun A yoo mai
kha? B: mai yoo khrap. pai sanarmbin. A: khun A yoo mai kha? B: mai yoo
khrap. pai rohng raem Oriental.

Exercise 8

khun Sakorn mai yoo thee London. yoo thee krungthep.
khun Steve mai yoo thee rohng raem Oriental. yoo thee barn.
khun Saowalak mai yoo thee apartmen. yoo thee opfit.
khun Ann mai yoo thee krungthep. yoo thee Chieng Mai.

Exercise 9

1 Saowalak tham ngarn thee London shai mai? **2** Steve tham ngarn thee
rohng raem Oriental shai mai? **3** Sakorn mai yoo thee opfit shai mai?
4 Steve pai krungthep shai mai? **5** wannee Saowalak mai mar tham
ngarn shai mai? **6** Steve pai opfit shai mai?

Exercise 10

1 shai kha. **2** shai kha. **3** mai shai kha. **4** mai shai kha. **5** shai kha.
6 mai shai kha.

Exercise 11   (suggested answers)

1   shai khrap. **2**   mai shai khrap. **3**   mai shai khrap. **4**   mai shai khrap.
5   shai khrap.

Exercise 12   (suggested answers)

pai sanarmbin mai khrap?
pai rohng raem shai mai?
mai yoo thee sanarmbin.
mai pai rohng raem khrap.

Exercise 13

1   sawatdee khrap. khun Ken yoo mai khrap? **2**   khorthoht kha. **3**   mai
pen rai. **4**   (examples) pai opfit shai mai? pai sanarmbin shai mai? pai
rohng raem shai mai? pai krungthep shai mai? pai apartmen shai mai?
5   khun malee yoo mai khrap? mai yoo kha. yoo thee opfit kha. wannee
khun pai opfit shai mai? mai shai kha. wannee yoo thee barn.

Vocabulary building

tham	to do
wan	day
thoht	punishment
bin	to fly
nee	this
ngarn	work
khor	to ask for

Exercise 14

dee   mee   mar   narn   pai   bart

Exercise 15

ดี มา ไป มี นาน บาท

Comprehension

Sakorn: not at work. Saowanee: airport. Saowalak: Paris. Manat: Hilton.

Lesson 2

Exercise 1

pai talart	pai opfit	pai krungthep	pai Chieng Mai
pai London	pai sanarmbin	pai rohng raem	pai apartmen

Exercise 2

pai talart mai khrap? pai opfit mai khrap? pai krungthep mai khrap? pai Chieng Mai mai khrap? pai London mai khrap? pai sanarmbin mai khrap? pai rohng raem mai khrap? pai apartmen mai khrap?

Exercise 3

1 mai pai. pai rohng raem **2** mai pai. pai opfit. **3** yoo thee krungthep. **4** mai pai. pai talart. **5** mai pai. pai thieo **6** pai sanarmbin.

Exercise 4 (example)

khun pai rohng raem shai mai kha?
mai shai khrap. pai sanarmbin. khun la khrap?
pai opfit kha.

Exercise 5

MALEE: sawatdee kha, khun Akorn. AKORN: sawatdee khrap, khun Malee. khun sabai dee mai? MALEE: sabai dee khorpkhun kha. khun la kha? AKORN: sabai dee khrap. MALEE: pai nai kha? AKORN: pai sanarmbin kha. khun la kha? MALEE: pai opfit kha. shohk dee na khrap. AKORN: khorpkhun khrap. laeo cher kan na khrap.

Exercise 6

1 yoo thee nai? **2** khun pai nai? **3** pai thee nai? **4** yoo thee nai? **5** pai nai?

Exercise 7 (examples)

1 sabai dee khorpkhun khrap. **2** khorpkhun khrap. shohk dee na khrap. **3** pai opfit. **4** yoo thee barn. **5** mai pen rai.

Exercise 8   (examples)

1   mai pai talart reuh? **2**   mai pai apartmen reuh? **3**   pai krungthep reuh?
4   pai tham ngarn reuh? **5**   mai pai sanarmbin reuh? **6**   mai pai rohng
raem Hilton reuh?

Exercise 9

1   Suchart tham ngarn thee rohng raem Hilton reuh? **2**   Malee yoo thee
barn shai mai? **3**   Saowalak mai yoo thee opfit shai mai? **4**   Suchart mai
tham ngarn thee sanarmbin reuh? **5**   Sakorn pai sanarmbin reuh?
6   Malee mai pai talart reuh?

Exercise 10

1   pai tham ngarn mai? **2**   khun Saowanee tham ngarn thee sanarmbin
shai mai? **3**   wannee khun Dusit pai tham ngarn shai mai? **4**   phom pai
rohng raem. pai duey kan mai? **5**   Saowalak yoo thee talart shai mai?

Exercise 11   (examples)

1   shai kha. **2**   mai yoo kha. pai tham ngarn. **3**   mai shai kha. yoo thee
London. **4**   mai shai kha. **5**   mai shai kha tham ngarn thee rohng raem
Hilton. **6**   mai pai. yoo thee barn.

Exercise 12

1   phom pai talart. pai duey kan mai? **2**   phom pai sanarmbin. pai duey
kan mai? **3**   phom pai seuh khorng. pai duey kan mai? **4**   phom pai kin
karfae. pai duey kan mai? **5**   phom pai opfit. pai duey kan mai? **6**   phom
pai London. pai duey kan mai?

Exercise 13

MALEE: sawatdee kha Sue. SUE: sawatdee kha Malee. khun sabai dee reuh?
MALEE: sabai dee, khorpkhun kha. SUE: pai nai kha? MALEE: pai seuh
khorng kha. pai duey kan mai? SUE: dee see kha.

Exercise 14

1   shan pai seuh khorng kha. pai duey kan mai? **2**   pai kin karfae thee
rohng raem Hilton. dee see khrap. **3**   shohk dee na khrap. laeo cher kan na
khrap. **4**   mai pai thieo khrap. pai thura.

Vocabulary building

1 sabai dee, sawatdee shohk dee **2** talart, opfit, sanarmbin, rohng, raem barn, apartmen.

Exercise 15

tham rai kin ngarn kan bin rak mark

Exercise 16

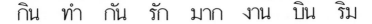

กิน ทำ กัน รัก มาก งาน บิน ริม

Comprehension

1 Saowalak is going to the airport. She's going to London. Akorn is going to the Hilton hotel. **2** Manat is in London. He's gone shopping.

Lesson 3

Exercise 1

1 pen khon thai. **2** pen khon angkrit. **3** pen khon amerikan. **4** pen khon farangset. **5** pen khon cheen. **6** pen khon malesian.

Exercise 2

1 khun mar chark Paris reuh? **2** khun mar chark krungthep reuh? **3** khun mar chark Washington reuh? **4** khao mar chark Kuala Lumpur reuh? **5** khun mar chark London reuh? **6** khun mar chark pakin reuh?

Exercise 3 (examples)

1 shai kha. **2** mai shai kha. pen khon amerikan. **3** mai shai kha. pai thieo London. **4** mai shai kha. mar chark Los Angeles. **5** mai shai kha. pen khon amerikan. **6** mar chark Los Angeles. **7** shai kha.

Exercise 4

1 Yves mai shai kon cheen. pen khon farangset. **2** Wan Omar mai shai khon angkrit. pen khon malesian. **3** Saowalak mai shai khon lao. pen khon thai. **4** Steve mai shai khon thai. pen khon angkrit. **5** Wei Lin mai shai khon farangset. pen khon cheen.

Exercise 5

1 mar chark angkrit. **2** mar chark meuang thai. **3** mar chark yeepun. **4** mar chark amerikar. **5** mar chark itarlee. **6** mar chark meuang thai.

Exercise 6 (examples)

Ken pai thieo meuang thai.
Manat pai thura thee yeepun.
Suchart yoo thee meuang lao.
Ena mar chark amerikar.

Exercise 7

1 pai talart thammai? **2** mar London thammai? **3** pai sanarmbin thammai? **4** pai krungthep thammai? **5** pai rohng raem thammai?

Exercise 8 (examples)

1 pai seuh khorng. **2** mar tham ngarn. **3** pai krungthep. **4** pai thieo. **5** pai tham ngarn.

Exercise 9 (examples)

mar chark London.
yoo thee London thammai?
pai London shai mai?
mai pai London shai mai?

Exercise 10

Dialogue 1 A: pai nai khrap? B: pai krungthep kha. A: pai thamnmai. B: pai thura. A: shohk dee na khrap. B: khorpkhun mark kha.
Dialogue 2 A: khun pen khon farangset shai mai? B: mai shai khrap. pen khon angkrit. khun la khrap? A: pen khon cheen.

Exercise 11

SUCHAT: khorthoht khrap khun pen khon amerikan shai mai khrap? LISA: mai shai kha. pen khon itarlian, kha. mar chark Milan. khun mar chark Chieng Mai reuh kha? SUCHAT: mai shai khrap. mar chark krungthep. khun mar krungthep thammai? mar thieo reuh? LISA: mai chai, kha. mar thura. SUCHAT: sanuk mai khrap? LISA: mai sanuk kha.

Exercise 12

1 dee mai? mai dee. **2** sao mai? mai sao. kae. **3** sanuk mai? mai sanuk. nar beua. **4** ruey mai? mai ruey. chon. **5** nar kliat mai? mai nar kliat. suey. **6** nar beua mai? mai nar beua. sanuk. **7** chon mai? mai chon. ruey. **8** suey mai? mai suey. nar kliat. **9** num mai? mai num. kae.

Exercise 13

1 pen khon dee mai? mai chai. pen khon mai dee. **2** pen khon sao mai? mai chai, pen khon kae. **3** pen khon ruey mai? mai chai. pen khon chon. **4** pen khon thai mai? mai chai. pen khon angkrit. **5** pen khon cheen mai? mai chai. pen khon lao. **6** pen khon chon mai? mai chai. pen khon ruey.

Exercise 14 (examples)

1 mee khrap. **2** mai mee khrap. **3** mee khrap. **4** mai mee khrap. **5** mee khrap. **6** mee khrap. **7** mai mee khrap.

Exercise 15 (examples)

khun tham ngarn thee krungthep shai mai? tham ngarn thee rohng raem reuh? tham ngarn thee nai? khun pen khon thai reuh? mar chark krungthep shai mai? mar chark thee nai?

Exercise 16

1 mee ngern mark. mee faen. mee look. mee barn. mee apartmen duey. mee pheuan mark mark. **2** mai mee ngern. mai mee barn. mai mee look. mai mee faen mai mee pheuan.

Exercise 17

1 khorthoht khrap khun mee faen mai? **2** khun mee look mai khrap? **3** khun mee ngern mai? **4** khun mee barn mai? **5** khun mee apartmen mai? **6** khun mee ngarn mai?

Exercise 18 (examples)

1 nar beua. **2** nar beua mark mark. **3** sanuk mark. **4** sanuk mark mark.

Exercise 19

1 Because she doesn't have any friends. **2** Because she doesn't have any money. **3** He doesn't have to work but he has a house in London and a flat in Paris as well as living in New York. He doesn't have a wife (or girlfriend) and he's going on holiday to Japan.

Exercise 20

khun Ken mar chark London	pen khon angkrit
khun Martin pen khon chon	mai mee ngern
khun Saowalak mai kae	pen khon sao
khao mai shai khon chon	pen khon ruey
yoo thee apartmen mai sanuk	nar beua

Exercise 21 (examples)

Dialogue 1 KEN: sawatdee khrap khun Manat. MANAT: sawatdee khrap khun Ken. pai nai khrap? KEN: pai opfit khrap. MANAT: faen yoo thee nai? KEN: yoo thee barn.

Dialogue 2 A: khun mee ngern mai? B: mee khrap. pen khon ruey. khun la khrap? A: mee nitnoi mai mark. phom pen khon chon.

Exercise 22

1 ngarn phom nar beua. mai mee pheuan mai mee ngern duey **2** khun mar chark thee nai? tham ngarn thee nai? ngarn sanuk mai? **3** faen khao pen khon cheen. mar chark Hong Kong. yoo thee London. tham ngarn thee Oxford. **4** khao pen khon sao, suey duey. tham ngarn thee rohng raem. mai mee ngern. faen pen khon kae. pen khon ruey mark. nar kliat. mee apartmen thee London, mee apartmen thee Rome, mee apartmen thee Paris duey.

Vocabulary building

1 workman **2** make-up **3** housework (home work) **4** workplace, office **5** make good **6** neighbour

Exercise 23

look lao soop khon suey cheen wan tham ngarn sao chon

Exercise 23

คน ยา สวย นม รวย ดู จีน ลง ลาว วัน

Comprehension

Suthaep works at the Oriental hotel. He is American, and says he has only a little money; his children have a beautiful flat in New York and a lot of money.

Dusit works at the airport; doesn't like his job; has a wife but no children.

What they have in common: Both their wives are in London.

How well do they know each other? They have obviously seen each other before as they ask how the other is; Suthaep, however, does not know where Dusit works while Dusit thinks Suthaep works in the Hilton. Dusit is also mistaken about Suthaep's nationality and neither knows anything about the other's family.

Lesson 4

Exercise 1

1 mee kao khon. **2** mee sip khon. **3** mee har khon. **4** mee sarm khon. **5** mee hok khon.

Exercise 2 (examples)

Suchart mee pheuan sorng khon; mee look chet khon; mee lookshai har khon, mee looksao sorng khon.

Exercise 3

mee faen kee khon?/mee look kee khon?/mee lookshai kee khon?/mee looksao kee khon?/mee pheuan kee khon?/thee opfit khun mee pheuan kee khon?/thee barn mee khon kee khon?

Exercise 4

Cholada aryu sorng khuap. Manop aryu see sip chet pee. Ena aryu yee sip sarm pee. Malee aryu sarm sip har pee. Alex aryu hok khuap.

Exercise 5

1 khun yoo thee rohng raem Oriental reuh rohng raem Hilton? **2** khun tham ngarn thee sanarmbin reuh thee rohng raem? **3** faen khun mar chark krungthep reuh Chieng Mai? **4** khun pen khon thai reuh khon lao? **5** thee barn mee khon see khon reuh har khon? **6** look khun pen phooshai reuh phooying?

Exercise 6

1 39. **2** 56. **3** 69. **4** 71. **5** 48. **6** 11.

Exercise 7

a) neung chet sarm see b) sorng hok paet hok c) kao see sorng see d) har sarm neung chet e) sorng chet see hok

Exercise 8

1 Twenty women; thirty men. **2** He has many friends; ninety-nine of them are women and one man who works at the airport.

Exercise 9

A: khorthoht, khrap, khun mee faen mai khrap? B: mee kha. mee look duey. A: khun mee look kee khon? B: har khon kha. A: pen phooshai reuh phooying? B: pen phooying. A: ching ching reuh!

Exercise 10

1 khun pen khroo reuh? **2** khun pen mor shai mai? **3** khun pen mae barn reuh? **4** khun pen lekharnukarn shai mai? **5** khun pen nak thurak-it shai mai? **6** khun pen tamruat shai mai?

Examples of answers: **1** mai shai khrap. pen mor. **2** mai shai khrap. pen tamruat.

Exercise 11 (example)

Suporn pen tamruat. pen khon kae. aryu har sip chet pee. nar kliat duey. mar chark Khon Kaen. tham ngarn thee krungthep.

Exercise 12 (examples)

1 plao kha. sanuk. **2** mai shai kha. pen khon chon. **3** shai kha. pen khroo. **4** mai mee. **5** shai kha. pen khon farangset. **6** mai shai kha. **7** plao kha. keng nitnoi.

Exercise 13 (examples)

khun mae khao pen mor shai mai?
khun phor khun pen khon lao reuh?
looksao khun pen nak thurakit shai mai?

Exercise 14

1 looksao phom ko pen nak thurakit. **2** lookshai phom ko yoo thee amerikar. **3** khun mae phom ko pai sanarmbin. **4** ngarn khun phor phom ko nar beua. **5** look phom ko keng.

Exercise 15 (examples)

look sao shan pen mae barn.
mor shan keng.
khun pen mor shai mai?

Exercise 16 (example)

pen khon farangset. aryu chet sip har pee. faen pen khon itarlian. aryu yee sip paet pee. mee look har khon.

Exercise 17

1 khit war pen khon angkrit. **2** khit war mai mee. **3** khit war mee look see khon. **4** khit war yoo thee London. **5** khit war tham ngarn thee sanarmbin. **6** khit war pen khon chon.

Exercise 18 (example)

1 DOCTOR: khun mee look kee khon? FRIEND: mee look sorng khon kha. DOCTOR: aryu thaorai? FRIEND: phooying hok khuap, phooshai see khuap kha. DOCTOR: look yoo thee nai? FRIEND: phooying yoo kap khun mae shan thee London phooshai yoo thee krungthep. **2** khun mae khun pen lekharnukarn shai mai? **3** A: look khun pai rohng rian shai mai? B: plao kha. yoo thee barn kap pheuan shan sabai sabai.

Vocabulary building

1 kliat **2** bin **3** rian **4** rohng **5** beua **6** sanarm **7** rak **8** ching

Exercise 19

phom shan sarm hok morng talart sabai dee sip hok hok sip

Exercise 20

หก ผม สอง ฉัน ตก มอง

Exercise 21

phom pai sanarmbin. khon cheen mar tham ngarn.
shan rak khon cheen mark. thammai look tham ngarn narn?

Comprehension

Her husband is a doctor and works in Bangkok. She has three children, all
girls. So does the doctor. Both have children aged two, four, and six. Both
Jo and the doctor's wife are from Manchester.

Lesson 5

Exercise 1

nee rohng rian. nee opfit phom. lang nan barn phom. nan rohng raem
Shangri-La. nan thanarkharn. nohn sanarmbin. nohn talart. nohn rohng
phayarbarn

Exercise 2 (examples)

1 mee rohng raem yee sip haeng. **2** mee talart sorng haeng. **3** mee
thanarkharn har haeng. **4** mee rohng phayarbarn sarm haeng. **5** mee
sanarmbin sorng haeng. **6** mee wat sarm sip haeng.

Exercise 3

1 sanarmbin nai? **2** rohng phayarbarn nai? **3** thanarkharn nai?
4 rohng rian nai? **5** rohng raem nai? **6** wat nai ?

Exercise 4

1 tham arai? **2** kin arai? **3** seuh arai? **4** hen arai? **5** khit arai?
6 pen arai?

Exercise 5

1 khrai pai sanarmbin? **2** khrai pai rohng raem? **3** khrai pai rohng
phayarbarn? **4** khrai pai kin karfae? **5** khrai pai seuh khorng? **6** khrai
pai thanarkharn?

Exercise 6

They disagree on what the building is. B thinks it's a hospital. C thinks it's
the American bank. C thinks it's beautiful; B disagrees.

Exercise 7

1 barn khun Malee yai. **2** barn khun Saowalak lek. **3** faen khorng
Saowalak pen nak thurakit. **4** faen khorng Saowanee num. **5** faen
khorng Saowalak kae. **6** faen khorng Saowanee pen tamruat.

Exercise 8

1 mee sanarm yar mai? **2** mee thee chort rot mai? **3** mee thohrasap
mai? **4** mee ae mai? **5** mee too yen mai?

Exercise 9

1 barn pen yangngai barng? yai mark. **2** rot pen yangngai barng? kao.
mai suey. **3** faen pen yangngai barng? suey khrap. **4** horng khrua pen
yangngai barng? lek lek. **5** horng nang len pen yangngai barng? nar yoo.
6 horng narm pen yangngai barng? sa-art. **7** look pen yangngai barng?
nar rak.

Exercise 10

1 har larn bart **2** paet meun bart **3** sip chet larn bart **4** sorng phan see
roi har sip bart **5** sorng larn chet saen neung meun bart **6** see larn kao
saen khon **7** sip kao larn khon **8** neung saen chet meun har phan khon

Exercise 11 (examples)

> barn kao tae suey
> rohng raem phaeng tae dee
> rot mai tae sokkaprok
> rohng phayabarn yai tae mai phaeng
> khao pen tamruat tae mai dee
> faen khorng khun Saowalak pen khroo tae mai keng
> khao pen khon ruey tae mai dee
> phooying suey tae mai keng
> khao pen mor tae mai mee ngern

Exercise 12

1 classroom **2** workshop **3** lover **4** driver **5** toy

Exercise 13 (examples)

1 barn yai. mee horng norn sarm horng horng nang len sorng horng horng
narm sarm horng mee sanarm yar yai mark. **2** barn suey mark. mee thee
chort rot yai. mee sanarm yar suey. . . . **3** barn phaeng. horng khrua lek.
horng narm sokkaprok. klai mark.

Exercise 14 (examples)

yai mai? pen yangngai barng? mee thohrasap mai? mee ae mai?

Exercise 15 (examples)

khrai pai seuh rot? thanarkharn yoo nai? khun pai thanarkharn thammai?

Vocabulary building

> List 1
>
> | | |
> |---|---|
> | mar | pai |
> | mark | nitnoi |
> | thura | thieo |
> | nar beua | nar son chai |
> | kae | num |
> | nar rak | nar kliat |
> | ruey | chon |
> | phooshai | phooying |

looksao	look shai
nakrian	khroo
mae	pho
sa-art	sokkaprok
mai	kao
len	tham ngarn

List 2

talart	seuh khorng
khao	horng khrua
sanuk	nar son chai
ruey	ngern
suey	nar rak
rohng rian	khroo
mor	rohng phayarbarn
lekharnukarn	thee tham ngarn
teuk	horng khrua

Exercise 16

1 thee nee mee thanarkharn har haeng pai thanarkharn nai? **2** khortho-ht khrap mai sarp. **3** rot nee khorng khrai? **4** pen yangngai barng? mai mai? phaeng mai? **5** thee chort rot pen yangngai barng?

Exercise 17

see phor mae welar hen yen lek phaeng kae tae

Exercise 18

พ่อ เย็น แพง เล่น เล็ก แต่ พูด

Comprehension

It costs five thousand three hundred bart. There are three bedrooms, two comfortable sitting rooms and four bathrooms. There's a garage, and the garden is small but pretty. It's near the hospital and it belongs to a friend of Malee's who is in London.

Lesson 6

Exercise 1

1 mee bia mai? **2** mee phak mai? **3** mee kung mai? **4** mee kai mai?
5 mee phak ruam mai? **6** mai plar mai? **7** mee narm mai?

Exercise 2

1 mai mee kha. **2** mee kha. **3** mai mee kha. **4** mai mee kha. **5** mee
kha. **6** mai mee kha. **7** mee kha.

Exercise 3 (examples)

1 shorp mark. **2** shorp nitnoi. **3** mai shorp. **4** mai shorp. **5** shorp
mark. **6** mai shorp. **7** shorp nitnoi.

Exercise 4

1 shorp karfae mai? **2** shorp ngarn khorng khun mai? **3** shorp seuh
khorng mai? **4** shorp meuang thai mai? **5** shorp aharn yeepun mai?
6 shorp rian nangseuh mai?

Exercise 5 (examples)

khor bia khuat neung. khor phak ruam. khor tom yam kai. khor khao phat
kai. khor phonlamai ruam. khor narm khaeo neung. khor phak phat. khor
thom yam plar.

Exercise 6

1 khor narm sorng khuat. **2** khor bia sarm kaeo. **3** khor karfae see
thuey. **4** khor phonlamai ruam har charn. **5** khor khao phat kung sarm
charn. **6** khor tom yam kung see charn.

Exercise 7

pai nai mai?	mai pai nai.
pai kin arai mai?	mai kin arai.
thee barn mee khrai mai?	mai mee khrai.
tham arai mai?	mai tham arai.

Exercise 8

1 thee barn mee khrai barng? **2** thee talart seuh arai barng? **3** pai nai barng? **4** thee barn mee phonlamai arai barng? **5** thee talart mee phak arai barng? **6** thee rarn aharn mee plar arai barng?

Exercise 9

1 He's going to the Thai restaurant because he's thirsty. **2** He only likes it a little as it's very spicy. He doesn't like **tom yam** but he likes the fruit very much.

Exercise 10 (examples)

1 mee khon cheen noi khon. mee khon amerikan lai khon. mee khon yeepun barng khon. **2** thee A mee rohng phayabarn noi haeng. mee rohng raem barng haeng. mee rarn aharn lai haeng.

Exercise 11

1 rarkhar phonlamai thaorai? **2** rarkhar tom yam pla thaorai? **3** rarkhar saparot thaorai? **4** rarkhar mamuang thaorai? **5** bia rarkhar thaorai? **6** karfae rarkhar thaorai? **7** narm rarkhar thaorai?

Exercise 12

1 khor kluey sarm bai **2** khor mamuang see bai **3** khor saparot har bai **4** khor taeng moh sorng bai **5** khor malakor sarm bai **6** khor som see bai

Exercise 13

1 aroi mai? **2** warn mai? **3** phet mai? **4** mai shorp reuh? **5** hiu mai? **6** hiu narm mai? **7** prieo mai? **8** aroi mai? **9** nao mai? **10** rorn mai?

Exercise 14

The papayas were expensive because there were not very many of them. The oranges were not sweet because of the rain (and also because of the heat). There were no water melons because it had rained too much.

Exercise 15

STEVE: rarkhar kung thaorai khrap? STALLHOLDER: kiloh la 250 bart khrap. STEVE: thammai phaeng khrap? STALLHOLDER: mai phaeng rok kha STEVE: aroi mai khrap? STALLHOLDER: aroi mark kha. seuh mai kha? STEVE: seuh kiloh neung.

Vocabulary building

1 khao. All the others are fruits. **2 kung**. All the others are meats. **3 shorp**. All the others are foods. **4 bai**. It is the only classifier. **5 thohras-ap**. The others are receptacles. **6 thee chort rot**. The others are all to do with food. **7 kai**. The others are all words for groups of things. **8 klai**. The others can all apply to foods.

Exercise 16

kung phooshai horng norn horng len horng khrua horng narm
narm som taeng moh shohk dee lookshai khuat khorng len
khap khor malakor manao maphrao

Exercise 17

โรงแรม กุ้ง โชคดี ขวด

น้ำส้ม มะละกอ มะม่วง

Comprehension

1 On the menu: fried rice with prawns; fried rice with chicken; spicy soup; pork fried rice; water melon, pineapple, papaya and mangoes. **2** She likes bananas. She does not like prawns, pork, spicy food, Thai fruits. **3** They order prawn fried rice, a cup of coffee, a bottle of water, one mixed fruit.

Lesson 7

Exercise I

1 yar chort trong nee. **2** yar lieo sai. **3** yar lieo kwar. **4** yar chort trong kharm rohng rian. **5** yar lieo kwar pharn rohng phayarbarn.

Exercise 2

A **1** chort thee rohng raem Orbis. **2** chort thee pamnamman Esso.
3 chort thee satharnthoot angkrit. **4** chort thee rohng nang. **5** chort
thee rohng phayarbarn. B (Examples) pharn rohng raem Orbis lieo sai.
pharn satharnthoot angkrit lieo kwar. korn rohng nang lieo sai. korn rohng
phayarbarn lieo kwar.

Exercise 3 (example)

1 khun dern pharn rohng raem Shangri-La pramarn sorng narthee laeo ko
hen satharnthoot.

Exercise 4

1: Italian Embassy
2: Suchart's house

Exercise 5

1 lieo kwar laeo ko lieo sai. thanarkharn yeepun yoo tharng kwar.
2 dern trong pai. rohng nang yoo tharng sai. **3** dern trong pai. **4** lieo sai
laeo ko lieo kwar. satharnthoot farangset yoo tharng sai. **5** dern trong pai.
rarn aharn yoo lieo kwar.

Exercise 6 (example)

A: barn khorng khun yoo thee nai khrap? B: yoo klai rohng phayarbarn
khrap. A: rohng phayarbarn nai khrap? B: rohng phayarbarn Central
khrap. A: yoo trong kharm rohng phayarbarn shai mai? B: mai shai khrap
tae mai klai. A: yoo korn reuh pharn rohng phayarbarn? B: pharn rohng
phayarbarn khrap. A: yoo tharng sai reuh tharng kwar? B: yoo tharng kwar.
A: dern pharn rohng phayarbarn kee narthee khrap? B: pramarn yee sip
narthee khrap.

Exercise 7

I was standing outside the Rex cinema trying to find my way to the
Japanese Embassy. A passer-by told me it was twenty-five minutes' walk
past the American Embassy, opposite the French bank. When I got there I
was told that the building opposite the French bank was the Japanese
school. The Japanese Embassy was opposite the Rex cinema.

Exercise 8

1 pai thanarkharn mar. **2** pai seuh rot mar. **3** pai seuh khorng mar.
4 pai rohng phayarbarn mar. **5** pai rarn aharn cheen mar. **6** pai
krungthep mar. **7** pai thieo shai tale mar.

Exercise 9

A: pai nai mar kha? B: pai talart mar kha. A: pai thammai kha? B: pai seuh
khorng kha. A: seuh arai kha? B: seuh khao kha. A: pai yangngai kha?
B: pai reua kha.

Exercise 10

khreuang bin sia welar thaorai? reua sia welar thaorai? rot fai sia welar
thaorai? rot me sia welar thaorai? pai rot taeksee sia welar thaorai?

Exercise 11

khreuang bin sia welar har shaumohng. reua sia welar sarm shuamohng khreung. rot fai sia welar sip shuamohng. rot me sia welar chet shuamohng khreung. rot taeksee sia welar yee sip har narthee.

Exercise 12

1 khun yoo thee Paris kee pee? **2** khun dern kee wan? **3** khun tham ngarn thee thanarkharn kee pee? **4** khun yoo thee rohng nang kee narthee? **5** khun yoo thee rohng phayarbarn kee shuamohng? **6** khun tham ngarn thee satharnthoot farangset kee arthit?

Exercise 13

1 pai nai mar? **2** pai har khrai? **3** khrai yoo thee barn lang nan? **4** pai rot sia welar thaorai? **5** khar rot me thaorai? **6** pai yangngai? **7** yoo kee arthit?

Exercise 14 (example)

SUCHART: pai nai mar khrap? ANNA: pai Paris mar kha. SUCHART: sanuk mai?ANNA: mai sanuk kha.SUCHART: khun tham arai? ANNA: pai seuh khorng kha. SUCHART: khun yoo thee nohn kee wan khrap? ANNA: wan neung thaonan kha. SUCHART: pai yangngai khrap? ANNA: pai rot tua kha. SUCHART: rot tua sia welar thaorai khrap? ANNA: sia welar chet shuamohng kha. SUCHART: shar na khrap. khar tua phaeng mai khrap? ANNA: phaeng kha. sorng phan bart kha.

Exercise 15 (examples)

1 yoo thee thanon X. **2** klai mark. **3** mai chai. yoo klai satharnthoot cheen. **4** pai rot me. **5** phaeng mark. **6** sia welar khrung shuamohng. **7** khit war rot mai tit. **8** narn mark. sia welar sorng shuamohng. **9** yoo tharng kwar.

Vocabulary building

1

reo	shar
kwar	sai
korn	pharn

nao   rorn
prieo   warn

2 (examples)
khreuang bin, reua, rot taeksee, rot tit,
shuamohng, sia welar, arthit, wan, deuan

Exercise 16

1 chort trong kharm satharnthoot yeepun. yar lieo kwar pharn pam narm-man. **2** pai thieo mar. mai sanuk. nar beua mark. pai rot fai. sia welar sarm sip hok shuamohng. **3** pai taeksee mai narn. leo. mai phaeng. pai rot me narn mark. **4** khun dern wan la kee shuamohng?

Exercise 17

1 fon tok fai fai far dern pen khon farang afrikan afrikar yar im itarlee rerm ngern
2 **1** Opposite the petrol station. **2** After the hotel. **3** By the sea. **4** Walk past the hotel, then straight on. **5** Tarksin Street.

Exercise 18

คุณเดินผ่านโรงแรมแล้วเลี้ยวขวาบ้านผม
อยู่ตรงข้ามโรงพยาบาล

Comprehension

1 Because he can get a nice house cheaply. **2** It's big; it has a garden and a garage. It's two years old and is air conditioned. **3** The train is quicker than his car because the traffic's bad. And as his car is old it uses a lot of petrol.

Lesson 8

Exercise 1

1 and **6** might meet at the market. **2** and **4** might meet at the hospital. **3** and **5** might meet at the airport.

Exercise 2

1 cha pai seuh arai? **2** cha pai thammai? **3** cha pai nai? **4** cha pai har khrai? **5** cha pai kin khao thee nai? **6** cha pai thammai?

Exercise 3

1 cha klap barn. **2** cha pai thieo. **3** cha pai har mor. **4** cha pai seuh rot. **5** cha pai kin khao.

Exercise 4 (examples)

yang mai klap opfit. yang mai kin khao. yang mai pai thanarkharn. yang mai seuh buree.

Exercise 5

1 kin laeo. **2** kin laeo. **3** soop laeo. **4** pai laeo. **5** pai laeo. **6** deuhm laeo.

Exercise 6

A: khun Naowalak yoo mai kha? B: yang mai mar khrap. eek sip narthee cha mar laeo.A: phrungnee khao cha pai rohng phayarbarn shai mai kha? B: mai sarp khrap.

Exercise 7

1 Manat's wife is unwell. She has a cold.

Example 1 JANET: *norng sao* khun pen yangngai barng kha? MANAT: mai sabai khrap. JANET: pen arai kha? MANAT: *puat thorng* khrap. *Example 2* JANET: *khun mae* khun yang mai sabai yoo reuplao kha? MANAT: shai khrap. JANET: pen arai khrap? MANAT: *pen wat* khrap.

Exercise 8 (examples)

khao phak yoo thee nai? sheuh arai? tham ngarn thee nai? aryu thaorai?

Exercise 9 (examples)

1 yang (taeng ngarn laeo). **2** yang mai kin. **3** deuhm laeo. **4** yang mai khap. **5** yang mai seuh.

Exercise 10

khun kin khao laeo reu yang? khun pai thanarkharn laeo reu yang? khun seuh buree laeo reu yang?

Exercise 11

1 pai khrap. **2** mai dai seuh. **3** mai dai pai. **4** mai dai pai. **5** mai norn. **6** shai khrap. **7** mai dai pai. **8** phoot khrap. **9** mai mao khrap.

Exercise 12

khun pai thanarkharn reuplao? khun pai har mor reuplao? khun pai kin khao reuplao? khun pai thieo reuplao?

Exercise 13

Saowalak is smoking. Steve is going to look at the garden. Saowanee is sitting near Saowalak.

Exercise 14   (examples)

A: rot thee shan seuh phaeng. barn thee phom doo suey. thanarkharn thee looksao phom pai mai dee. B: phooying thee seuh rot phom keng. phooshai thee mar doo barn shan pen khon mao. khon thee phoot kap Steve mai dee.

Exercise 15

A: khorthoht khrap. khon nan sarmee khorng khun shai mai? B: mai shai kha. yang mai taeng ngarn. A: khon nan khrai khrap? A: khon thee soop buree shai mai kha? B: mai shai khrap. khon thee phoot kap Steve. B: khit war sheuh Manat. tharm thammai? A: khit war khao pen mor.

Exercise 16

1 mai shai kha. khon phorm. **2** mai shai kha. khon tia. **3** mai shai kha. phooying nar kliat. **4** mai shai kha. khon uwan. **5** mai shai kha. khon sao. **6** mai shai kha. phooshai soong.

Exercise 17 (examples)

1 phom sheuh John. phom kae. uwan. tham ngarn thee London. **2** pen khon soong. phorm. sai waen tar. nar kliat mark. khit war mao.

Exercise 18 (examples)

Dialogue 1 A: khon nan sheuh arai? B: sheuh John. pen mor. pen khon keng. hen khon nan mai? A: hen kha. B: pen sarmee khun Saowalak. pen khon mao. *Dialogue 2* A: phom sheuh John khrap. khun pen khroo shai mai? B: mai shai kha. pen mae barn. A: pheuan khun pen khroo shai mai? B: mai shai kha. mai shai pheuan kha. pen mae khorng shan. pen tamruat. A: khun sheuh arai? B: sheuh Mary kha.A: khun mai shai khon thai reuh khrap? B: mai shai pen khon thai kha. pen khon angkrit.

Exercise 19

1 shern kha. nee sarmee shan. **2** sarmee khun pen yangngai barng? yang tham ngarn nak reuh? **3** deuhm Pepsi mai? **4** khun khit theung sarmee mai? **5** khun mar khon dieo shai mai? cha pai har Malee phrungnee shai mai?

Vocabulary building

1 yindee. **2** klap. **3** theung. **4** yang. **5** sia. **6** norn. **7** rot. **8** welar. **9** lieo. **10** trong. **11** khao. **12** tok. **13** khorng

Exercise 20

1 deuhm lao pheuan nangseuh malakor warn leuhm waen tar seuh buree **2** He hasn't come home yet. He's going to buy the book tomorrow. Chartree has got married.   I miss you.   I'm going to see my son who is 12.

Exercise 21

จะกลับบ้านพรุ่งนี้   วันนี้ผมไปโรงหนัง

ดูหนังจีนหนังสนุกมาก

Comprehension

Suporn is thin, has a pretty wife, is old and works at the Japanese Embassy. Sombat has bought a house in Tarskin Street and is married with four children. He works at the Esso petrol station. Suthaep has glasses, is often drunk, and is a policeman. Manop went to the USA, is working in oil, and is returning to Bangkok tomorrow.

Lesson 9

Exercise 1

1 khun seuh rot meuarai? **2** khun taeng ngarn meuarai? **3** khun pai amerikar meuarai? **4** khun pai har Steve meuarai? **5** khun pai har khun phor khun thee yeepun meuarai? **6** khun khai barn meuarai?

Exercise 2

1 seuh rot pee thee laeo. **2** taeng ngarn deuan thee laeo. **3** pai amerikar arthit thee laeo. **4** pai har Steve meuawannee. **5** pai har khun phor phom pee thee laeo. **6** khai barn deuan thee laeo.

Exercise 3

1 khai sorng pee thee laeo. **2** seuh sarm pee thee laeo. **3** taeng ngarn hok deuan thee laeo. **4** pai sarm arthit thee laeo. **5** pai see wan thee laeo. **6** seuh sarm deuan thee laeo.

Exercise 4

cha hai narlikar faen phom.
cha hai buree khun phor phom.
cha hai nangseuh look sao phom.
shai hai parkkar khun mae pheuan phom.
cha hai rom khun mae phom.
cha hai too yen looksao phom.
cha hai khreuang bin pheuan phom.
cha hai khorng len looksao pheuan phom.

Exercise 5   (examples)

khun mae hai narlikar shan. khun phor hai nangseuh shan. faen hai krapao shan.

Exercise 6 *(examples)*

khun mae phom hai parkkar pheuan phom. khun phor shan hai krapao satarng faen shan.

Exercise 7

A: parkkar A: seuh B: seuh thee talart kha B: wan thee laeo A: phaeng mai kha

Exercise 8

sip sorng pee thee laeo khai rarn aharn. seuh rohng raem. sip et pee thee laeo khai rohng raem pai amerikar. sip pee thee laeo seuh reua lae khreuang bin. har pee thee laeo khai reua khai khreung bin seuh rohng raem sorng haeng rarn aharn sarm haeng barn sorng lang. sarm pee thee laeo khai rohng raem khai rarn aharn khai barn lang lek. pee thee laeo seuh rarn aharn lek.

Exercise 9 *(examples)*

1 mee rot sarm sip khan. **2** mee rot mortersai see sip khan. **3** mee rot me har khan. **4** mee rot taeksee sip et khan. **5** mee rot tua sip har khan.

Exercise 10

1 seuh seua nork sorng tua. **2** seuh seua neung tua. **3** seuh kraprohng sarm tua. **4** seuh karng keng see tua. **5** seuh krapao sorng bai. **6** seuh rorng thao sarm khoo.

Exercise 11

1 khun seuh nangseuh kee lem? **2** khun seuh nangseuh phim kee shabap? **3** khun seuh rot kee khan? **4** khun seuh rot mortersai kee khan? **5** khun seuh parkkar kee darm? **6** khun seuh seua kee tua?

Exercise 12 *(examples)*

1 see dam. **2** see daeng. **3** see khieo. **4** see nam tarn. **5** see khao. **6** see nam ngern. **7** see dam.

Exercise 13

1 hai rom phom see khrap. **2** hai narlikar phom see khrap. **3** hai nangseuh phim phom see khrap. **4** hai nangseuh phom see khrap. **5** hai buree phom see khrap. **6** hai ngern phom see khrap. **7** hai parkkar phom see khrap.

Exercise 14

A: khun seuh arai barng khrap? B: seuh kraprohng sorng tua. khun shorp see khieo reuh see daeng? A: shorp see khieo khrap. phaeng mai khrap? B: phaeng mark kha. har roi bart.

Exercise 15

1 He lost his wallet. **2** It was small, brown and old. **3** He lost it in the toilet yesterday.

Exercise 16

A: parkkar khorng phom hai khrap. B: parkkar khun pen yangngai kha? A: see dam. suey duey khrap. B: hai meuarai kha? A: hai sarm wan thee laeo khrap. B: thee nai kha? A: thee rarn aharn khrap.

Vocabulary building

A **1** orange juice **2** telephone kiosk **3** joke **4** birthplace **5** wallet **6** salesman **7** caterer **8** pedestrian **9** visitor **10** lover **11** light reading, novel.
B (examples) khorng len; seuh khorng; rohng phayarbarn; rohng rian; horng narm; horng nang len.
C **1** chai dee **2** dee chai **3** chai rorn **4** chai yen **5** sia chai

Exercise 17

1 khorpkhun mark khrap. khun chai dee mark. **2** khun hai nangseuh phanrayar khun kee lem? **3** hai seua sorng tua khrap. **4** shorp see nam ngern mai shorp see khieo.

Exercise 18

chai yen   lieo kwar khon dieo   pai thieo   look sao shan rian nangseuh
wan kert   **2**   He bought some toys for his son and some shoes, trousers
and a shirt. He received an umbrella from his mother and money from his
father.

Exercise 19

เกิดวันที่ วัน ๒๑ เดือน ๓ ปี ๖๓ อายุ
๒๗ ชื่อ ชาตรี มาจาก กรุงเทพ เกิดที่
กรุงเทพ ที่อยู่ ๐๓ตากสิน กรุงธน
แต่งงานแล้ว ✓ ยังไม่แต่งงาน

Comprehension

1 She has lost a handbag **2** It was a pretty black leather one made in Italy.
It contained a ring, her glasses, a pen, a skirt, a book, a newspaper and
some toys. **3** They saw a woman wearing the skirt and carrying the handbag and the same book.

Lesson 10

Exercise 1

1 wan arthit phom len korp. **2** wan sao phom len tenit. **3** wan chan
phom pai talart. **4** wan suk phom pai wainarm. **5** wan phareuhat phom
tham kapkhao. **6** wan phut phom doo theewee. **7** wan angkarn phom
rian nangseuh.

Exercise 2 (examples)

(STEVE) **1** len korp thuk arthit. **2** wai narm arthit la sorng khrang. **3** pai
thieo pee la sorng khrang. **4** soop buree barng khrang barng khrao. **5** kin
lao deuan la khrang dieo. **6** doo thee wee arthit la sorng sarm khrang.
7 arn nangseuh thuk wan. **8** len phai barng khrang barng khrao.
(Suporn) **1** len korp barng khrang barng khrao. **4** soop buree thuk wan.
5 kin lao wan la sorng khuat. **6** doo theewee wan la sip shuamohng.

Exercise 3 (examples)

1 cha seuh rarn aharn eek hok deuan. cha seuh rohng raem pee nar. cha khai rarn aharn eek sorng pee. **2**   cha pai meuang thai deuan nar. cha pai doo wat. cha pai Paris eek see deuan. cha pai rarn aharn farangset.

Exercise 4

In common: they like Chinese food; they like watching sport on TV; they both like shopping; they both buy a lot of clothes. Some examples of how they differ: A doesn't like cooking, B does; A likes Thai music while B likes western music; A goes to the restaurant every day, B goes rarely.

Exercise 5 (examples)

1 nar sia dai. **2**   shohk dee na khrap. khun cha tham arai? **3**   suey mai? **4**   mai pen rai khrap. **5** suey mark. **6**   thammai mai shorp? **7**   dee see khrap. pai nai mar? **8**   khun khit theung khao mai?

Exercise 6

1 phom pai amerikar pee nar. **2**   phom cha pai tham ngarn thee London. **3** khun phor phom hai rot phom. **4**   meuawarnnee narlikar phom hai. **5** phom cha pai seuh rot mai. **6**   phom shorp len tenit.

Exercise 7

A: khun shorp dontree mai kha? B: shorp khrap. A: look sao shan ko shorp kha. khao len dontree thuk wan. khun len dontree reuplao kha? B: len meuankan tae barng khrang barng khrao thaonan mai mee welar warng.

Exercise 8

1 mai dai khrap. torng pai rohng phayarbarn. **2**   mai dai khrap. torng pai seuh khorng. **3** mai dai khrap. torng pai tham ngarn. **4**   mai dai khrap. torng pai har pheuan. **5**   mai dai khrap. torng pai har mor.

Exercise 9

1 There were no buses. There was a lot of traffic and the taxi driver couldn't go fast. **2** Examples: khorthoht thee mar shar khrap. fon tok. torng tham ngarn nak.

Exercise 10

A: wan chan nar B: mai warng B: torng A: khun warng mai khrap B: khorthoht kha mai warng. pai har khun mae shan thee rohng phayarbarn.

Exercise 11 (examples)

harm kin lao, harm soop buree. torng pai thieo. mai torng tham ngarn nak.

Exercise 12 (examples)

1 shai. **2** mai torng. **3** shai. **4** mai torng. **5** shai. **6** mai torng.

Exercise 13

1 shuey phom seuh seua phar dai mai khrap? **2** hai phom roi bart dai mai khrap? **3** phom yeuhm har roi bart dai mai khrap? **4** phom yeuhm rot khun dai mai khrap? **5** seuh nangseuh hai phom dai mai khrap? **6** phom yeuhm karset dai mai khrap?

Exercise 14

1 mai dai khrap harm soop buree. **2** mai dai khrap. harm chort thee nee. **3** mai dai khrap. harm pai tharng nee. **4** mai dai khrap. harm chort trong kharm satharnthoot. **5** mai dai khrap. harm lieo kwar. **6** mai dai khrap. harm dern trong pai.

Exercise 15

1 thanarkharn amerikan pert kao mohng shao pit bai sarm mohng. **2** rarn aharn cheen pert sip et mohng shao pit see thum. **3** rarn aharn thai pert sip mohng shao pit har thum. **4** rarn aharn farangset pert thiang pit thiang kheuhn. **5** rohng rian St James pert chet mohng shao pit bai see mohng.

Exercise 16

1 torn tee har ko dai khrap. **2** torn chet mohng shao ko dai khrap. **3** torn kao mohng shao ko dai khrap. **4** torn bai mohng ko dai khrap. **5** torn hok mohng yen ko dai khrap. **6** torn sorng thum ko dai khrap.

Exercise 17

1 torn shao mai warng khrap. torn bai warng. khun tharm thammai khrap? **2** phom ko cha pai rap pheuan thee sanarmbin meuankan. khun shohk dee mark na khrap. **3** torng pai chet mohng shao. dai mai khrap? **4** phom cha pai rap khun hok mohng shao.

Exercise 18

1 (Example) thuk wan arthit len korp. pai len tao mohng shao klap barn bai see mohng. **2** khun shorp len keelar shai mai? pai wai narm boi mai? **3** torng pai sanarmbin rap pheuan. phom yeuhm rot dai mai khrap? mai torng pai sanarmbin kap phom. pheuan phom torng pai rohng phayarbarn bai sarm mohng. torng mai mar shar.

Vocabulary building

A **1** **warng ngarn** = out of work **2** **warng** = free **3** **mai warng** = occupied **4** **warng** = empty **5** **welar warng** = free time, leisure **6** **khorng-warng** = snack **7** **ngarn warng** = vacancy B **1** broken, waste; **nar sia dai** = what a pity **2** **sia chai** = sorry **3** lose one's reputation, good name **4** waste **5** lose one's head

Exercise 19

1 tamruat   aharn   wan angkarn   wan arthit   wan chan
bia   nangseuh phim

2

Sunday,	read a novel;
Monday,	went to work;
Tuesday,	went for a walk;
Wednesday,	played cards with a friend;
Thursday,	played music;
Friday,	went swimming;
Saturday,	fetched a friend from the airport.

3
Monday, 8 a.m. – 5 p.m.; Friday, 9 a.m – 6 p.m.; Saturday, 10 a.m. – 4 p.m.; Sunday, closed.

Comprehension questions

1 Steve works ten or eleven hours a day. He drinks about two bottles of spirits a week. He smokes twenty to thirty cigarettes a day and plays golf two or three times a year. Apart from that he plays cards, goes to the cinema and enjoys eating. **2** The doctor advises him to play more sports, not to smoke or drink for two weeks, to go for walks with his wife and forget about playing cards and to see him again in two weeks' time.

Lesson 11

Exercise 1

1 khun phoot pharsar yeepun dai mai? **2** khun phoot pharsar angkrit dai mai? **3** khun phoot pharsar farangset dai mai? **4** khun phoot pharsar thai dai mai? **5** khun phoot pharsar cheen dai mai? khun arn pharsar yeepun dai mai? khun khian pharsar thai dai mai?

Exercise 2

1 Ken phoot pharsar yeepun khlorng lae phoot pharsar thai keng. **2** Steve phoot pharsar thai mai keng. phoot pharsar farangset nitnoi phoot tae barng kham. arn mai dai. khian mai dai. **3** Janet phoot pharsar farangset, pharsar itarlian lae pharsar yeepun khlorng tae arn mai dai khian mai dai. **4** James arn pharsar yeepun lae pharsar cheen khian dai duey tae phoot mai dai.

Exercise 3

1 khun khap rot pen mai? **2** khun wainarm pen mai ? **3** khun len korp pen mai? **4** khun phoot pharsar yeepun pen mai? **5** khun len dontree thai pen mai? **6** khun tham kapkhao pen mai? **7** khun shai kormpiuter pen mai?

Exercise 4

1 khap rot me mai dai. khap rot dai. **2** phoot pharsar cheen mai dai. phoot pharsar farangset pen. **3** tham kapkhao farangset mai pen. tham kapkhao angkrit dai. **4** shai kormpiuter mai pen. phim deet dai. **5** len dontree thai mai pen. len dontree farang pen. **6** khian pharsar yeepun mai pen. khian pharsar cheen pen.

Exercise 5

1 Tawat khap rot mai keng. **2** Saowalak sorn nangseuh mai keng.
3 Saowanee tham kapkhao mai keng. **4** Suporn len keelar mai keng.
5 Manat len dontree mai keng. **6** Steve phoot pharsar thai mai keng.
7 Janet arn pharsar cheen mai keng. **8** Don khian nangseuh mai keng.
9 John thai roop mai keng.

Exercise 6

1 khun khap rot keng. **2** khun phoot pharsar angkrit keng. **3** khun khian pharsar angkrit keng. **4** khun tham kapkhao keng. **5** khun len dontree keng. **6** khun wainarm keng. **7** khun thai roop keng.

Exercise 7

1 perhaps he's ill or has been banned from driving. **2** he's never learned.
3 perhaps it's just one of those days. **4** perhaps he has a bad cold.
5 perhaps she has a bad wrist. **6** he's forgotten his camera.

Exercise 8

1 soop buree thee rohng phayarbarn dai mai? **2** phoot angkrit dai mai?
3 thai roop dai mai? **4** deuhm karfae dai mai? **5** pai doo barn dai mai?
6 nang thee nee dai mai? **7** arn nangseuh phim dai mai?

Exercise 9

JANET: khun Suporn phoot pharsar angkrit keng kha. SUPORN: khorpkhun khrap. phoot nitnoi mai khlorng. JANET: khun rian pharsar angkrit thammai? SUPORN: pai tham ngarn thee London khrap. JANET: khun rian kap khroo shai mai? SUPORN: shai khrap. rian nangseuh wan la hok shuamohng.

Exercise 10   (examples)

1 khun khoei pai yeepun mai? khun khoei pai meuang thai mai? **2** khun khoei rian pharsar cheen mai? khun khoei rian pharsar lao mai? **3** khun khoei len dontree thai mai? khun khoei len korp mai?

Exercise 11   (examples)

mai khoei len korp. mai khoei shai kormpiuter. mai khoei len dontree.

Exercise 12   (examples)

1   khao khoei pen tamruat. **2**   khoei deuhm lao mark. **3**   khoei yoo thee
Paris. **4**   khoei rian pharsar yeepun. **5**   khoei doo thee wee nitnoi.
6   khoei pen khon ruey.

Exercise 13   (examples)

1   khoei len dontree khoei khap rot phaeng mark. khoei kin lao mark.
khoei pai thieo yeepun thuk pee. **2**   khoei pen khon chon. khoei yoo barn
lek lek. khoei tham ngarn wan la sip sorng shuamohng.

Exercise 14

1   khun len korp mar narn laeo reu yang? khun mar angkrit mar narn laeo
reu yang? khun rian dontree mar narn laeo reu yang? **2**   khun mar Chieng
Mai mar narn laeo reu yang? khun song pharsar angkrit mar narn laeo reu
yang? khun rian pharsar cheen mar narn laeo reu yang? khun len tenit thuk
wan mar narn laeo reu yang?

Exercise 15

1   khun len korp mar narn thaorai? khun mar angkrit mar narn thaorai?
khun rian dontree mar narn thaorai? **2**   khun mar Chieng Mai mar narn
thaorai? khun song pharsar angkrit mar narn thaorai? khun rian pharsar
cheen mar narn thaorai? khun len tenit thuk wan mar narn thaorai?

Exercise 16   (examples)

khun cha yoo meuang thai narn thaorai? khun cha yoo angkrit narn
thaorai?

Exercise 17

1   phom khoei khap rot reo mark. torn nee khap shar. **2**   phom khoei
soop buree mark mark. torn nee mai soop. **3**   khoei deuhm lao arthit la see
khuat. torn nee deuhm barng khrang barng khrao. **4**   khoei shai ngern
mark. torn nee mai shai mark. **5**   khoei len phai thuk wan. torn nee len
nitnoi. **6**   khoei doo thee wee wan la paet shuamohng. torn nee doo thee
wee deuan la sorng sarm khrang.

Exercise 18

1 False **2** False **3** True **4** True **5** False **6** True **7** False **8** False **9** True

Exercise 19

1 tham kapkhao cheen mai pen tae tham kapkhao farangset dai. **2** khun rian len dontree cheen mar narn thaorai? **3** (examples) khoei sai waen tar. torn nee mai sai. khoei shorp len keelar thuk wan. torn nee len nitnoi.

Vocabulary building

A 1 khoei. All the others are to do with languages. **2** thai roop. All the others relate to time. **3** phoot len. All the others are things you devote your free time to. **4** sia. The others are items of clothing. **5** nang. The others are objects of one sort or another.

B

ngai	yark
pit	pert
cham dai	leuhm
reo	shar
laeo	yang mai
phrungnee	meuawannee
samee	phanrayar
tia	soong
uwan	phorm

Exercise 20

1 klap kwar klai nar kliat sokkaprok phonlamai khorng khwan kraprohng khlorng tarng prathet khrorpkhrua **2** No smoking. No entry. No photography. No parking. No passing. **3** Secretary, English-speaking, working hours 8–6, apply within, experience, salary 2000 bart; Cook, Chinese cooking, Telephone 25 82 010, 500 bart a week **4** At the moment I am a housewife. I used to be a secretary. I can speak Chinese; At the moment I am working in Bangkok. I am a businessman. I used to be a policeman. Fifteen years ago I studied in London.

Comprehension

1 Tana is interested in people (she likes meeting people and chatting to colleagues) and she has some office experience fourteen years ago which she enjoyed. She has never studied accounts, though. She claims to be fluent in English (she lived in the United States for five years) though she can only write it a little. She has almost forgotten her German. **2** He knows that she's working in a petrol station. **3** She says she is divorced and her children live with her mother.

Lesson 12

Exercise 1 (examples)

1 mai shorp nang cheen. **2** shorp aharn farangset. **3** mai shorp khon amerikan. **4** shorp dontree thai. **5** shorp see daeng. **6** mai shorp wai narm.

Exercise 2

1 pai mai dai **2** khap rot mai dai **3** yark tham tom yam **4** arn pharsar cheen mai pen. **5** yark phop khon thai **6** yark pai shai tale

Exercise 3 (examples)

yark pai doo wat. yark pai wai narm. yark dern len thee Chieng Mai. yark rian pharsar thai. yark kin aharn thai.

Exercise 4

1 phaeng mark kern pai. **2** dai ngern mai phor. **3** yark kern pai. **4** leo mai phor. **5** nao kern pai. **6** phaeng kern pai.

Exercise 5

1 torng karn parkkar. **2** khun torng karn arai? **3** torng karn ao rom. **4** khao torng karn narlikar. **5** torng karn seua nork. **6** torng karn rot.

Exercise 6

Dialogue 1 A: hiu. B: yark kin arai? C: yark kin mamuang. *Dialogue 2* A: hiu narm. B: yark deuhm arai? C: yark deuhm bia. *Dialogue 3* A: pai

seuh khorng. B: yark seuh arai? A: yark seuh kraprohng. *Dialogue 4*
A: yark rian nangseuh. B: yark rian nangseuh arai? A: yark rian dontree.
Dialogue 5 A: yark cha pen khroo. B: yark cha song arai? A: yark cha song
pharsar angkrit. Dialogue **6** A: yark khai khorng. B: yark khai arai? A: yark
khai nangseuh.

Exercise 7 (examples)

1 phro war nao mark. **2** phro war narm tuam. **3** phro war fon tok.
4 phro arkart yae. **5** phro mai sabai. **6** phro war rorn mark kern pai.

Exercise 8

The weather was terrible. It rained every day. His wife forgot the umbrella
and on top of everything it was cold.

Exercise 9

1 yark doo muey thee thee wee. **2** mee panhar reuang rot. **3** mee nat
thee sanarmbin. **4** mee panhar reuang thohrasap. **5** torng pai sorp. **6**
torng pai len dontree kap pheuan shan. **7** faen mai sabai.

Exercise 10

1 cher kan yen nee. **2** cher kan phrungnee torn bai. **3** cher kan arthit
nar. **4** cher kan eek sarm wan. **5** lar korn na khrap. cher kan eek hok
deuan. **6** lar korn na kha. laeo phop kan mai na khrap.

Exercise 11

1 wang war khong mai. **2** wang war khong mai. **3** wang war yang ngan.
4 wang war khong mai. **5** wang war yang ngan. **6** wang war khong mai.
7 wang war khong mai.

Exercise 12

1 wang war cha hai khorng khwan phom **2** wang war cha hai ngarn mai
phom **3** wang war thee barn narm mai thuam **4** wang war cha tham
ngarn mark **5** wang war mai mee panhar

Exercise 13 (examples)

A kamlang rian nangseuh. B kamlang len dontree. C kamlang doo thee wee. D kamlang tham ngarn. E kamlang arn nangseuh phim. F kamlang phim deet.

Exercise 14

1 kamlang cha pai talart seuh khorng. **2** kamlang cha pai sanarmbin. **3** kamlang pai len korp **4** kamlang cha len dontree **5** kamlang cha pai ngarn **6** kamlang cha rian pharsar farangset **7** kamlang cha sorp khap rot

Exercise 15

1 khun kamlang cha pai sorp khap rot shai mai khrap? **2** mai narn rok. akart mai dee duey. nao mark. fon tok thuk wan. len korp mai dai. pai wai narm mai dai. **3** yark pai thieo amerikar. yark seuh tua phrungnee. thee amerikar yark seuh rot. yark yoo thee rohng raem phaeng.

Vocabulary building

1 mee welar mark. mai torng reep. **2** khun warng mai? mai warng kha. mee nat. **3** torng reep. khit war cha pai shar. **4** rot mai tit. khit war mar leo. **5** A: mar har khun Suporn. B: khorthoht kha mai yoo. **6** phom mar shar. mai dai phop khao. **7** sip mohng laeo. thammai mar tham ngarn sai?

Exercise 16

1 idea **2** truth **3** want **4** love **5** speed **6** meaning **7** hope **8** happiness

Exercise 17

karn khar	trade, business
karn ngern	finance
karn chark pai	departure
karn shern	invitation
karn dern tharng	travel
nak karn meuang	politician
karn tok long	agreement
karn thot rorng	experiment
karn pai thieo	excursion

Exercise 18

1 arkart narm thuam panhar muey futborn mee sheuh **2** There is a problem with the plane because the weather is bad. **3**   I'm staying in a nice hotel. The weather is starting to get cold. It's raining every day. I go shopping and I'm spending a lot of money. I haven't been to the beach. I miss you.

Comprehension

1   He wanted to find out if Suporn had finished the book he was writing about boxing. **2**   He was working hard for an exam (which he failed) and has been trying to buy a flat. **3**   He missed a meeting with a famous boxer because he had to go by bus and he was held up by the traffic.

Lesson 13

Exercise 1

	Cost	Size	Comfort	Distance	Food: cost	Food: quality
Orbis	✓	✓	✓	✓		
Rama					✓	✓

Exercise 2

1   B keng kwar. **2**   C soong kwar. **3**   B nak kwar. **4**   C kae kwar. **5**   C soong kwar. **6**   A keng kwar.

Exercise 3

1   phoot lae arn pharsar yeepun keng kwar B. B   khian pharsar yeepun dee kwar A. **2**   B phoot lae khian pharsar angkrit keng kwar C tae C arn pharsar angkrit dee kwar B. **3**   A khian pharsar angkrit dee kwar C. A khian pharsar yeepun dee kwar C.

Exercise 4

B suey kwar C. B yai kwar A lae C. rot fai phaeng kwar rot me. rot me narn kwar rot fai. khreuang bin saduak kwar rot fai.

Exercise 5

1 B: shorp see dam mark kwar. B: see daeng yai mark kern pai.
2 (examples) A: shorp barn lang nai mark kwar? barn mai reuh barn kao? B: shorp barn mai mark kwar. A: thammai? B: thee chort rot yai kwar.

Exercise 6

1 deuan kumpharphan nao. deuan mokkarar nao mark. deuan singharkhom rorn. **2** deuan meenarkhom nao mai? deuan mesaryon rorn mai? deuan phreutsapharkhom fon tok mai? deuan mithunaryon mee lom mai? deuan korrakadarkhom rorn mai? deuan singharkhom narm tuam mai?

Exercise 7 (examples)

yark pai shai tale deuan mesaryon. pai nai dee? rorn mai? fon tok mai? pai yangngai dee? pai khreuang bin phaeng mai?

Exercise 8

1 rian arai ko dai. **2** pai yangngai ko dai. **3** kin meuarai ko dai. **4** len arai ko dai. **5** rohng raem nai ko dai. **6** mar har khrai ko dai.

Exercise 9 (examples)

1 khun roochak Chīeng Rai mai? khun khoei pai Chieng Rai mai?
2 khun khoei yoo thee rohng raem Hilton mai? khun khit war rohng raem Hilton dee mai? **3** khun shorp too yen yeepun reuh too yen angkrit mark kwar kan? khun khit war too yen yeepun dee kwar too yen angkrit mai?
4 khun mee thura arthit nar shai mai? ar thit nar khun warng mai kha?
5 khun mar yoo thee London meuarai? khun yoo thee London mar narn thaorai laeo?

Exercise 10

1 Suchart (though he drinks most). **2** Suchart (he's strongest).
3 Suchart (though his Chinese is not as good as Suporn's). **4** Manop (he's the best driver and second in English). **5** Suchart likes walking.
6 Suporn (Manop smokes most, Suchart drinks most).

Exercise 11

1 B keng thee sut. C soong thee sut. A nak thee sut. C kae thee sut. **2** A suey thee sut. B yai thee sut. C klai thee sut. khreuang bin phaeng thee sut. rot me narn thee sut. khreuang bin saduak thee sut.

Exercise 12 (examples)

khong cha pai doo phu khao khong cha pai dern len. khong cha pai wai narm. khong cha pai doo wat. khong cha kin aharn cheen.

Exercise 12

khuan cha pai rot fai. khuan cha mar har phom. mai khuan pai shai tale.

Exercise 14

A: pai Ayuthaya yangngai dee khrap? B: khun khuan cha pai rot fai. sadu-ak kwar. A: rot me pen yangngai barng khrap? B: yae mark kha. khong cha narn mark. A: sia welar narn thaorai khrap? B: khong cha sia welar see shuamohng kha.

Exercise 15

A: phrungnee khun pai nai mai? B: yang mai nae kha. barng thee pai Oxford reuh barng thee pai Cambridge. khun khoei pai Cambridge mai kha? A: mai khoei khrap tae roochak Oxford. B: khit war Cambridge suey. A: phom khit war Oxford suey kwar Cambridge lae sanuk kwar. B: Oxford ngiap sangop shai mai? A: mai khoi ngiap khrap tae thee Cambridge mee nak thorng thieo mark kwar Oxford. Cambridge lek kwar duey.

Exercise 16

1 A soong kwar B. B kae thee sut. C len dontree keng kwar B. **2** khun khoei pai London deuan kumpharphan shai mai? **3** phom khong cha pai meuang thai deuan nar. khuan cha seuh arai mai? **4** seuh see arai ko dai.

Vocabulary building

arkart	lom
keelar	muey
khorngwarn	phonlamai

meuang	farangset
khreuang deuhm	bia
aharn	khao
meua	moo
phonlamai	kluey
see	daeng
khreuang khrua	too yen
khreuang khian	parkkar

Exercise 17

1 Car for hire. Two hundred bart a day. International driving licence necessary. **2** House for rent. Five thousand a month. Three bedrooms. Telephone. Air conditioned. Garage. Near British Embassy. **3** I have been here three months. The weather is still terrible. I rest every day. It's very boring. Tourists like the peace and quiet but I think it's not fun. I don't like western food. I'm homesick.

Comprehension

Ko Samui is the best. It's quiet and not very big. There are hills, you can hire a motorbike and there are plenty of restaurants. It's furthest and the ticket costs more than for Ko Samit. The journey is more comfortable than for Ko Samit. Ko Samit is smaller and there are fewer tourists. It might get boring. Hotels are about the same price as in Ko Samui. The beaches are prettier but the journey takes longer. Phuket is nice, too. It's the biggest. There are more bars, discos and restaurants and the hotels are the most expensive. Some of the beaches are nice, some are dirty. They have about the same weather and the travel agent doesn't think it'll rain this month.

Lesson 14

Exercise 1 (examples)

1 khao pai laeo. **2** khao pai nai? **3** khao pai meuarai? **4** khao pai thanarkharn laeo. **5** khao pai rot taeksee shai mai? **6** prokkati khao len korp. **7** khao seuh rot shai mai?

Exercise 2 (examples)

1 khun sarp mai war rarn khai nangseuh yoo thee nai? **2** khun sarp mai war rarn tat phom yoo thee nai? **3** khun sarp mai war satharn thoot angkrit yoo thee nai? **4** khun sarp mai war satharnee rot fai yoo thee nai? **5** khun sarp mai war sa wainarm yoo thee nai? **6** khun sarp mai war rarn khai rorng thao yoo thee nai? **7** khun sarp mai war rarn khai seua phar yoo thee nai?

Exercise 3

khun sarp mai war khrai cha mar? khun sarp mai war cha mar meuarai? khun sarp mai war cha mar kee khon? khun sarp mai war cha mar thammai? khun sarp mai war cha yoo narn thaorai?

Exercise 4

1 khun sarp mai war khao len keelar thuk wan reuplao? **2** khun sarp mai war khao len phai thuk wan reuplao? **3** khun sarp mai war khao shorp dern len reuplao? **4** khun sarp mai war khao song pharsar angkrit reuplao? **5** khun sarp mai war khao len dontree reuplao? **6** khun sarp mai war khao soop buree mark mark reuplao?

Exercise 5

1 art cha pai len tenit. **2** art cha pai paet mohng shao. **3** art cha pai rot khao. **4** art cha phop pheuan khon cheen khao. **5** art cha pai kin khao thee rarn aharn farangset. **6** art cha klap barn har mohng yen.

Exercise 6

1 mai sarp war khao shorp len phai reuplao. **2** mai sarp war khao pai sa wainarm meuawarnnee reuplao. **3** mai sarp war khao pai talart seuh rom reuplao. **4** mai sarp war khao pai rot taeksee reuplao. **5** mai sarp war khao cha klap opfit korn thiang reuplao. **6** mai sarp war khao phoot pharsar yeepun dai reuplao.

Exercise 7

A: khun sarp mai khrap war Suport yoo thee nai? B: pai satharnee rotfai laeo kha. A: khun sarp mai war satharnee rotfai yoo thee nai? B: mai sarp kha. A: khun sarp mai war khao pai meuarai? B: pai har thum kha.

A: phom phop khao dai meuarai? B: shan mai sarp war khao cha klap meuarai.

Exercise 8

A: khorthoht khrap rot tua pai Chieng Mai khan nai sarp mai khrap? B: khan nan khrap. A: khorpkhun khrap. khun sarp mai war ork meuarai? B: har tum khrap. A: khun sarp mai khrap war sia welar narn thaorai? B: yang mai nae. khit war sia welar see shuamohng.

Exercise 9

1 she recommends going by air by Thai International. **2** It leaves at 8 a.m. and arrives at about noon. She thinks it does not stop at Kuala Lumpur. **3** It's slow (it takes two to three days). **4** very few people use it.

Exercise 10 (examples)

khun tharm khao reuplao war khao seuh arai? khun tharm khao reuplao war pen yangngai? khun tharm khao reuplao war yai mai? khun tharm khao reuplao war khao seuh thee nai? khun tharm khao reuplao war khao seuh meuarai? khun tharm khao reuplao war rarkhar thaorai?

Exercise 11

khun bork khao mai war khao pai thieo thee nai? khun bork khao mai war khao cha klap barn meuarai? khun bork khao mai war khao phop khrai?

Exercise 12

1 Suchart says he can't play golf today. **2** Saowalak says she will telephone you tomorrow. **3** Malee asks whether you can go to her house on Saturday. **4** Manat wants to know if you know where the exam is taking place. **5** The Chinese Embassy called. You have an appointment with Mr Wang at eleven o'clock tomorrow morning. **6** Sunnee wants to know when the train leaves.

Exercise 13

khun Suporn yoo mai kha? mai yoo kha. pai satharnthoot cheen. khun tharm khao war shan phop khao phrungnee dai mai kha? khao bork war phrungnee mai mar thamngarn kha. khao bork mai war mar tham ngarn meaurai? bork war khong cha mar wan chan nar kha.

Exercise 14

1 cha thai roop eek meua pai thieo. **2** cha seuh rot mai meua mee ngern mark mark. **3** cha dai ngarn mai meua pai London. **4** cha dai bai khap kee meua khap rot pen. **5** cha shao rot meua pai Chieng Mai. **6** cha taeng ngarn meua mee ngern.

Exercise 15

1 pai rohng phayarbarn meua rian nangseuh thee rohng rian Sayarm. **2** rian thai roop meua rian nangseuh thee maharwitthayarlai. **3** pai thieo amerikar meua rian nangseuh thee maharwitthayarlai. **4** taeng ngarn meua tham ngarn thee thanarkhan amerikan. **5** mee ubat het meua pai thieo yeepun. **6** yoo nai khuk meua tham ngarn thee satharnthoot angkrit.

Exercise 16

1 yoo thee meuang farangset tangtae rian chop. **2** tham ngarn thee satharnee rotfai tangtae chop maharwitthayarlai. **3** rian kormpiuter tangtae pai amerikar. **4** song banshee tangtae ork chark borrisat ILC. **5** yar tangtae klap krungthep. **6** pen khon khrua tangtae taeng ngarn.

Exercise 17

Current job: secretary, MPA Company. She has worked there since leaving university. She has studied computer studies and Japanese. She studied English when she lived in America.

Exercise 18

1 mai sarp war khao rian nangseuh thee nai. mai sarp war khao rian nangseuh narn thaorai. mai sarp war khao rian nangseuh arai. mai sarp war khao tham arai tangtae chop maharwitthayarlai. **2** khun tharm khao mai war khao pen khrai? khao bork war arai? khun tharm khao mai war khao yark phop khrai? **3** khun sarp mai war khreuang bin ork meuarai? khun sarp mai war khar tua thaorai? **4** phom mee nat kap Suporn bai nee thee rohng raem Oriental. khun bork khao mai war rot fai theung shar phro war narm tuam. khun tharm khao dai mai war phop khao phrungnee dai mai khrap? khun tharm khao dai mai khrap war khao cha mar kin khao kap phom phrungnee torn yen reuplao?

Vocabulary building

phop	cher
art	khong
khit	songsai
nao	yen
kin	deuhm
faen	samee
pen	dai
sanuk	nar son chai
sao	num
pee	khuap
kao	kae
phoot	bork
duey tua eng	khon dieo

2
1 dern mar **2** dern pai **3** klap mar **4** klap pai **5** khap rot pai **6** rot mar

Exercise 19

1 swimming pool chemist's bookshop shoe shop clothes shop university Japanese restaurant American Embassy ladies' toilet gentlemen's toilet railway station boxing stadium **2** I have to go to the ... company for some urgent business. Telephone your office before mid-day as there's a problem with the air ticket.

Comprehension

1 He has been very busy since he returned from America. He had a car accident, though he wasn't hurt. And he has problems of some sort with his house. **2** He can't see Ken tomorrow because he's playing golf in the morning and he has meetings after that. Then he goes to see his parents for two or three days. He will be able to see Ken when he returns.

Lesson 15

Exercise 1

1 reuang bai anuyart. **2** reuang sin khar song ork. **3** reuang sin khar song khao. **4** reuang song khao borarn watthu. **5** reuang song ork borarn watthu. **6** reuang bai khap kee. **7** reuang ubat het thee mahawitthayarlai. **8** reuang nangseuh dern tharng.

Exercise 2

1 pai krungthep phrungnee dai thar khun mee tua laeo. khap rot dai thar khun mee bai khap khee sarkon. dai ngarn dee dai thar khun phoot pharsar angkrit pen. sorp pharn dai thar khun arn nangseuh mark. pai tarng prathet dai thar khun mee nangseuh dern tharng. pai praisanee song chotmai dai thar khun khian chotmai laeo. **2** (example) pai praisanee song chotmai mai dai thar khun yang mai khian chotmai.

Exercise 3

thar khun mar wan angkharn phom yoo thee mahawitthayarlai. thar khun mar wan phareuhat phom yoo thee Chieng Mai. thar khun mar wan suk phom yoo thee borrisat MCA. thar khun mar sao arthit nar phom yoo thee Khon Kaen. thar khun mar arthit nar phom yoo thee London. thar khun cha yoo deuan nar phom yoo thee Paris.

Exercise 4 (examples)

1 cha seuh nangseuh hai thar pharn rarn khai nangseuh. **2** cha seuh tua rotfai hai thar pharn satharnee rot fai. **3** cha ao hai thar pharn satharnthoot yeepun. **4** cha seuh hai thar pharn rarn khai yar. **5** cha seuh hai thar shan pharn sanarmbin. **6** cha song hai thar pharn praisanee.

Exercise 5 (examples)

1 phom song khun pharsar angkrit thar khun song pharsar thai phom. **2** phom hai yeuhm nangseuh thar khun hai phom yeuhm parkkar khun. **3** phom shuey khun khian nangseuh reuang muey thar khun shuey phom khian chotmai. **4** phom shuey khun tham khwarm sa-art barn thar khun tham kapkhao hai phom. **5** rap pheuan khun thee sanarmbin thar khun rap pheuan shan thee rohng raem. **6** phom hai yeuhm rom thar khun hai phom yeuhm narlikar khun. **7** song chotmai hai thar khun seuh parkkar hai phom.

Exercise 6

1 khor phoot kap khun Manat noi dai mai khrap? **2** mee khon thee tham ngarn thee opfit thee shuey phom dai mai khrap? **3** reuang bai anuyart. **4** mai dai khrap. phrungnee pai thieo. **5** eek sorng arthit dai mai khrap? **6** khun sarp mai war khun Manat rap chotmai chark phom laeo reu yang?

Exercise 7

1 Manat mai sabai tangtae wan chan. **2** yang mai nae. phanrayar bork war khao khuan cha klap opfit arthit nar. **3** thar phanrayar khao thohrasap mar cha bork khao hai. mee reuang arai? **4** thee nee ko mee panhar kormpiuter meunkan. mai mee khon warng arthit nee.

Exercise 8

1 phom son chai khreuang ngern/khreuang thorng/borarn watthu/phar mai/dontree/muey/keelar/khuk. **2** phom son chai cha song ork borarn watthu/song khao phar mai/seuh khreuang thorng/khai khreuang ngern.

Exercise 9 (example)

futborn chark itarlee dee thee sut nai lohk.

Exercise 10

She bought two skirts, a red one and a white one. The starting price was five hundred and four hundred bart respectively. She paid seven hundred bart for the two.

Exercise 11

1 rarkhar narlikar thaorai? **2** khit war phaeng khrap. **3** thar phom seuh har reuan rarkhar thaorai? **4** 150 bart dai mai khrap? **5** tok long khrap. seuh narlikar sip reuan.

Exercises 12, 13 and 14

These are left to your own imagination.

Vocabulary building

arn ork khian dai	to be literate
ork nangseuh	to publish a book
doo ork	to be able to tell just by looking, ascertain
tharng ork	exit
ork siang	to pronounce, vote
fang pharsar angkrit mai ork	understand a language when spoken

Exercise 15

1 Be careful   Danger   No Smoking   Please take off your shoes   Thank you very much   Don't forget to switch off the light   Don't forget to turn off the gas   Urgent   Passport **2** Hello. How are you? I miss you. Since you went back I've had a lot of work. I've not had any holiday. I've done the passport already. Tomorrow I'm going to the British Embassy about the visa. I might buy the ticket next week. I'm waiting for your letter. I will probably get your letter before you get mine. I hope you've been able to sell the toys we bought in Bangkok and that you made a good profit. I will buy some more but they are more expensive now. I will send them to you on Friday and telephone on Saturday. Good luck. Good bye.

Comprehension

1   Antiques: Suporn thinks there would be too many problems (there are a lot of fakes, you have to get a permit, you can't take out Buddhas). Gold and silver: there are too many people doing these already. Silk: the best as Thai silk is cheap and the best in the world. **2**   Ken will take five hundred for forty bart each; Suporn will send them as quickly as possible.

English–Thai glossary

The numbers indicate the lessons in which the word is introduced.

about	**pramarn** 7, **rêuang** 12	ask	**thǎrm** 8
abroad	**tàrng prathêt** 11	at	**thêe** 1
accident	**ubàt hèt** 14	August	**deuan sǐnghǎrkhom** 13
accounts	**banshee** 11		
ache	**pùat** 8	bag	**krapǎo** 9
advice	**naé nam** 15	banana	**klûey** 6
aeroplane	**khrêuang bin** 7	Bangkok	**krungthêp** 1
after	**phàrn** 7	bank	**thanarkharn** 5
afternoon	**torn bài** 10	bathroom	**hôrng nárm** 5
age	**aryú** 4	be	**pen** 3
ago	**thêe laéo** 9	be, to be somewhere	**yòo** 1
air conditioning	**ae** 5		
airport	**sanǎrmbin** 1	because	**phró wâr** 12
all	**tháng** 10	bedroom	**hôrng norn** 5
alone	**khon dieo** 8	beef	**néua** 6
already	**laéo** 8	beer	**bia** 6
always	**saměr** 10	before	**kòrn** 7
America	**amerikar** 3	before now	**mêua kòrn** 11
American	**amerikan** 3	big	**yài** 5
and	**laéo ko** 4, **laé** 4	birth	**kèrt** 9
angry	**kròht** 8	black	**dam** 9
antique	**borarn wátthù** 15	blue	**sěe nám ngern** 9
any other	**yàrng euhn** 10	boat	**reua** 7
appointment	**nát** 12	book	**nángsěuh** 9
April	**deuan mesǎryon** 13	book (reserve)	**chorng** 13
		boring	**nâr bèua** 3
arrive	**thěung** 14	borrow	**yeuhm** 10
as well	**dûey** 2	bottle	**khùat** 6

boxing	**muey** 12	vehicles	**khan** 9
boy	**phôoshai** 4	clean	**sa-àrt** 5
boyfriend	**faen** 3	clever	**kèng** 4
brother (elder)	**phêe shai** 8	clock	**narlikar** 9
brother (younger)	**nórng shai** 8	close(d)	**pìt** 10
		clothes	**sêua phâr** 9
brothers and sisters	**phêe nórng** 8	clothes shop	**rárn khǎi sêua phâr** 14
brown	**sěe nám tarn** 9	coffee	**karfae** 2
Buddha figure	**phrá** 15	cold	**nǎo** 6
building	**teùk** 5	cold; have a cold	**yen** 5; **pen wàt** 8
bus	**rót me** 7	colour	**sěe** 9
businessman	**nák thúrákìt** 4	come	**mar** 1
but	**tàe** 5	comfortable	**sadùak**
buy	**seúh** 2	company	**borrisàt** 14
		computer	**kormpiutêr** 11
calm	**chai yen** 9	cook	**tham kàpkhâo** 10
can (know how to do something)	**pen** 11	cool	**yen** 5
		cup	**thûey** 6
		cupboard	**tôo** 5
can (possible)	**dâi** 10		
car	**rót** 5	daughter	**lôok sǎo** 4
careful	**rawang** 15	December	**deuan thanwark-hom** 13
cassette	**karset** 10		
chat	**khui** 11	delicious	**aròi** 6
cheap	**thòok** 13	dessert	**khǒrng wǎrn** 6
chemist's	**rárn khǎi yar** 14	difficult	**yârk** 11, **yûng** 15
chicken	**kài** 6	dirty	**sòkkapròk** 5
child	**lôok** 3	disgusting	**nâr klìat** 3
children	**lôok** 3	divorced	**yàr** 11
Chinese	**cheen** 3	doctor	**mǒr** 4
cigarette	**burèe** 8	drink	**kin** 2, **dèuhm**
cinema	**rohng nǎng** 7	drink alcohol	**kin lâo** 10
classifiers		drive	**khàp** 5
books	**lêm** 9	driving licence	**bai khàp khèe** 13
buildings	**hǎeng** 5	drunk	**mao** 8
cigarettes	**tua** 9		
clothing	**tua** 9	early (i.e. ahead of schedule)	**reo** 10
fruit	**bai** 6		
houses	**lǎng** 5	early (in the morning)	**sháo** 10
newspapers	**shabàp** 9		
pens	**dârm** 9	earn	**dâi ngern**

easy	**ngâi** 11		food	**ahǎrn** 6
eat	**kin** 2		football	**fútborn** 12
eight	**pàet** 4		for	**hâi** 9
either	**dûey** 2		for (the purpose	**phêua** 13
eleven	**sìp èt** 4		of)	
Embassy	**sathǎrn thôot** 7		forbidden	**hârm** 10
England	**angkrìt** 3		foreign	**tàrng prathêt** 11
English	**angkrìt** 3		foreigner,	**faràng** 3
enjoyable	**sanùk** 3		Westerner	
enough	**phor** 12		forget	**leuhm** 10
enter	**khâô**		four	**sèe** 4
evening	**torn yen** 10		free	**wârng**
every	**thúk** 10		French	**faràngsèt** 3
exam, take an	**sòrp** 12		Friday	**wan sùk** 10
exam			fridge	**tôô yen** 5
excuse me	**khǒrthôht** 1		fried	**phàt** 6
expensive	**phaeng** 5		friend	**phêuan** 3
export (noun)	**sǐn khár òrk** 15		fruit	**phǒnlamái** 6
export (verb)	**sòng òrk** 15		fun	**sanùk** 3
eye	**tar** 8			
			garden	**sanǎrm yâr** 5
fail	**sòrp tòk** 12		German	**yerraman** 11
fall	**tòk** 6		girl	**phôôyǐng** 4
family	**khrôrpkhrua** 11		girlfriend	**faen** 3
famous	**mee shêuh** 12		give	**hâi** 9
far	**klai** 5		glass	**kâeo** 6
fare	**khâr tǔa** 7		glasses,	**wâen tar** 8
fat	**ûwan** 8		spectacles	
father	**phôr** 4		go	**pai** 1
February	**deuan**		go on business	**pai thúrá** 2
	kumpharphan		go somewhere	**pai thîeo** 2
	13		for pleasure	
fetch	**ráp** 10		gold	**(khrêuang)**
few, a	**nói** 6			**thorng** 15
film	**nǎng** 7		golf	**kórp** 10
finish	**chòp** 14		good	**dee** 2
finished	**sèt** 12		good at	**kèng** 4
fish	**plar** 6		goodbye, say	**lar** 12
five	**hâr** 4		green	**sěe khǐeo** 9
flat	**apártmén** 1			
floods	**nárm thûam** 12		hair, get one's	**phǒm** 14, **tàt**
fluently	**khlôrng** 11		hair cut	**phǒm** 14

happy	**dee chai** 9, **sùk** 9	Japan	**yêepùn** 3
hardly at all	**mâi khôi** 11	Japanese	**yêepùn** 3
have	**mee** 3	July	**deuan korrák-**
have to	**tôrng** 10		**adarkhom** 13
head	**hŭa** 8	June	**deuan**
hello	**sawàtdee** 1		**míthunaryon** 13
help	**shûey** 10		
here	**thêe nêe** 8	kilo	**kiloh** 6
hire	**shâo** 13	kind	**chai dee** 9
home; come, go	**bârn** 1; **klàp**	kitchen	**hôrng khrua** 5
home	**bârn** 8	know	**sârp** 5, **róochàk**
hope	**wăng** 11		7, **róo** 15
hospital	**rohng pha-**	know how to	**pen** 11
	yarbarn 5	do something	
hot	**rórn** 6		
hot-tempered	**chai rórn** 9	language	**pharsăr** 11
hotel	**rohng raem** 1	Laotian	**lao** 3
hour	**shûamohng** 7	last	**thêe laéo** 9
house	**bârn** 1	late (at night)	**deùhk** 10
housewife	**mâe bârn** 4	late (behind	**shár** 10
how	**yangngai** 5	schedule)	
how many	**kèe** 4	late (in the	**săi** 10
how much	**thâorài** 4	morning)	
hundred	**rói** 4	lazy	**khêe kìat** 12
hungry	**hĭu** 6	leather	**năng** 9
hurry	**rêep** 12	leave	**òrk** 14
husband	**sărmee** 8, **faen** 3	left	**sái** 7
		lend	**yeuhm** 10
if	**thâr** 15	letter	**chòtmăi** 15
import (noun)	**sĭn khár khâo** 15	like	**shôrp** 6
import (verb)	**nam khâo** 15	little, a	**nítnòi** 3
in	**thêe** 1, **nai** 14	live	**yòo** 1
interesting	**nâr sŏn chai** 5	long time, a; take	**narn** 7
international	**sărkon** 13	a long time	
invite	**shern** 8	look	**doo** 5
island	**kò** 7	lose	**hăi** 9
Italian	**ìtarlian** 3	loss	**khart thun** 15
Italy	**ìtarlêe** 3	lot, a	**mârk** 1
		lovely	**nâr rák** 3
jacket	**sêua nôrk** 9	luck	**shôhk** 2
January	**deuan mokkarar**		
	13	Malaysian	**malesian** 3

man	**phôoshai** 4	next	**nâr** 10
mango	**mamûang** 6	night	**torn meûht** 10
March	**deuan meenark-**	nine	**kâo** 4
	hom 13	not enough	**mâi phor** 12
market	**talàrt** 2	not yet	**yang mâi** 8
marry, be	**tàeng ngarn** 8	November	**deuan phreút-**
married			**sachìkaryon** 13
May	**deuan phreút-**	now	**dǐeo neé** 11, **torn**
	sapharkhom 13		**née** 11
maybe	**barng thee** 15		
mean	**mǎi khwarm** 12	occasionally	**barng khráng**
meat	**néua sat** 6		**barng khrao** 10
medicine	**yar** 14	October	**deuan tularkhom**
meet	**cher** 2, **phóp** 12		13
meeting	**prashum** 14	office	**opfit** 1
midday	**thîang** 10	often	**bòi bòi, bòi** 10
midnight	**thîang kheuhn** 10	oil	**námman** 7
minute	**narthee** 7	OK	**tòk long** 10
miss someone	**khít thěung** 8	old	**kào** 5, **kàe** 3
mixed	**ruam** 6	on one's own	**dûey tua eng** 11
moment, at the	**dǐeo née, torn**	one	**nèung** 4
	née 11	only	**thâonán** 7
Monday	**wan chan** 10	open	**pèrt** 9
money	**ngern** 3	opportunity	**ohkàrt** 11
month	**deuan** 7	opposite	**trong khârm** 7
more	**kwàr** 13	orange	**sôm** 6
mornïng	**torn sháo** 10		
most, the most	**thêe sùt** 13	papaya	**malakor** 6
mother	**mâe** 4	park	**chòrt** 5
motorcycle	**rót mortersai** 7	pass	**phàrn** 7
mountain	**phu khǎo** 13	passport	**nángseǔh dern**
move	**yái** 10		**tharng** 15
move house	**yái bârn** 10	pen	**pàrkkar** 9
much	**mârk** 1	permit	**bai ànúyârt** 15
music	**dontree** 10	people	**khon** 3
must	**tôrng** 10	person	**khon** 3
		petrol	**námman** 7
name (. . .	**shêuh** 8	petrol station	**pám námman** 7
name is . . .)		photograph,	**thài rôop** 11
near	**klâi** 5	(take a)	
new	**mài** 5	photograph	
newspaper	**nángseǔh phim** 9	picture	**rôop** 9

pineapple	**sàparót** 6	seaside	**shai tale** 7
plate	**charn** 6	secretary	**lekhǎrnúkarn** 4
play	**lên** 5	see	**hěn** 5
play cards	**lên phâi** 10	see (visit, call on)	**hǎr** 8
policeman	**tamrùat** 4	sell	**khǎi** 6
poor	**chon** 3	send	**sòng** 15
pork	**mǒo** 6	September	**deuan kanyaryon**
post office	**praisanee** 15		13
prawn	**kûng** 6	seven	**chèt** 4
present	**khǒrng khwǎn** 9	shirt	**sêua**
pretty	**sǔey** 3	shoe	**rorng tháo** 9
price	**rarkhar** 7	shoe shop	**rárn khǎi rorng**
prison	**khúk** 14		**tháo** 14
probably	**art** 14, **khong cha**	shopping	**seúh khǒrng** 2
	13	short	**tîa** 8
problem	**panhǎr** 12	should	**khuan cha** 13
profit	**kamrai** 15	shower	**àrp nárm** 10
pupil	**nákrian** 4	sidestreet	**soi** 7
		silk	**phâr mǎi** 15
quick	**reo** 7	silver	**(khreûang)**
quiet	**ngîap** 13		**ngern** 15
quiet and	**ngîap sangòp** 13	sister (elder)	**phêe sǎo** 8
peaceful		sister (younger)	**nórng sǎo** 8
		sit	**nâng** 5
rain	**fǒn** 6	sitting room	**hôrng nâng lên** 5
ready	**sèt** 12	six	**hòk** 4
really	**chingching** 4,	skirt	**kraprohng** 9
	chang (loei)	sleep	**norn** 5
receive	**ráp** 6, **dâi** 9	slow	**shár** 10
red	**sěe daeng** 9	small	**lék** 5
request	**khǒr**	so	**laéo** 2
rest	**phákphòrn** 13	some	**barng** 11
restaurant	**rárn ahǎrn** 6	sometimes	**barng thee** 10
rice	**khâo** 2	son	**lôok shai** 4
rich	**ruey** 3	sorry	**sǐa chai** 9
right	**kwǎr** 7	sour	**prîeo** 6
room	**hôrng**	speak	**phôot** 11
		spend (money)	**shái ngern**
same, the same	**měuankan** 10	spicy	**phèt** 6
Saturday	**wan sǎo** 10	spicy soup	**tôm yam** 6
say	**bòrk** 9	sport	**keelar** 10
school	**rohng rian** 4	station	**sathǎrnee** 14

stay	**phák** 7, **yoo** 1	thirsty	**hǐu nárm** 6
stick, get stuck	**tìt** 7	this	**née**
still	**yang** 8	thousand	**phan** 5
stomach; upset stomach	**thórng** 8, **thórng sia** 8	three	**sǎrm** 4
		Thursday	**wan pháréuhàt** 10
straight	**trong** 7		
straight ahead	**trong pai** 7	ticket	**tǔa** 7
street, road	**thanǒn** 7	time	**welar** 10
strong	**khǎeng raeng** 9	tired	**nèuai** 11
student	**nákrian** 4	tiring	**neuai** 11
study	**rian nángsěuh** 10	today	**wannée** 1
Sunday	**wan arthít** 10	together	**dûey kan** 2
sure	**nâe chai** 14	toilet	**hôrng nárm** 5
sure!	**nâe norn** 7	tomorrow	**phrûngneé** 8
sweet	**wǎrn** 6	too	**kern pai** 12, **kô** 4
swim	**wâi nárm** 10	too much	**mârk kern pai** 12
swimming pool	**sà wâinárm** 14	tourist	**nák thôrng thîeo** 13
take	**nam** 15, **ao** 6	toy	**khǒrng lên** 9
take time	**sǐa welar** 7, **shái welar** 14	trousers	**karng keng** 9
		try	**thot lorng** 6
talk	**phôôt** 8	Tuesday	**wan angkarn** 10
tall	**sǒong** 8	turn	**liéo** 7
taxi	**rót taéksêê** 7	TV	**thee wee** 10
teach	**sǒrn** 11	twenty	**yêe sìp** 4
teacher	**khroo** 4	two	**sǒrng** 4
telephone	**thohrasàp** 5	type	**phim dèet** 11
tell	**bòrk** 9		
ten	**sìp** 4	ugly	**nâr klìat** 3
tennis	**tenít** 10	umbrella	**rôm** 9
terrible	**yâe** 12	understand	**khâo chai** 11, **róo rêuang** 15
Thai	**thai** 3		
Thailand	**meuang thai** 3	university	**mahǎrwíttha- yarlai** 14
thank you	**khòrpkhun** 1		
that (e.g. that man)	**nán** 5	unwell	**mâi sabai** 8
		urgent	**dùan** 14
that (e.g. think that)	**wâr** 4	use	**shái** 11
		usually	**pròkkatì** 10
thin	**phǒrm** 8		
things	**khǒrng** 2	vegetables	**phàk** 6
think	**khít** 4	very	**mârk**
think (deduce)	**sǒngsǎi** 12	visit	**hǎr** 8

wait	**ror** 14	which (relative)	**thêe** 8
waiter, waitress	**khon sèrp** 11	white	**sěe khǎo** 9
walk	**dern** 7	who?	**khrai** 5
walk for pleasure	**dern lên** 10	who (relative)	**thêe** 8
wallet	**krapǎo satarng** 9	why?	**thammai** 3
want	**tôrng karn** 12, **yàrk** 12	wife	**phanrayar** 8, **faen** 3
watch	**narlikar** 9	wind	**lom** 12
water	**nárm** 5	with	**kàp** 4
water melon	**taeng moh** 6	woman	**phôoyǐng** 4
way	**tharng** 7	word	**kham** 11
wear	**sài** 8	work (to)	**tham ngarn** 1
weather	**arkàrt** 12	work	**ngarn** 1
Wednesday	**wan phút** 10	world	**lôhk** 15
week	**arthít** 7	write	**khǐan** 11
week-end	**sǎo arthít** 13		
well, to be	**sabai dee** 2	year	**pee** 4, **khuap** 4
what	**arai** 5	yellow	**sěe leǔang** 9
what for?	**thammai** 3	yesterday	**mêuawarnnée** 9
what time?	**kèe mohng** 10	you	**khun** 2
when?	**mêua rài** 9	young (for a female)	**sǎo** 3
where?	**nǎi, thêe nǎi** 2		
where exactly	**trong nǎi** 7	young (for a male)	**nùm** 3
which?	**nǎi** 5		

Thai–English glossary

The numbers indicate the lessons in which the word is introduced.

ae	air conditioning 5	**barng thee**	sometimes 10, maybe 15
ahǎrn	food 6	**bàrt**	unit of Thai currency 5
amerikan	American 3		
amerikar	America 3	**bia**	beer 6
angkrìt	English 3, England 3	**bòi**	often 10
		bòi bòi	often 10
ao	take, have, get 6	**borarn wátthù**	antique 15
apártmén	flat 1	**bòrk**	say, tell 9
arai	what 5	**borrisàt**	company 14
arkàrt	weather 12	**burèe**	cigarette 8
aròi	delicious 6		
àrp nárm	shower 10	**chai dee**	kind 9
art	probably 14	**chai rórn**	hot-tempered 9
arthít	week 7	**chai yen**	calm, even-tempered 9
aryú	age 4		
		chang (loei)	really, very
baèp née	in this fashion 12	**charn**	plate 6
		cheen	Chinese 3
bai	classifier for fruit 6	**cher**	meet 2
		chèt	seven 4
bai ànúyârt	permit 15	**chingching**	really 4
bai khàp khee	driving licence 13	**chon**	poor 3
		chòp	finish, complete 14
banshee	accounts 11		
bârn	house 1	**chorng**	book (reserve) 13
barng	some 11		
barng khráng barng khrao	occasionally 10	**chòrt**	park 5
		chòtmǎi	letter 15

dâi	can, be possible 10; receive, get, earn 9	**eèk sǒrng pee**	in two years 10
dam	black 9	**faen**	boyfriend, girlfriend, husband, wife 3
dârm	classifier for pens 9		
dee	good 2	**faràng**	foreigner, Westerner 3
dee chai	happy 9	**faràngsèt**	French 3
dern	walk 7	**fǒn**	rain 6
dern lên	walk for pleasure 10	**fútborn**	football 12
deuan	month 7	**haeng**	classifier for buildings 5
deuan kanyaryon	September 13		
deuan korrák-adarkhom	July 13	**hâi**	for 9, give
		hǎi	lose 9
deuan kumpharphan	February 13	**hǎr**	see, visit, call on 8
deuan meenarkhom	March 13	**hâr**	five 4
		hârm	forbidden 10
deuan mesǎryon	April 13	**hěn**	see 5
deuan míthunaryon	June 13	**hǐu**	hungry 6
		hǐu nárm	thirsty 6
deuan mokkarar	January 13	**hòk**	six 4
deuan phréut-sachìkaryon	November 13	**hôrng**	room
		hôrng khrua	kitchen 5
deuan phréut-sapharkhom	May 13	**hôrng nâng lên**	sitting room 5
		hôrng nárm	bathroom, toilet 5
deuan sǐnghǎrkhom	August 13		
deuan thanwarkhom	December 13	**hôrng norn**	bedroom 5
		hǔa	head 8
deuan tularkhom	October 13	**ìtarlée**	Italy 3
deùhk	late (at night) 10	**ìtarlian**	Italian 3
diěo née	now, at the moment 11	**kàe**	old 3
		kâeo	glass 6
dontree	music 10	**kài**	chicken 6
doo	look 5	**kamrai**	profit 15
dùan	urgent 14	**kâo**	nine 4
dûêy	as well, either 2	**kào**	old 5
dûêy kan	together 2	**kàp**	with 4
dûêy tua eng	on one's own 11	**karfae**	coffee 2

karng keng	trousers 9		**khuan cha**	should 13
karset	cassette 10		**khuap**	year 4
kèe	how many 4		**khùat**	bottle 6
kèe mohng	what time? 10		**khui**	chat 11
keelar	sport 10		**khúk**	prison 14
kèng	clever, good at 4		**khun**	you 2
kèrt	birth 9		**kiloh**	kilo 6
khǎeng raeng	strong 9		**kin**	eat, drink 2
khǎi	sell 6		**kin lǎo**	drink alcohol 10
kham	word 11		**klai**	far 5
khan	classifier for		**klâi**	near 5
	vehicles 9		**klàp bârn**	go come home 8
khâo	enter		**klûey**	banana 6
khâo	rice 2		**kô**	too 4
khâo chai	understand 11		**kò**	island 7
khàp	drive 5		**kormpiutêr**	computer 11
khâr	price 7		**kòrn**	first 12
khâr tǔa	fare 7		**kòrn**	before 7
khart thun	loss 15		**kórp**	golf 10
khêe kìat	lazy 12		**krapǎo**	bag 9
khǐan	write 11		**krapǎo satarng**	wallet 9
khít	think 4		**kraprohng**	skirt 9
khít thěung	miss someone 8		**kròht**	angry 8
khlôrng	fluently 11		**krungthêp**	Bangkok
khon	person, people 3		**kûng**	prawn 6
khon dieo	alone 8		**kwàr**	more 13
khon sèrp	waiter, waitress		**kwǎr**	right 7
	11			
khong cha	probably 13		**láe**	and 4
khǒr	request		**láeo**	so 2
khǒrng	things 2		**láeo**	already 8
khǒrng khwǎn	present 9		**láeo ko**	and 4
khǒrng lên	toy 9		**lǎng**	classifier for
khǒrng wǎrn	dessert 6			houses 5
khòrpkhun	thank you		**lao**	Laotian 3
khǒrthôht	excuse me		**lar**	to say goodbye
khrai	who 5			12
khrêuang bin	aeroplane 7		**lék**	small 5
khrêuang ngern	silver		**lekhǎrnúkarn**	secretary 4
khrêuang thorng	gold		**lêm**	classifier for
khroo	teacher 4			books 9
khrôrpkhrua	family 11		**lên**	play 5

lên phâi	play cards 10
leuhm	forget 10
liéo	turn 7
lôhk	world 15
lom	wind 12
lôôk	child, children 3
lôôk săo	daughter 4
lôôk shai	son 4
mâe	mother 4
mâe bârn	housewife 4
mahărwít-thayarlai	university 14
mài	new 5
mâi khôi	hardly at all 11
măi khwarm	mean 12
mâi phor	not enough 12
mâi sabai	not well 8
malakor	papaya 6
malesian	Malaysian 3
mamûang	mango 6
mao	drunk 8
mar	come 1
mârk	a lot, much 1
mârk kern pai	too much 12
mee	to have 3
mee shêuh	famous 12
mêua kòrn	before now 11
mêua rài	when? 9
meuang thai	Thailand 3
mĕuankan	the same 10
mĕuawarnneé	yesterday 9
mŏo	pòrk 6
mŏr	doctor 4
muey	boxing 12
nâê	to be sure 13
nâê chai	sure 14
naé nam	advice 15
nâê norn	sure, of course 7
năi	where 2
nai	in 14

năi	which 5
nák thôrng thîeo	tourist 13
nák thúrákìt	businessman 4
nákrian	student, pupil 4
nam	take
nam khâô	import (verb)
námman	petrol, oil 7
nán	that 5
năng	film 7
nâng	sit 5
năng	leather 9
nángsĕuh	book 9
nángsĕuh dern tharng	passport 15
nángsĕuh phim	newspaper 9
năo	cold 6
nâr	next 10
nâr bèua	boring 3
nâr klìat	ugly, disgusting 3
nâr rák	lovely 3
nâr sŏn chai	interesting 5
narlikar	watch, clock 9
nárm	water 5
nárm thûam	floods 12
narn	(take) a long time 7
narthee	minute 7
nát	appointment 12
née	this
néua	beef 6
néua sat	meat 6
nèuai	tired 11
nèung	one 4
ngâi	easy 11
ngern	money 3, silver 15
ngîap sangòp	quiet and peaceful 13
nítnòi	a little 3
nói	a few 6
norn	sleep 5
nórng shai	younger brother 8

nùm	young (for a male) 3
ohkàrt	opportunity 11
opfit	office
òrk	leave 14
pàet	eight 4
pai	go
pai thiêô	go somewhere for pleasure 2
pai thúrá	go on business 2
pám námman	petrol station 7
panhǎr	problem 12
pàrkkar	pen 9
pee	year 4
pen	to be 3
pen	can, know how to do something 11
pen wàt	have a cold 8
pèrt	open 9
phaeng	expensive 5
phàk	vegetables 6
phák	stay 7
phákphòrn	rest 13
phan	thousand 5
phanrayar	wife 8
phâr mǎi	silk
phàrn	after 7
phàrn	pass 12
pharsǎr	language 11
phàt	fry, fried 6
phêê nórng	brothers and sisters 8
phêê sǎo	elder sister 8
phèt	spicy 6
phêua	for (the purpose of) 13
phêuan	friend 3
phim dèet	type 11
phǒnlamái	fruit 6

phôôshai	boy, man 4
phôôt	talk, speak 8
phôôying	girl, woman 4
phóp	meet 12
phor	enough 12
phôr	father 4
phǒrm	thin 8
phrá	Buddha figure 15
phró wâr	because 12
phrûngnée	tomorrow 8
phu khǎo	mountain 13
pìt	close(d) 10
plar	fish 6
praisanee	post office 15
pramarn	about 7
prashum	meeting 14
priêô	sour 6
pròkkatì	usually 10
pùat	ache 8
ráp	fetch, receive 10
ráp	receive 6
rárn ahǎrn	restaurant 6
rárn khǎi rorng tháo	shoe shop 14
rárn khǎi sêua phâr	clothes shop 14
rárn khǎi yar	chemist's 14
rawang	be careful 15
rêêp	hurry 12
reo	quick 7, early (i.e. ahead of schedule) 10
reua	boat 7
rêuang	about, on the subject of 12
rian nángsěuh	study 10
rohng nǎng	cinema 7
rohng phayarbarn	hospital 5
rohng raem	hotel
rohng rian	school 4

rói	a hundred 4	sèe	four 4
rôm	umbrella 9	sĕe	colour 9
róo	to know 15	sĕe daeng	red 9
róo rêuang	to understand 15	sĕe khảo	white 9
róochàk	know 7	sĕe khiěo	green 9
rôop	picture 9	sĕe luěng	yellow 9
ror	wait 14	sĕe nám ngern	blue 9
rórn	hot 6	sĕe nám tarn	brown 9
rorng tháo	shoe 9	sèt	ready, finished 12
rót	car 5		
rót me	bus 7	sêua	shirt
rót mortersai	motorcycle 7	sêua nôrk	jacket 9
rót taéksêe	taxi 7	sêua phâr	clothes 9
ruam	mixed 6	seúh	buy 2
ruey	rich 3	seúh khỏrng	shopping 2
		shabàp	classifier for newspapers 9
sà waînárm	swimming pool 14	shái	use 11
sa-àrt	clean 5	shai thale	seaside 7
sabai dee	to be well 2	shái welar	take time 14
sadùak	comfortable	shâo	hire 13
sái	left 7	sháo	early (in the morning) 10
sài	wear, put 8		
sǎi	late (in the morning) 10	shár	late (behind schedule) 10, slow 10
sak wan nèung	one day 11		
saměr	always 10	shern	to invite, please 8
sanǎrm yâr	garden 5		
sanǎrmbin	airport 1	shêuh	to be called 8
sangòp	peaceful	shôhk	luck 2
sanùk	enjoyable, fun 3	shôrp	like 6
sǎo	young (for a female) 3	shûamohng	hour 7
		shûey	help 10
sǎo arthít	weekend 13	sǐa chai	to be sorry 9
sàparót	pineapple 6	sǐa welar	take time 7
sǎrkon	international 13	sǐn khár khảo	import (noun) 15
sǎrm	three 4	sǐn khár òrk	export (noun) 15
sǎrmee	husband 8	sìp	ten 4
sârp	know 5	sìp èt	eleven 4
sathǎrn thôot	Embassy 7	soi	sidestreet off a **thanon** 7
sathǎrnee	station 14		
sawàtdee	hello	sòkkapròk	dirty 5

sôm	orange 6		**thêe**	at, in 1
sòng	send 15		**thêe laéo**	last, ago 9
sòng òrk	export (verb) 15		**thêe nêe**	here 8
sŏngsăi	to think (deduce) 12		**thêe sùt**	the most 13
sŏong	tall 8		**thee wee**	TV 10
sŏrn	teach 11		**thĕung**	arrive 14
sŏrng	two 4		**thîang**	midday 10
sòrp	exam, take an exam 12		**thîang kheuhn**	midnight 10
			thohrasàp	telephone 5
sòrp tòk	fail 12		**thòok**	cheap 13
sŭey	pretty 3		**thórng**	stomach 8
sùk	happy 9		**thorng**	gold
			thórng sĭa	upset stomach, diarrhoea 8
taè	but 5		**thot lorng**	try 6
taeng moh	water melon 6		**thŭey**	cup 6
taèng ngarn	to marry, be married 8		**thúk**	every 10
			tîa	short 8
talàrt	market 2		**tìt**	to stick, get stuck 7
tamrùat	policeman 4			
tar	eye 8		**tìt tòr**	contact, get in touch with 14
tàrng prathêt	abroad, foreign 11			
tàt phŏm	get one's hair cut 14		**tòk**	fall 6
			tòk long	OK 10
tenít	tennis 10		**tôm yam**	spicy soup 6
tèuk	building 5		**tôo**	cupboard 5
thai	Thai 3		**tôo yen**	fridge 5
thài rôop	(take a) photo-graph 11		**torn bài**	afternoon 10
			torn mêuht	night 10
tham kàpkhâo	cook		**torn née**	now, at the moment 11
tham ngarn	to work 1			
thammai	what for, why? 3		**torn sháo**	morning 10
			torn yen	evening 10
thanarkharn	bank 5		**tôrng**	must, have to 10
tháng	all 10		**tôrng karn**	want 12
thanŏn	street, road 7		**trong**	straight 7
thâonán	only 7		**trong khârm**	opposite 7
thâorài	how much 4		**trong năi**	where exactly 7
thâr	if 15		**trong pai**	straight ahead 7
thărm	ask 8		**tŭa**	ticket 7
tharng	way 7		**tua**	classifier for clothing (or
thêe	who, which 8			

	cigarettes) 9	yae	terrible 12
ubàt hèt	accident 14	**yaì**	big 5
ûwan	fat 8	**yaí**	move, transfer 10
		yaí bârn	move house 10
wâen tar	glasses 8	**yang**	still 8
wâi nárm	swim 10	**yang mâi**	not yet 8
wan angkarn	Tuesday 10	**yangngai**	how 5
wan arthít	Sunday 10	**yar**	medicine 14
wan chan	Monday 10	**yàr**	divorced 11
wan phâréuhàt	Thursday 10	**yârk**	difficult 11
wan phút	Wednesday 10	**yàrk**	want 12
wan sǎo	Saturday 10	**yàrng euhn**	any other 10
wan sùk	Friday 10	**yêe sìp**	twenty 4
wǎng	hope 11	**yêepùn**	Japanese 3,
wǎng wâr yang	I hope so 11		Japan 3
ngán		**yen**	cool, cold 5
wanneé	today 1	**yerraman**	German 11
wâr	think that 13	**yeuhm**	lend, borrow 10
wâr	that 4	**yòo**	to be some-
wǎrn	sweet 6		where, stay,
wârng	free		live 1
welar	time 10	**yûng**	difficult